Des Moines, May 20, 2008.

"Let us, each of us, now embrace with solemn duty and awesome joy what is our lasting birthright. With common effort and common purpose, with passion and dedication, let us answer the call of history and carry into an uncertain future that precious light of freedom."

— President Barack Obama
Second Inaugural Address
JANUARY 21, 2013

*President Obama in the Old Family Dining Room
at the White House, August 24, 2016.*

The New York Times

OBAMA

THE CALL OF HISTORY

PETER BAKER

CALLAWAY

NEW YORK
2017

Distributed by ABRAMS

"All the News
That's Fit to Print"

The New York Times

Late Edition
Today, limited sunshine, a shower, high 63. **Tonight,** cloudy, scattered showers, patchy fog, low 55. **Tomorrow,** rain ends, remaining cloudy, high 62. Weather map, Page B19.

VOL. CLVIII . . No. 54,485 + © 2008 The New York Times NEW YORK, WEDNESDAY, NOVEMBER 5, 2008 $5 beyond the greater New York metropolitan area. $1.50

OBAMA

RACIAL BARRIER FALLS IN DECISIVE VICTORY

08 ONLINE

■ *The latest state-by-state results: the presidential contest and House, Senate and governors' races.*
■ *The Caucus blog: updates from The Times's political staff.*

■ *Interactive graphics: the electoral map, voter profiles and analysis.*
■ *Video, audio and photos: reactions from the voters and the campaigns.*
nytimes.com

PRESIDENT-ELECT

THE LONG CAMPAIGN

Journey to the Top

The story of Senator Barack Obama's journey to the pinnacle of American politics is the story of a campaign that was, even in the view of many rivals, almost flawless. After a somewhat lackluster start, Mr. Obama and his team delivered. They developed a strategy to secure the nomination, and stuck with it even after setbacks. PAGE P1

SENATE

NORTH CAROLINA

Elizabeth Dole Is Out

After leading by a double-digit margin, the Republican Senator Elizabeth Dole, left, was defeated by State Senator Kay R. Hagan. In the campaign's final week, Mrs. Dole came under criticism for an advertisement that linked Ms. Hagan to a group called the Godless Americans. PAGE P12

VIRGINIA

Mark Warner Wins

Extending the Democrats' advantage in the Senate, former Gov. Mark R. Warner of Virginia easily won his race to replace John W. Warner (no relation), a retiring Republican. PAGE P12

NEW HAMPSHIRE

Sununu Is Defeated

Another leading Republican, Senator John E. Sununu, was ousted by a wide margin by Jeanne Shaheen, the former New Hampshire governor whom he beat in 2002. PAGE P12

HOUSE

CONNECTICUT

G.O.P. Stalwart Falls

Representative Christopher Shays, the last Republican House member from New England and a political Houdini who escaped previous Democratic attempts to topple him, was defeated by a political novice, Jim Himes. PAGE P15

NEW YORK

LEGISLATURE

Democrats Take Senate

Democrats won a majority in the New York State Senate, putting the party in control of both houses of the Legislature and the governor's office for the first time since the New Deal. Voters ousted two Republican senators whose combined years in office spanned more than half a century. PAGE P15

FOR HOME DELIVERY CALL 1-800-NYTIMES

DOUG MILLS/THE NEW YORK TIMES

President-elect Barack Obama with his wife, Michelle, and their daughters in Chicago on Tuesday night.

Democrats in Congress Strengthen Grip

By ADAM NAGOURNEY

Barack Hussein Obama was elected the 44th president of the United States on Tuesday, sweeping away the last racial barrier in American politics with ease as the country chose him as its first black chief executive.

The election of Mr. Obama amounted to a national catharsis — a repudiation of a historically unpopular Republican president and his economic and foreign policies, and an embrace of Mr. Obama's call for a change in the direction and the tone of the country.

But it was just as much a strikingly symbolic moment in the evolution of the nation's fraught racial history, a breakthrough that would have seemed unthinkable just two years ago.

Mr. Obama, 47, a first-term senator from Illinois, defeated Senator John McCain of Arizona, 72, a former prisoner of war who was making his second bid for the presidency.

To the very end, Mr. McCain's campaign was eclipsed by an opponent who was nothing short of a phenomenon, drawing huge crowds epitomized by the tens of thousands of people who turned out to hear Mr. Obama's victory speech in Grant Park in Chicago.

Mr. McCain also fought the headwinds of a relentlessly hostile political environment, weighted down with the baggage left to him by President Bush and an economic collapse that took place in the middle of the general election campaign.

"If there is anyone out there who still doubts that America is a place where all things are possible, who still wonders if the dream of our founders is alive in our time, who still questions the power of our democracy, tonight is your answer," said Mr. Obama, standing before a huge wooden lectern with a row of American flags at his back, casting his eyes to a crowd that stretched far into the Chicago night.

"It's been a long time coming," the president-elect added, "but tonight, because of what we did on this date in this election at this defining moment, change has come to America."

Mr. McCain delivered his concession speech under clear skies on the lush lawn of the Arizona Biltmore, in Phoenix, where he and his wife had held their wedding reception. The crowd reacted with scattered boos as he offered his congratulations to Mr. Obama and saluted the historical significance of the moment.

"This is a historic election, and I recognize the significance it has for African-Americans and for the special pride that must be theirs tonight," Mr. McCain said, adding, "We both realize that we have come a long way from the injustices that once stained our nation's reputation."

Not only did Mr. Obama capture the presidency, but he led his party to sharp gains in Congress. This puts

Continued on Page P3

THE CHALLENGE

No Time for Laurels; Now the Hard Part

By PETER BAKER

WASHINGTON — No president since before Barack Obama was born has ascended to the Oval Office confronted by the accumulation of seismic challenges awaiting him. Historians grasping for parallels point to Abraham Lincoln taking office as the nation was collapsing into Civil War, or Franklin D. Roosevelt arriving in Washington in the throes of the Great Depression.

The task facing Mr. Obama does not rise to those levels, but that these are the comparisons most often cited sobers even Democrats rejoicing at their return to power. On the shoulders of a 47-year-old first-term senator, with the power of inspiration yet no real executive experience, now falls the responsibility of prosecuting two wars, protecting the nation from terrorist threat and stitching back together a shredded economy.

Given the depth of these issues, Mr. Obama has little choice but to "put your arm around chaos," in the words of Leon E. Panetta, the former White House chief of staff who has been advising his transition team.

"You better damn well do the tough stuff up front, because if you think you can delay the tough decisions and tiptoe past the graveyard, you're in for a lot of trouble," Mr. Panetta said. "Make the decisions that involve pain and sacrifice up front."

What kind of decision maker and leader Mr. Obama will be remains unclear even to many of his supporters. Will he be willing to use his political capital and act boldly, or will he move cautiously and risk being paralyzed by competing demands from within his own party? His performance under the harsh lights of the campaign trail suggests a figure with remarkable coolness and confidence under enormous pressure, yet also one who rarely veers off the methodical path he lays out.

"It leads you to wonder whether passivity is the way he approaches most things," said John R. Bolton, President Bush's former ambassador to the United Na-

Continued on Page P4

THE MOMENT

After Decades, A Time to Reap

By KEVIN SACK

ALBANY, Ga. — Rutha Mae Harris backed her silver Town Car out of the driveway early Tuesday morning, pointed it toward her polling place on Mercer Avenue and started to sing.

"I'm going to vote like the spirit say vote," Miss Harris chanted softly.

I'm going to vote like the
spirit say vote,
I'm going to vote like the
spirit say vote,
And if the spirit say vote I'm
going to vote,
Oh Lord, I'm going to vote
when the spirit say vote.

As a 21-year-old student (on right in photo), she had bellowed that same freedom song at mass meetings at Mount Zion Baptist Church back in 1961, the year Barack Obama was born in Hawaii, a universe away. She sang it again while marching on Albany's City Hall, where she and other black students demanded the right to vote, and in the cramped and filthy cells of the city jail, which the Rev. Dr. Martin Luther King Jr. described as the worst he ever inhabited.

For those like Miss Harris who withstood jailings and beatings and threats to their livelihoods, all because they wanted to vote, the short drive to the polls on Tuesday culminated a lifelong journey from a time that is at once unrecognizable and eerily familiar here in southwest Georgia. As they exited the voting booths, some in wheelchairs, others with canes, these foot soldiers of the civil rights movement could not suppress either their jubilation or their astonishment at having voted for an African-American for president of the United States.

"They didn't give us our mule and our acre, but things are better," Miss Harris, 67, said with a gratified smile. "It's time to reap some of the harvest."

When Miss Harris arrived at the city gymnasium where she votes, her 80-year-old friend Mamie L. Nelson greeted her with a hug. "We marched, we sang and now it's happening," Ms. Nelson said. "It's really a feeling I

Continued on Page P6

THE PROMISE

For Many Abroad, An Ideal Renewed

By ETHAN BRONNER

GAZA — From far away, this is how it looks: There is a country out there where tens of millions of white Christians, voting freely, select as their leader a black man of modest origin, the son of a Muslim. There is a place on Earth — call it America — where such a thing happens.

Even where the United States is held in special contempt, like here in this benighted Palestinian coastal strip, the "glorious epic of Barack Obama," as the leftist French editor Jean Daniel calls it, makes America — the idea as much as the actual place — stand again, perhaps only fleetingly, for limitless possibility.

"It allows us all to dream a little," said Oswaldo Calvo, 58, a Venezuelan political activist in Caracas, in a comment echoed to correspondents of The New York Times on four continents in the days leading up to the election.

Tristram Hunt, a British historian, put it this way: Mr. Obama "brings the narrative that everyone wants to return to — that America is the land of extraordinary opportunity and possibility, where miracles happen."

But wonder is almost overwhelmed by relief. Mr. Obama's election offers most non-Americans a sense that the imperial power capable of doing such good and such harm — a country that, they complain, preached justice but tortured its captives, launched a disastrous war in Iraq, turned its back on the environment and greedily dragged the world into economic chaos — saw the errors of its ways over the past eight years and shifted course.

They say the country that weakened democratic forces abroad through a tireless but often ineffective campaign for democracy — dismissing results it found unsavory, cutting deals with dictators it needed as allies in its other battles — was now shining a transformative beacon with its own democratic exercise.

It would be hard to overstate how fervently vast

Continued on Page P4

TABLE OF CONTENTS

10   Prologue

18   Chapter 1: 'This Winter of Our Hardship'

40   Chapter 2: 'Bring Our Troops Home'

62   Chapter 3: 'Time to Turn the Page'

82   Chapter 4: 'A Shellacking'

100   Chapter 5: 'Justice Has Been Done'

124   Chapter 6: 'Fought Our Way Back'

148   Chapter 7: 'Governing By Crisis'

174   Chapter 8: 'Red Line'

194   Chapter 9: 'Haunted By Those Deaths'

220   Chapter 10: 'Could Have Been Me'

238   Chapter 11: 'Never Fear to Negotiate'

262   Chapter 12: 'A Personal Insult'

308   Epilogue

314   Index

319   Acknowledgments

PROLOGUE

On a chilly evening the night before the election that would determine his successor, President Barack Obama addressed a boisterous crowd on the lawn of Independence Hall in Philadelphia. He was near the end of a momentous eight-year journey, full of triumph and tribulation, success and setback. He was grayer than that heady day at Grant Park in Chicago when he first won the presidency and scarred from the many battles that would follow. The country he had hoped to transform was on the verge of replacing him with someone who was his polar opposite in temperament, philosophy and goals.

As he stood in front of a giant American flag addressing supporters in what would be the last campaign rally of his presidency that night in November 2016, Obama reflected on the path that had taken him from his first appearance on the national stage, a convention speech decrying the divisions of a Red America and a Blue America, to this moment when the divisions seemed as deep as they had ever been. A journalist, he noted, had just asked him about the contrast between that ideal and the reality he was leaving behind. "Maybe your vision was misguided, he suggested, or at least very naïve," the president recalled the reporter asking. And it was a fair question.

"I had to acknowledge that I hadn't fully counted on the obstruction we'd see when I first came into office and was to save the economy," he said. "I didn't anticipate the way social media would magnify our divisions and muddy up facts. None of us knew then how deep the Great Recession would cut and how many people would suffer and how it would make so many people anxious about their futures and their kids' futures, even after the economy recovered. But despite all that, I told him, the answer is yes, I still believe in hope. I'm still as optimistic as ever about our future."

The presidency of Barack Hussein Obama was all about hopes – those that were realized and those that were dashed. He righted the economic ship that was in danger of capsizing, brought home the vast majority of the 180,000 troops who were fighting overseas, authorized the mission that dispatched Osama bin Laden, enacted policies to stem climate change, imposed new regulations on Wall Street banks, rescued the auto industry and created a new health care system that provided coverage to 20 million Americans. But the progressive, post-racial, bridge-building society he had promised gave way to an angry, jeering, us-against-them nation to be led by a new president who relished reality-show name calling with racial overtones. Domestic achievements like health care were in danger of being reversed and rather than bringing peace to a raucous Middle East, Obama left the region even more turbulent than he found it. He finished his presidency near the peak of his popularity, admired for his steady dignity in contrast to his voluble and impulsive successor, and yet voters rejected his chosen heir.

At times, Obama seemed like an enigma, even to those around him. Historians and commentators constantly tried to categorize him – when he took office, he self-consciously emulated Abraham Lincoln, arriving in Washington along the same route and using the old railsplitter's Bible to take the oath. He was compared in those early days to a latter-day Franklin Roosevelt, George Washington or John Kennedy. As the years passed, and the hardships piled up and the poll numbers fell and the hope faded into gridlock, other comparisons came to mind. Some likened him to Lyndon Johnson for sending a temporary surge of troops to Afghanistan or Jimmy Carter for seeming feckless in the face of challenges from Russia to Iran or even George W. Bush for his embrace of drone warfare and certain counter-terrorism tactics of his predecessor. "Sometimes I think the only president we haven't been compared to is Franklin Pierce," one aide noted wryly.

As it happened, the difficulty in defining Barack Obama and the tumultuous eight years of his presidency stemmed in part from the fact that he was like none of his predecessors, at least not precisely. As Obama himself noted during the 2008 campaign, he did not "look like all the presidents on the dollar bills." His first line in the history books was written the day he won office as the first African-American president, but he was determined to offer more than simply a new complexion in the Oval Office. Beyond his status as a breaker of racial barriers, he managed to captivate and confuse his nation simultaneously, presenting himself as a champion of the progressive idea that government could be a force for good in society while at the same time promising to be a non-ideological consensus builder who would reach across the aisle. "I am like a Rorschach test," he observed at one point. People saw in him what they wanted to see.

He was just as opaque to those of us in the White House press corps who covered him day in and day out. While many politicians lay it all out there, like his famously unfiltered vice president, Joseph Biden, Obama was as reserved in private as he was in public. He did not shoot the breeze. He did not let his guard down. He did not dispense playful nicknames as Bush did or spin out colorful Ozark yarns as Bill Clinton did. If Obama came back to the press cabin on Air Force One, it was to deliver a message or to ruminate out loud on the serious, substantive issues confronting him or perhaps to chide a reporter whose story he did not like. Where other pols might put a hand on your shoulder or ask after your kids, he saw that as frivolous and fake.

Not that he was necessarily cold. While Maureen Dowd famously compared him to Mr. Spock, the hyperlogical half-Vulcan from *Star Trek*,

Obama had a human side. He was a fierce, trash-talking competitor on the basketball court and golf course, enjoyed a range of music on his iPad and stayed up late watching ESPN's *SportsCenter*. And he could deliver a one-liner with impeccable timing. He had a hard time disguising his exasperation with Washington and he openly flouted its conventions. He was a family man who made sure to leave the Oval Office by 6:30 p.m. in time for dinner at home. He doted on his two daughters and took his motorcade, complete with the ever-present ambulance and press vans, to watch their school basketball games. At his most emotional moment, we watched him cry in the White House briefing room over the shooting massacre of school children in Newtown, Connecticut.

But he faced crises that would daunt even Lincoln, taking the oath at a time when the country was perched on the edge of an economic abyss while fighting two wars overseas and still facing a potent terrorist threat. Over the course of his tenure, the Middle East would undergo profound changes amid civil war and the rise of a vicious new terrorist group while Europe would slide back into another cold war with a revanchist Russia. At home, Obama confronted deep schisms over his initiatives on health care, immigration, climate change, gun control and government spending. A conservative Tea Party backlash cost him both houses of Congress in midterm elections. Perhaps most painfully for Obama, racial tensions exploded with a series of police shootings and riots that belied the promise of his election.

The country was in a sour mood even before Obama arrived and remained so for his entire presidency – the last time a majority of Americans in Gallup polls was satisfied with the way things were going in the country was in 2004. At one point during Obama's first term, only 11 percent of Americans were happy with the country's direction. And so the candidate of hope and change ended up presiding over an era of paralysis and polarization.

It said something about the period that even an unvarnished triumph like the commando raid that finally caught up to and killed Osama bin Laden lifted moods only briefly. An economic recovery that produced millions of jobs, cut unemployment in half and vaulted markets beyond even their pre-crash heights nonetheless left many Americans behind and feeling resentful.

Obama arrived in office with great faith in the power of his oratory to inspire and in the power of his good sense to solve problems, only to discover the limits of both. The speeches that he scrawled out by hand on yellow legal pads may have thrilled supporters on the campaign trail, but they ultimately failed to move entrenched forces at home or abroad and, indeed, over time gave way to professorial lectures from the White House podium. The notion that reasonable people could settle their disputes if only he could get them to the table seemed contradicted everywhere from Capitol Hill to the Kremlin to Jerusalem. Haunted by the devastation in Syria and frustrated by his inability to fully extricate from Iraq and Afghanistan, Obama set about transforming America's relationships with two longstanding enemies, Iran and Cuba.

Like his predecessors, Obama regularly noted that the easy issues never made it to his desk, only the hard ones. It got to the point that he and his first White House chief of staff, Rahm Emanuel, joked that they should move to Hawaii and open a T-shirt shack with only one size and one color (medium, white) so they would not ever have to make another decision. It became such a running joke that during meetings on especially thorny issues with no good options, Emanuel would turn to Obama.

"White," he would say.

"Medium," Obama would reply.

If the trials of his time took a personal toll beyond the graying hair he always joked about, Obama did not show it. Through all manner of challenges, he carried himself with a calm poise and grace under pressure. He rarely rushed into decisions, sometimes to a fault. A night owl, he sat alone late in the White House residence after the family had retired, reading briefing papers, watching sports or playing Words With Friends. The only indulgence he permitted himself during these solitary hours was a handful of almonds – exactly seven of them, no more, no less, the president's chef joked to Michael Shear of *The New York Times*. Obama felt compelled to deny such fastidiousness but it seemed all too plausible. Either way, it was a self-discipline that, for all the controversies, allowed him to emerge from eight years in office without a hint of personal scandal.

Still, it was a humbling journey. Full of confidence to the point of hubris, Obama started out promising that his election would be the moment "when the rise of the oceans began to slow and our planet began to heal." By the low point of his second term, he had radically revised his expectations. Perhaps there were no more Lincolns. Perhaps even a president could not single-handedly change the world, he concluded, but he could at least push it in the right direction.

He had learned, he told the writer David Remnick, that as president "you are essentially a relay swimmer in a river full of rapids, and that river is history." Switching metaphors, Obama said, "At the end of the day, we're part of a long-running story. We just try to get our paragraph right."

This is his paragraph.

Doug Mills/New York Times

Christie's Image/Handout/
European Pressphoto Agency

2009   2010

Nov Dec Jan Feb Mar Apr May Jun Jul Aug Sep Oct Nov Dec Jan Feb Mar Apr May Jun Jul Aug Sep Oct Nov Dec

NOVEMBER 2008
Barack Obama is elected the 44th President of the United States.

JANUARY 2009
Barack Obama is inaugurated, vowing to "begin again the work of remaking America."

JUNE 2009
President Obama delivers speech in Cairo reaching out to Muslim world.

OCTOBER 2009
President Obama is awarded the Nobel Peace Prize.

JANUARY 2010
A 7.0 earthquake just outside the capital city of Port-au-Prince devastates Haiti.

Damon Winter/New York Times

MARCH 2010
Congress passes the Patient Protection and Affordable Health Care Act, which came to be known as Obamacare.

JULY 2010
President Obama signs the Dodd-Frank financial regulatory reform bill into law.

NOVEMBER 2010
Mid-term elections are a disaster for President Obama as Republicans gain 63 seats in the House of Representatives.

FEBRUARY 2009
Congress passes a $787 billion economic stimulus package.

JULY 2009
President Obama hosts "beer summit" bringing together Henry Louis Gates, an African-American professor at Harvard, with the white police officer who mistakenly arrested him in his own home.

NOVEMBER 2009
Nidal Hasan, an Army major and psychiatrist, kills 13 active and retired soldiers in a shooting spree at Fort Hood in Texas.

APRIL 2010
President Obama signs arms control treaty with Russia.

AUGUST 2010
Elena Kagan is confirmed as a Supreme Court justice.

DECEMBER 2010
President Obama signs legislation repealing the "don't ask, don't tell" ban on gays and lesbians serving openly in the military.

FEBRUARY 2009
President Obama orders withdrawal of American forces from Iraq by the end of 2011.

AUGUST 2009
Sonia Sotomayor is confirmed as the first Hispanic to serve on the Supreme Court.

DECEMBER 2009
President Obama orders 30,000 more troops sent to Afghanistan but promises to begin withdrawing forces in 2011.

APRIL 2010
The Deepwater Horizon oil rig explodes in the Gulf of Mexico off the coast of Louisiana, killing 11 workers and causing a massive offshore oil spill that takes three months to stop and becomes the largest in American history.

Doug Mills/New York Times

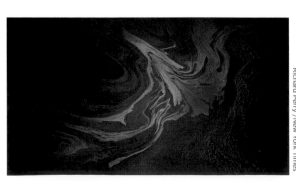

Richard Perry/New York Times

2011 2012 2013

Dec | Jan | Feb | Mar | Apr | May | Jun | Jul | Aug | Sep | Oct | Nov | Dec | Jan | Feb | Mar | Apr | May | Jun | Jul | Aug | Sep | Oct | Nov | Dec | Jan | Feb

DECEMBER 2010
Protests in Tunisia set off demonstrations across the Middle East and North Africa in what came to be known as the Arab Spring.

MARCH 2011
Arab Spring unrest escalates to armed conflict in Syria, setting off a years-long civil war with hundreds of thousands of casualties and millions of refugees.

SEPTEMBER 2011
Anwar al-Awlaki, an American-born imam and recruiter for Al-Qaeda, is killed in a U.S. drone strike in Yemen.

DECEMBER 2011
Last American troops leave Iraq more than eight years after the invasion that toppled Saddam Hussein.

FEBRUARY 2012
Trayvon Martin, an unarmed black 17-year-old, is shot and killed by George Zimmerman, the watch coordinator of a gated community in Florida, setting off demonstrations across the country.

JUNE 2012
Rejecting a legal challenge from conservatives, the Supreme Court upholds the constitutionality of the core element of Obamacare.

SEPTEMBER 2012
Christopher Stevens, the ambassador to Libya, and three other Americans are killed when Islamic militants attack the U.S. diplomatic compound in Benghazi.

FEBRUARY 2011
Egypt's longtime autocratic president, Hosni Mubarak, a key U.S. ally, resigns under pressure from President Obama.

MARCH 2011
President Obama orders military intervention in Libya to prevent mass killings of civilians.

OCTOBER 2011
Muammar Qaddafi, by then deposed as Libyan leader, is caught and killed by opposition forces.

NOVEMBER 2012
President Obama is re-elected, defeating Republican Mitt Romney.

MAY 2011
Navy Seals kill Osama bin Laden after he is tracked to a secret compound in Pakistan, ending a decade-long manhunt.

Moises Saman for The New York Times

DECEMBER 2012
A lone gunman kills 20 children and six adults at the Sandy Hook Elementary School in Newtown, Connecticut, prompting President Obama to seek gun control.

Luke Sharrett for The New York Times

Tauseff Mustafa/AFP/Getty Images

2013   2014

Oct | Nov | Dec | Jan | Feb | Mar | Apr | May | Jun | Jul | Aug | Sep | Oct | Nov | Dec | Jan | Feb | Mar | Apr | May | Jun | Jul | Aug | Sep | Oct | Nov | Dec

JANUARY 2013
President Obama reaches deal with congressional Republicans extending Bush-era tax cuts permanently for all but those making more than $400,000 a year.

APRIL 2013
Bombs planted by two Chechen brothers near the finish line of the Boston Marathon kill three people and injure 100.

AUGUST 2013
Egyptian military ousts President Mohamed Morsi and cracks down on the Muslim Brotherhood.

OCTOBER 2013
A budget dispute between the president and congressional Republicans shuts down the federal government for 17 days.

Gabriella Demczuk/
New York Times

JANUARY 2014
Islamic extremists known as the Islamic State overrun Iraqi army forces to capture the cities of Falluja and Ramadi.

JUNE 2014
The Environmental Protection Agency announces far-reaching rule to slash power plant pollution.

AUGUST 2014
The Islamic State releases videos of the beheadings of American journalists James Foley and Steven Sotloff.

NOVEMBER 2014
Republicans sweep mid-term elections, capturing the Senate to go along with their House majority.

APRIL 2013
Senate blocks President Obama's gun control proposals.

SEPTEMBER 2013
After declaring a "red line" against the use of chemical weapons, President Obama aborts a threatened military strike on Syria for gassing civilians and instead agrees to Russian plan to destroy Syria's chemical stockpiles.

MARCH 2014
President Vladimir Putin of Russia annexes Crimea and sets in motion a separatist war in eastern Ukraine. President Obama and European leaders respond with sanctions.

JUNE 2014
Islamic State forces capture Mosul, the second-largest city in Iraq.

Doug Mills/
New York Times

AUGUST 2014
Eighteen-year-old Michael Brown is shot and killed by a police officer in Ferguson, Missouri, touching off violent demonstrations.

NOVEMBER 2014
President Obama reaches agreement with China setting limits on greenhouse emissions.

JUNE 2013
Edward Snowden, a former National Security Agency contractor, releases documents disclosing widespread collection of Americans' telephone records and surveillance of foreign leaders.

OCTOBER 2013
Health care plan debuts to widespread failures of its web site, undercutting its credibility.

AUGUST 2014
President Obama orders new campaign of American airstrikes against the Islamic State in Iraq.

SEPTEMBER 2014
President Obama expands the air war against the Islamic State for the first time to Syria.

NOVEMBER 2014
President Obama asserts executive authority to shield up to five million illegal immigrants from deportation.

Kayana Szymczak for The New York Times

2015   2016   2017

Stephen Crowley/New York Times

Damon Winter/New York Times

Dec Jan Feb Mar Apr May Jun Jul Aug Sep Oct Nov Dec Jan Feb Mar Apr May Jun Jul Aug Sep Oct Nov Dec Jan Feb Mar

DECEMBER 2014
President Obama restores diplomatic relations with Cuba after more than half a century of hostility between the two nations.

JUNE 2015
A 21-year-old self-proclaimed white supremacist opens fire on a Bible service at the Emanuel African Methodist Episcopal Church in Charleston, South Carolina, killing nine African-Americans.

SEPTEMBER 2015
Pope Francis visits the White House.

NOVEMBER 2015
President Obama rejects Keystone pipeline and reaches agreement with other world leaders in Paris on a global accord to fight climate change.

MARCH 2016
President Obama nominates Merrick Garland to succeed the late Justice Antonin Scalia but Senate Republicans, citing the president's lame-duck status, refuse to consider the nomination.

JUNE 2016
A deadlocked Supreme Court blocks President Obama's plan to allow five million illegal immigrants to avoid deportation.

JULY 2016
An African-American sniper kills five police officers in Dallas, fueling more racial tension across the nation.

DECEMBER 2016
The president imposes sanctions on Russia after intelligence agencies conclude that the Kremlin tried to influence the U.S. elections on Trump's behalf by hacking Democratic Party computers.

JANUARY 2015
Terrorists storm the Paris offices of Charlie Hebdo, a satirical weekly magazine, killing 11 people.

JUNE 2015
Supreme Court finds a constitutional right to same-sex marriage.

Zach Gibson/The New York Times

OCTOBER 2015
President Obama abandons plan to withdraw all troops from Afghanistan by the end of his term.

DECEMBER 2015
A married couple with extremist Islamic leanings opens fire at a public health department holiday party in San Bernardino, California, killing 14 people and seriously injuring 22.

MARCH 2016
President Obama travels to Cuba and meets with President Raul Castro.

Stephen Crowley/New York Times

JUNE 2016
British vote to leave the European Union, part of a wider revolt against the established order.

NOVEMBER 2016
While losing the popular vote, Donald J. Trump defeats Clinton in the Electoral College to claim the presidency in what many see as a repudiation of President Obama.

JANUARY 2017
Obama commutes the sentence of Chelsea Manning and pardons James Cartwright, both convicted of leaking national secrets.

MARCH 2015
Prime Minister Benjamin Netanyahu of Israel addresses the U.S. Congress to castigate President Obama's negotiations with Iran.

JULY 2015
The United States and five other powers reach agreement with Iran to curb its nuclear program.

NOVEMBER 2015
Terrorists mount coordinated attacks in Paris, killing 130 people and wounding 368.

JUNE 2016
An American-born man pledging allegiance to the Islamic State kills 49 people and wounds 53 in an Orlando gay nightclub before being killed in a shootout with police.

JULY 2016
Obama addresses the Democratic National Convention to kick off months of campaigning for Hillary Clinton to succeed him.

DECEMBER 2016
At odds with Trump and Netanyahu, Obama declines to block a United Nations resolution condemning Israeli settlements in the West Bank.

Doug Mills/New York Times

CHAPTER I

'This Winter of Our Hardship'

The new president tackles the worst global economic crisis in 80 years while simultaneously seeking to overhaul the nation's health care system.

President Obama and Treasury Secretary Timothy F. Geithner at the White House, February 3, 2009.

For all intents and purposes, Barack Obama's presidency got underway more than a month before he actually took the oath of office on the steps of the United States Capitol. It was a bitterly cold Chicago day just a little more than a week before Christmas of 2008. A storm enveloped the city and made for an arduous journey for a team of economic advisers trudging through nine inches of snow to a meeting with the president-elect. Gathering in a generic government office being used for the transition, they sat with Obama around a set of sectional tables pushed together. A video screen on the wall beamed in other advisers from Washington.

The advisers delivered to Obama the sort of sobering news that would make anyone wonder why he wanted the job in the first place. Not only was the economy in free fall, which Obama knew – it was much, much worse than anyone had realized, and quite likely to get worse still. As in another Great Depression. Massive unemployment. Bread lines. A banking system on the verge of collapse. The auto industry as well. Actually, the advisers told Obama, it could turn out to be even grimmer than the Great Depression. More American families were tied to the markets than in 1929. Household wealth was falling faster than ever before. The American business sector was more dependent on the financial system.

In any White House, certain moments become etched into its creation myth, part of the narrative told again and again to explain a presidency. For Obama, the meeting on December 16, 2008, was one such moment. In the space of a couple hours, any residual feelings of euphoria over his historic election quickly vanished in a haze of statistics and forecasts that, when added up, spelled potential calamity for millions of Americans. In the years that followed, Obama's closest aides would look back at that meeting both to underscore the gravity of the situation that he faced coming into office and to understand the decisions that would flow from it. Even before putting his hand on Abraham Lincoln's Bible, Obama was forced to make critical choices about how he would respond to the crisis and what kind of presidency he wanted to have.

Little had prepared him for this moment. He might have been a former president of the Harvard Law Review and one-time community organizer with a compelling personal story, but Obama was then just four years out of the Illinois state legislature with no executive experience to speak of and little exposure to the sorts of monumental issues that cross the desk in the Oval Office every day of the week. At age forty-seven, he now had the fate of the world's last superpower resting on his shoulders. Calm and cerebral, he gave no indication to advisers that day of feeling overwhelmed, but some of them

September 29, 2008.

later felt that way themselves and they were convinced it left a mark on their leader. "That was a formative event," said David Axelrod, Obama's senior adviser. "Here's the incoming president with his economic team essentially being confronted with as bleak a report as anyone has gotten in generations."

None of this was what Obama anticipated when he first set out on his path to the White House. As he kicked off his campaign, he was running as the anti-Iraq war candidate, the apostle of hope and change, the unifier of Blue America and Red America, the antidote to eight years of George W. Bush. At the time Obama announced his candidacy, the economy was humming along, its fatal flaws unnoticed by most policymakers. But by the time he prevailed over John McCain in November 2008, Obama was confronted with an economic emergency the likes of which had not occurred since before he was born. He had no time for anything but on-the-job training.

In that fateful December meeting, he was presented with proposals for an economic stimulus package intended to jump-start the economy. This was a page out of John Maynard Keynes, pumping government money into the economy to promote growth, a mainstay of Democratic economic theory for decades. Christina Romer, tapped to chair the President's Council of Economic Advisers, told him the job would require $1.2 trillion in government spending and tax cuts, a jaw-dropping figure that was so inconceivable politically that she had been talked out of even putting it in the memo listing options. Instead, she and the other economic advisers recommended an $800 billion package, even then the largest in the nation's history. The stimulus would come on top of the hundreds of billions of dollars that Bush had already committed to save the banks in his final weeks in office and the billions more that would be required to keep the auto industry from falling apart.

Protesters in New York City, September 14, 2009.

But Obama did not want to simply be reactive. He had a long agenda of ambitious initiatives. He wanted to overhaul the health care system to cover millions of Americans without insurance coverage, revise immigration rules to provide a path to citizenship for many of those in the country illegally and put in place a new market-oriented system called cap-and-trade designed to curb the greenhouse gas emissions blamed for climate change. Rebuilding the economy while doing all of that would be a tall order for any president. Aides wondered whether Obama wanted to scale back some of his aspirations just to focus on the crisis immediately at hand.

No, he said. "I want to pull the Band-Aid off quickly, not delay the pain."

If nothing else, there would be plenty of pain.

The magnitude of the challenge facing him was evident a month later when he stood before as many as two million Americans gathered on a chilly day on Washington's National Mall on January 20, 2009, to be sworn in as the forty-fourth president of the United States. The celebration of his ascension was tempered by the task awaiting him.

The New York Stock Exchange, December 29, 2008.

Obama, the son of a black man from Kenya and a white woman from Kansas, inherited a White House built partly by slaves. The moment captured the imagination of much of the world as Obama recited the oath with his hand on the same Bible that Lincoln used at his first inauguration 148 years earlier. The sight of a black man climbing the highest peak electrified people across racial, generational and partisan lines.

But in his eighteen-minute Inaugural Address, Obama offered a grim assessment of "this winter of our hardship," a nation rocked by home foreclosures, shuttered businesses, lost jobs, costly health care, failing schools, energy dependence, climate change, two overseas wars and the threat of Islamic terrorism. It was time, he said, to "begin again the work of remaking America."

"Now there are some who question the scale of our ambitions, who suggest that our system cannot tolerate too many big plans," he acknowledged. "Their memories are short, for they have forgotten what this country has already done, what free men and women can achieve when imagination is joined to common purpose and necessity to courage."

Barack Obama was an unlikely avatar for that national purpose for all sorts of reasons beyond the color of his skin. Tall and thin, he had probing eyes that seemed to see everything and the cool, detached demeanor of a college professor. For a man with relatively little experience at the highest echelons of public life, he projected a preternatural self-assurance that even aides thought sometimes bordered on cockiness but that served him well through the ordeals of a marathon campaign in which he managed to take down two of the biggest names in American politics, first Hillary Clinton and then John McCain.

Born in Hawaii and abandoned by his father, Obama grew up far removed from the American mainland and the core American experiences of his generation. He was too young and geographically distant to undergo the traumas of the Vietnam and civil rights eras that left their marks on Clinton, McCain and other modern political leaders. Indeed, Obama was the first American president born too late to have served in the killing fields of Southeast Asia, and yet he spent a formative period of his own childhood living in Indonesia with his white mother, Ann Dunham, an anthropologist, as she moved to Jakarta to build a new life with a new husband.

After she sent him back home to Hawaii to live with her parents, Barry, as he was known then, attended Punahou Academy, the island's premier prep school, played basketball, earned academic honors, smoked marijuana with his friends and could not help but notice he was one of just a handful of black students in class. A little aimless and unsure of his place in the universe, he headed to the mainland for an education, first at Occidental College in Los Angeles and then as a transfer student at Columbia University in New York. After a period as a community organizer in Chicago, he earned his way into Harvard Law School, where he won election as the

Clockwise from top left: Baby Barack; mother and son in the 1960s; Stanley Dunham (left) with daughter Ann Dunham, grandchildren Maya and Barack; newlyweds in Hawaii, 1992; Harvard Law School; father and son in the 1970s.

Facing Republican insurgents, Obama responds, 'Elections have consequences, and Eric, I won.'

first African-American president of the prestigious law review in 1990 by assembling an odd-bedfellows coalition of liberals and conservatives and convincing both sides he would listen to their views with respect – the first but not the last time he would land on the pages of *The New York Times*. He went on to briefly work at a law firm and teach law part time at the University of Chicago, but a legal career was not in the offing as he was drawn to an exploration of race and his roots that generated an acclaimed early memoir, *Dreams From My Father*. His election to the Illinois State Senate led to an improbable candidacy for the United States Senate, propelled by a star turn at the Democratic National Convention of 2004 with his call for "a single American family."

Obama's stirring oratory underscored the key conundrums about his political identity. He could move audiences of tens of thousands in a football stadium to tears with his rhetoric, and yet in news conferences or policy talks come across as plodding and even patronizing. He could inspire strangers en masse but did not seem to especially enjoy them as individuals. He flashed an incandescent smile but was not a natural backslapper. He was an introvert who was drained after a public event to the point that some aides tried to make sure he had a few minutes alone to recharge before heading into his next appointment. He generated gales of anger among his many critics and yet was rarely roused to demonstrations of passion himself. He saw governance as the rational calculation of benefits and drawbacks in which different players could ultimately find mutual agreement.

Yet if Obama hoped to usher in a new era of bipartisanship as he took the oath, it would not last out the night. Even as he raced around town to ten inaugural balls that evening, about fifteen top Republicans, including rising stars like Representatives Eric Cantor of Virginia and Kevin McCarthy of California, gathered for dinner at the Caucus Room, a well-known Washington watering hole, to talk about how to rebound from their defeat. Central to their strategy would be standing against Obama's plans to expand government. The thinking was straightforward if calculating: Going along with Obama's plan, in addition to betraying their own conservative principles, would only ensure that Republicans remained the minority party. Opposing him, on the other hand, would pay off at the polls if he failed. And if he succeeded, the country would move on to other issues and not dwell on votes that did not matter.

For four hours, the Republican insurgents mapped out a campaign of resistance. "We've got to challenge them on every single bill and challenge them on every single campaign," McCarthy told the group, according to the author Robert Draper, who writes for *The New York Times Magazine*.

It did not take long for the first collision between the new president and his Republican opposition. With the economy bleeding 700,000 jobs a month, Obama would focus first on a massive stimulus package along the size that Christine Romer outlined, composed of public works spending, aid to beleaguered states, extended unemployment benefits and temporary tax breaks.

Obama assumed that at least some Republicans in Congress would embrace the plan, since it included tax cuts, but he overestimated their appeal. Three days after taking the oath, he invited to the White House congressional leaders from both parties, including Cantor and Representative John Boehner of Ohio, the House Republican minority leader, to talk about the recession.

Cantor came prepared and handed out a Republican plan. Obama preferred his own. The two exchanged words. Finally, Obama pulled out his trump card.

Twenty-four days after the inauguration, Congress passes a $787 billion stimulus package.

Eric Cantor on a break as Congress debated the stimulus bill, February 13, 2009.

"Elections have consequences," he said, "and Eric, I won."

Four days later, Obama planned to go to Capitol Hill to meet with the entire House Republican conference. As he prepared to leave the White House, an aide showed him a news story reporting that Boehner had just urged the conference to reject Obama's stimulus plan, without even waiting for him to make his case.

Miffed, Obama and the Democrats pushed through their program without Republicans. On February 13, just twenty-four days after the inauguration, the House passed a $787 billion package without a single Republican voting for it, and the Senate concurred with just three Republicans in favor. It was a remarkable achievement for a new president, passing the largest such economic package in American history in barely three weeks. The stimulus directed money to what Obama called "shovel-ready" road and bridge projects, clean-energy initiatives and the pockets of average taxpayers. It added red ink to the national debt but put many Americans back to work.

It also set the tone for the next eight years, poisoning relations between the president and his Republican opponents from the start. To Obama, it was a lesson in bad faith. The Republicans never intended to even consider working with him. To Republicans, it was a case study in a liberal "I won" president shoving his agenda down their throats. Neither side would forget.

As he embarked on his term, Obama assembled a team that blended his own most trusted advisers with veterans of Bill Clinton's administration as well as a few Republicans in search of that elusive spirit of bipartisanship.

"All the News That's Fit to Print"

The New York Times

Late Edition
Today, unseasonably mild, limited sun, high 60. **Tonight,** mild, rain arriving, low 48. **Tomorrow,** windy, clouds, a bit of sun, cooler, high 53. Weather map appears on Page B20.

VOL. CLVIII . . No. 54,583 NEW YORK, WEDNESDAY, FEBRUARY 11, 2009 $1.50

Bailout Plan: $2.5 Trillion and a Strong U.S. Hand

DOUG MILLS/THE NEW YORK TIMES

BANKING RESCUE, REDUX Treasury Secretary Timothy F. Geithner's speech and testimony drew a lukewarm response. Page B1.

Scant Details, and Wall Street Reacts With a 4.6% Plunge

By STEPHEN LABATON and EDMUND L. ANDREWS

WASHINGTON — The White House plan to rescue the nation's financial system, announced on Tuesday by Timothy F. Geithner, the Treasury secretary, is far bigger than anyone predicted and envisions a far greater government role in markets and banks than at any time since the 1930s.

Administration officials committed to flood the financial system with as much as $2.5 trillion — $350 billion of that coming from the bailout fund and the rest from private investors and the Federal Reserve, making use of its ability to print money.

Mindful of previous financial crises at home and abroad that became protracted because governments moved too slowly, Mr. Geithner pointedly criticized the Bush administration for not acting boldly and quickly enough.

But the initial assessment of the plan from the markets, lawmakers and economists was brutally negative, in large part because they expected more details.

Basic questions about how the various parts of the program would work, especially those involving the unsellable mortgages that banks are holding and preventing home foreclosures, were left for another day. Some Wall Street experts criticized the plan for relying too heavily on the same vague solutions proposed by the Bush administration.

The stock market, propped up for weeks on the expectation that Washington would finally deliver a comprehensive rescue plan, dipped almost as soon as Mr. Geithner began speaking in the morning. The Dow Jones industrial average fell 382 points, or 4.6 percent, by the time the market closed. Yields on Treasury bills dropped, indicating a flight from stocks to the safety of government bonds.

While traveling in Fort Myers, Fla., President Obama welcomed the news that the Senate voted 61-37 to approve its $838 billion economic stimulus bill Tuesday, but dismissed the market reaction to his bank rescue plan.

"Wall Street, I think, is hoping for an easy out on this thing and there is no easy out," Mr. Obama said in an interview with ABC News.

Many of the vital details of the program remain unsettled and are the subject of an intense behind-the-scenes debate.

The president himself had built up expectations that the plan would get ahead of the crisis — and not lurch from pillar to post as the Bush administration did last year, often in partnership with the New York Federal Re-

Continued on Page A22

TALKS ON STIMULUS Officials said the $838 billion economic plan could be finalized by the end of this week. PAGE A20

BREAKING RANKS The two Republican senators from Maine are wielding outsize power on the economic recovery plan. PAGE A20

A CLOSE BATTLE IN ISRAELI VOTE

Center and Right Vying to Form Government

By ETHAN BRONNER and ISABEL KERSHNER

JERUSALEM — Israel's centrist Kadima Party led by Foreign Minister Tzipi Livni and the more conservative Likud Party led by Benjamin Netanyahu were locked in a tight battle for leadership early Wednesday that left unclear the shape of the next Israeli government.

The close race all but guaranteed that the political jockeying to assemble a governing coalition would be intense and lengthy. And it left open the question of whether Ms. Livni, a supporter of a peace accord with the Palestinians, or the more hawkish Mr. Netanyahu would form the next government. Commentators predicted political chaos in the coming weeks. With 99 percent of the votes counted, Kadima was marginally ahead in the parliamentary elections, The Associated Press reported. But it was unclear if Kadima's lead would survive the final count, especially with the votes of soldiers still to be counted, or if the party could muster enough political partners for a stable coalition.

Mr. Netanyahu's party had been the front-runner in nearly all voter surveys for months, but the most recent public opinion polls showed the race tightening. In speeches to their followers early Wednesday, Mr. Netanyahu and Ms. Livni each claimed the right to form the next government.

With the latest vote tally in Tuesday's election, Kadima appeared to have 28 out of 120 parliamentary seats, and Likud appeared to have 27. The right-wing party Yisrael Beitenu of Avigdor Lieberman, which had been surging in recent weeks in the wake of Israel's three-week war in Gaza, stood at 15 seats, with the Labor Party of Defense Minister Ehud Barak at 13 seats.

Normally the leader of the party with the most votes is given the chance to form the next government, but the right-wing bloc, of which Likud is the largest par-

Continued on Page A12

'Vulture' Investors Eye Bad Assets, but Warily

By MICHAEL J. de la MERCED and ZACHERY KOUWE

Howard S. Marks is the sort of financier who Washington hopes will help fix the nation's tumbledown banks. Trouble is, he is not quite sure he wants the job.

Mr. Marks is a former banker who became a pioneer in the graveyard of Wall Street. He is one of the biggest players in distressed investing — putting money into risky investments that few others will touch.

But he and other potential investors are wary of the risk in this case.

With its plan to shore up banks that was announced on Tuesday, the Obama administration hopes to entice investors like Mr. Marks, who has $55 billion at his command, to buy troubled assets from the nation's banks and enable them to make the loans

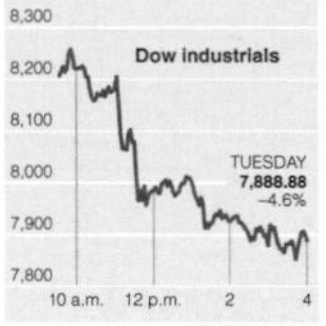

Source: Reuters THE NEW YORK TIMES

needed to jump-start the economy.

The administration hopes, in short, to counterbalance some of the fear gripping the financial world with a bit of old-fashioned greed.

To combat the bust, Washington wants to marshal some of the same financiers who grew rich during the boom: hedge fund managers and corporate buyout specialists.

But Mr. Marks and other investors like him said they were in no hurry to wade into this mess. Distressed investors — "vultures" is the Wall Street term for them — aim to buy investments on the cheap in hopes of reaping big returns.

Yet even for the vultures, the risks — political as well as financial — seem daunting. Some worry about being seen as profiteers who benefit at taxpayers' expense, even though the economy could get worse unless they swoop in.

"You have to ask whether this is an attractive deal," said Mr. Marks, the chairman of Oaktree Capital Management, a big money management firm in Los Angeles. It all depends on the price, the terms and the risks, he said. Wall Street, of course, wants

Continued on Page A22

KEY STEPS TO HELP BANKS AND CONSUMERS

Public-private investment fund for bad assets — **UP TO $1 TRILLION**
This fund would provide financing to private investors to encourage buying of mortgage-related and other troubled assets from banks.

Promotion of consumer and business lending — **UP TO $1 TRILLION**
A vast expansion of a previously announced program intended to support the market for student, auto, credit card and business loans. The program will provide financing to private investors who purchase these loans.

Additional capital for banks
Banks could tap the remaining funds in the $700 billion Troubled Asset Relief Program, or TARP. Institutions with more than $100 billion in assets would have to undergo a government "stress test." Recipients must show how they are preserving and strengthening lending.

Help for homeowners — **$50 BILLION**
Details of this effort to help millions of homeowners avoid foreclosure and renegotiate the terms of their mortgages are expected soon.

A complete list of all of the government's bailout efforts can be viewed at:
nytimes.com/business

In New Procedure, Artificial Arm Listens to Brain

By PAM BELLUCK

Amanda Kitts lost her left arm in a car accident three years ago, but these days she plays football with her 12-year-old son, and changes diapers and bearhugs children at the three Kiddie Cottage day care centers she owns in Knoxville, Tenn.

Ms. Kitts, 40, does this all with a new kind of artificial arm that moves more easily than other devices and that she can control by using only her thoughts.

"I'm able to move my hand, wrist and elbow all at the same time," she said. "You think, and then your muscles move."

Her turnaround is the result of a new procedure that is attracting increasing attention because it allows people to move prosthetic arms more automatically than ever before, simply by using rewired nerves and their brains.

The technique, called targeted muscle reinnervation, involves taking the nerves that remain after an arm is amputated and connecting them to another muscle in the body, often in the chest. Electrodes are placed over the chest muscles, acting as antennae. When the person wants to move the arm, the brain sends signals that first contract the chest muscles, which send an electrical signal to the prosthetic arm, instructing it to move. The process requires no more conscious effort than it would for a person who has a natural arm.

Researchers reported Tuesday in the online edition of The Journal of the American Medical Association that they had taken the technique further, making it possible to perform 10 hand, wrist and elbow movements, a big improvement over the typical prosthetic repertoire of bending the elbow, turning the wrist, and opening and closing the hand.

"It's dramatically impacted the field," said Stuart Harshbarger, a biomedical engineer at Johns Hopkins University who is the program manager for a military-financed prosthetics study that

Continued on Page A15

SHAWN POYNTER FOR THE NEW YORK TIMES

Amanda Kitts lost her arm in a car accident in 2006, but a new kind of prosthetic allows her to tie shoes at her day care center.

On the Trail of War Criminals, NBC News Stirs Up Criticism

By BRIAN STELTER

NBC News, which teamed up with local police officers to trap sex offenders for its successful but scandalous "To Catch a Predator" series, is now using similar tactics to hunt bigger game: war criminals.

But one of the first efforts, an investigation of a Maryland college professor on genocide charges, is already attracting criticism from federal officials months before the program would be broadcast.

For more than a year, NBC has been investigating the possible perpetrators of human rights abuses in several countries, but the case of Leopold Munyakazi, a visiting professor of French at Goucher College in Towson, Md., is the only one that has become public.

In December, an NBC crew and a Rwandan prosecutor confronted Mr. Munyakazi with charges that he had participated in that country's genocide in 1994.

Reached by telephone on Tuesday evening, Mr. Munyakazi vigorously denied the allegations.

"I have never participated in genocide. I saved a number of people," said Mr. Munyakazi.

The Department of Homeland Security said it had significant concerns "that a program of this kind could negatively impact law enforcement's ability to investigate and bring cases against the perpetrators of these horrible crimes." The Justice Department had no comment about the professor's case.

Mr. Munyakazi is one of at least four subjects that NBC News producers focused on in apparent cooperation with the Rwandan government. Some human rights advocates are objecting to NBC's investigation, alleg-

Continued on Page A16

NATIONAL A14-22

Peanut Investigation Widens
The closing of a peanut plant in Texas after tests indicated possible salmonella contamination threatens to widen one of the largest food recalls ever. PAGE A14

Charges on Stevens Evidence
An F.B.I. agent said evidence was improperly concealed in the trial of former Senator Ted Stevens of Alaska. PAGE A14

NEW YORK A25-29

Still at Odds at New School
Efforts by Bob Kerrey, the president of the New School, to muster faculty support have gained little traction. PAGE A25

INTERNATIONAL A5-13

Iranian Leader's Overture
Iran's president took up President Obama's invitation for direct talks between the United States and Iran. PAGE A5

A Tamil Beat For Sri Lanka
The rapper M.I.A. has branded herself as the voice of Sri Lanka's Tamil minority. But her politics rankle some who question her views on the country's separatist rebels. PAGE A5

BUSINESS DAY B1-12

Corrective Ads About the Pill
As part of a settlement, Bayer is running ads that clarify the side benefits of a birth control pill. Regulators say earlier ads played down the risks. PAGE B1

White-Collar Job Cuts at G.M.
Nearing a deadline for a recovery plan, G.M. adds 10,000 white-collar job cuts to buyouts it offered the union. PAGE B10

ARTS C1-10

Bloody, Cruel, Omnipresent
The characters in Lynn Nottage's play "Ruined," set in Congo, can't shut out the war. Ben Brantley reviews. PAGE C1

SPORTSWEDNESDAY B13-18

Best (and Oldest) in Show
Stump, a 10-year-old Sussex Spaniel, became the oldest dog to be named Best in Show at Westminster. PAGE B15

Images from the dog show.
nytimes.com/sports

DINING D1-10

A Quicker Taste of Home
For New Yorkers who grew up in cultures where cooking was time-consuming, a more harried lifestyle requires adjustments for dinner. PAGE D1

Who's Got the Check?
In a recession, lunch mates are not grabbing for the check. PAGE D1

EDITORIAL, OP-ED A30-31

Thomas L. Friedman PAGE A31

0 354613 9

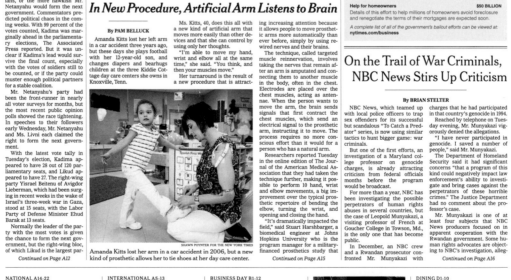

Most prominent among his selections was none other than his primary rival, Hillary Clinton, whom he tapped for secretary of state. He convinced Robert Gates, Bush's widely respected defense secretary, to stay on, and tapped Timothy Geithner, the Federal Reserve governor from New York who had been instrumental in fashioning the response to the financial crisis under Bush, to take over as Treasury secretary. Inside the White House, Obama installed Rahm Emanuel, a provocative and profane congressman from Chicago, as White House chief of staff and convinced Lawrence Summers, who was Bill Clinton's Treasury secretary, to accept the far less prestigious position of national economic adviser.

But not all of Obama's choices worked out well. He nominated Tom Daschle, the former Senate majority leader and a mentor to Obama, to be secretary of health and human services, a post he would use to shepherd through the new president's health care program. But reports that Daschle had failed to pay $128,000 in taxes for the use of a car and driver as he advised clients about how to influence government actions exemplified the very cashing-in culture that Obama had vowed to dismantle. Daschle withdrew and Obama admitted that he "screwed up" by thinking he could exempt someone from his standards just because he trusted him. As it happened, Daschle was not the only tax scofflaw on the Obama team. Geithner owed $34,000 in back taxes but still managed to win confirmation, perhaps because of the urgency of the economic situation. And an analyst Obama had hired from the McKinsey & Company management consultant firm dropped out after disclosing that she failed to pay taxes for a nanny. Asked later what surprised him most about becoming president, Obama said sardonically, "The number of people who don't pay their taxes."

It also took three tries to find a commerce secretary. His first choice, Governor Bill Richardson of New Mexico, was dropped because of an investigation into state contracts given to a political donor. (The probe resulted in no indictments, but not before derailing Richardson's trip to the Cabinet.) Obama's second choice, Senator Judd Gregg, a Republican from New Hampshire, accepted in the spirit of bipartisanship, but then quickly reversed himself and pulled out, citing "irresolvable conflicts" with the president's approach to the stimulus. Frustrated, Obama turned back to a Democrat, Gary Locke, the former governor of Washington State.

But Obama had little time to stew about such setbacks. Even with the stimulus in place, he faced the prospect of further aftershocks in the economy. One potential blow to the nation was the imminent collapse of the auto industry, with the Big Three automakers reporting their worst monthly sales in a quarter-century the same week Obama was elected. Two of the three, Chrysler and General Motors, were running on the fumes of last-minute loans issued by Bush to tide them over until Obama could take office and decide what to do.

The auto industry crisis would test the boundaries of Obama's activist approach and the acuity of his political instincts. When was it appropriate for the federal government to come to the rescue of private businesses? Did the auto sector play a critical too-big-to-fail role in the economy and therefore demand intervention as the banks did? What sort of conditions could the administration impose on the companies in exchange for assistance? How far did the government want to get into the business of making cars anyway? As it was, thanks to the broader bailout program initiated by Bush and continued by Obama, the government already owned a fair share of the nation's banking and insurance sectors.

'Nobody had ever done what we were about to do.'

Obama had little sympathy for the troubled automakers, seeing their troubles as a function of their own "failure to adapt to changing times," as he put it. But advisers convinced him that letting Chrysler and G.M. slide into an unstructured bankruptcy would set off a ripple effect through the whole chain of suppliers and vendors, leaving tens of thousands out of work and undercutting the goal of his own stimulus program. So Obama agreed to save the automakers as long as they submitted viable plans to Washington to overhaul themselves and return to profitability. He also forced out Rick Wagoner, the G.M. chief executive, making him a high-profile symbol of accountability. "All the advisers were divided; the public was absolutely against it," Rahm Emanuel said. "Nobody had ever done what we were about to do. And he picks the hardest option."

In case he did not have enough on his plate in his opening months as president, Obama soon was presented with another challenge – and opportunity. Justice David Souter, an anchor of the liberal wing of the Supreme Court, retired, opening a seat for Obama to fill. After culling through forty possible candidates and interviewing the top four finalists, Obama in May nominated Sonia Sotomayor, a federal appeals judge from New York who would become the first Hispanic member of the high court and only the third woman to sit on the bench.

Obama was impressed by Sotomayor's life story. She grew up the daughter of Puerto Rican parents living in a Bronx public housing project, worked her way into Princeton and Yale and served as a prosecutor, corporate litigator and federal district judge before joining the United States Court of Appeals for the Second Circuit in New York. Casting her as the embodiment of the American dream, Obama opened a confirmation campaign that he intended to wage over biography more than ideology.

But if the president assumed that Republicans would be loath to

Addressing a town meeting in Elkhart, Indiana, February 9, 2009.

oppose a Hispanic candidate for fear of alienating a growing voter bloc, he misjudged. Sotomayor, known for bracing candor and lively wit, found her past words coming back to haunt her. Republican senators focused on a lecture she delivered in 2001 describing how her background shaped her jurisprudence. "I would hope that a wise Latina woman with the richness of her experiences would more often than not reach a better conclusion than a white male who hasn't lived that life," she said then. At a conference four years later, she said that a "court of appeals is where policy is made." Taken together, the comments were interpreted by critics as a sign that she would try to impose her values and make policy from the bench rather than follow the letter of the law.

'We just put the first Latina on the Supreme Court. Pretty cool, huh?'

Given that Sotomayor would replace Souter, her appointment would not significantly shift the balance of power on the divided court, and she ultimately performed well at her confirmation hearings, explaining away her statements by insisting they did not mean she would put her thumb on the scale of justice. After a ten-week battle fueled by well-funded interest groups on both sides, the Senate confirmed Sotomayor, 68 to 31, on August 6, with nine Republicans joining every Democrat who participated in voting for her.

It was late on that Thursday when word of the vote arrived at the White House, where most officials had already begun to clear out. Obama strode out of the Oval Office and down the hall looking for someone with whom to savor the victory. He found David Axelrod and gave him a fist bump.

"We just put the first Latina on the Supreme Court," Obama exulted. "Pretty cool, huh?"

Still, he was a little disappointed not to find more aides. "He was frustrated because there weren't enough of us around," Axelrod said later. "He was seeking out people to celebrate with."

By that summer, there was little else to celebrate. Not content to simply put out economic fires, Obama was pressing ahead with a series of far-reaching initiatives that would fundamentally restructure American society. But progress had been slower than he had imagined.

His theory of the case was that the country was trapped in a bubble-and-bust cycle, cascading from one artificial, unsustainable boom to the next. He wanted not just to apply a short-term patch but to erect a more durable system with a stronger set of rules. He and his team even came up

With Senator Edward Kennedy at an Obama rally in Washington, DC, January 28, 2008.

F or health care,
a market-oriented
plan rather than a full
government takeover.

with a name for his program – the New Foundation, a rather awkward and self-conscious takeoff of Franklin D. Roosevelt's New Deal. Nearly every president since F.D.R. had tried to devise a pithy term to describe his collective ideas, some more successfully than others (think Lyndon B. Johnson's enduring Great Society versus Bill Clinton's quickly forgotten New Covenant). The New Foundation did not trip off the tongue any better than George W. Bush's Ownership Society, and it also quickly disappeared as a branding effort.

But the notions underlying it did not. Obama wanted to overhaul the nation's health care, energy, education and immigration systems and he wanted to move ahead while he still had political momentum. The fact that the country was in turmoil might actually make it easier, he reasoned, because the system would be so eager to avoid a repeat of the crisis that it would welcome change. As Rahm Emanuel put it, "You never want a serious crisis to go to waste."

The White House pushed ahead on several fronts as part of a "big-bang" strategy, but the area where it applied the most muscle was health care. More than 45 million Americans had no health insurance, costs were rising far faster than inflation and even many of those who did have coverage were frustrated by policies that left them on their own for their particular ailments. For more than a century, presidents from Theodore Roosevelt and Harry Truman to Richard Nixon and Bill Clinton had unsuccessfully sought to redesign the health care system with the goal of universal coverage. Obama was determined to succeed where they had failed.

In deciding how to proceed, Obama eschewed a full-scale government takeover of health care along the lines of Britain or Canada and instead, drawing on ideas once promoted by the conservative Heritage Foundation, designed a market-oriented program to help working families pay for private insurance. Insurance marketplaces would be set up in each state so that Americans could compare plans and purchase policies that met certain minimum standards. Those with less income would get subsidies to help make coverage affordable. Medicaid would be expanded to cover those who were poor but not so destitute to qualify otherwise. The plan would also require insurers to cover pre-existing conditions and allow adult children to be covered on their parents' plans.

For policy and political reasons, Obama jettisoned some of the promises he had made during the campaign. On the trail, he had castigated Hillary Clinton for proposing a mandate requiring everyone to have insurance, only to conclude now that he was in office that she was right after all, because the only way to pay for expanded coverage of the sick was to force the young and healthy to contribute into the system. He had likewise criticized John McCain for proposing to tax high-value insurance plans provided by employers, only to reverse course and adopt just such a tax as part of his program. Obama's vow to provide a "public option" – that is, a government-sponsored health plan to compete with private plans, in theory forcing everyone to lower costs – sounded like too much government for the moderates he was wooing, so he dropped it, much to the consternation of liberals. And to win over powerful opponents, Obama cut a deal with pharmaceutical giants agreeing to block the import of cheaper medicine from Canada in exchange for an $80 billion industry commitment to expand coverage, a tradeoff that upset reformers.

Rather than force the plan through Congress right away on the strength of his Democratic majorities, as he had done with the stimulus package, Obama let lawmakers take their time with it in hopes of attracting Republican support. But the delay nearly proved fatal. When Republican lawmakers returned home for the August recess, they found themselves under siege from conservative constituents livid that they might go along with such a major government intrusion into the private sector. Obama's chances were not helped by distortions of the plan, such as the widely spread myth that it would create "death panels" to decide which patients would receive treatment and which would be left to die. But the heat at those summer town hall meetings reflected a growing libertarian uprising against Obama's expansion of government that was dubbed the Tea Party movement after the Boston Tea Party. And even as Obama was on the defensive, he lost his most important ally, Senator Edward Kennedy of Massachusetts, the longtime liberal stalwart, who died of a brain tumor on August 25, just shy of his goal of finally passing universal health care legislation.

Losing a trusted ally and gaining a group of new antagonists.

Before Congress even returned to Washington, Obama's health care program seemed to be on life support. Rahm Emanuel went to the president day after day in August urging him to pull back and narrow his goals. Rather than push for a comprehensive plan that might go down to defeat, Emanuel advised, try instead for a "skinny" bill that focused on covering low-income children and families and would be easier to pass. Bill Clinton had adopted such an incremental strategy after his own sweeping health care proposal failed in the 1990s, and by the time he left office he had made important progress in providing medical services for children. If Obama insisted on pressing for the whole program, Emanuel warned, it would be at a cost to his other priorities. "That means a lot of this other stuff is going to get sidelined in the process," he said.

Obama met with the rest of his team to discuss the matter. He went around the room and, one by one, his advisers listed all of the obstacles to

Judge Sonia Sotomayor meets with President Obama and Vice President Joe Biden at the White House, May 26, 2009.

passing the more expansive health care plan. Finally, Obama came back to his legislative director, Phil Schiliro.

"So can we do this?" Obama asked.

"There's a path," Schiliro said. "But it's like the Clint Eastwood movie. Do you feel lucky?"

"My name is Barack Obama, I'm a black man and I'm president of the United States," he answered. "Of course I feel lucky."

'When you try to do big things and make big changes, it stirs passions and controversy.'

Having decided to press ahead for the full plan, Obama and his allies spent all that fall of 2009 grinding it out on Capitol Hill. Obama rallied Democrats and all but gave up on Republicans. He made it the central test of his presidency – and made clear to Democrats that they could not afford to let him fail. Emotions ran so high that when he delivered an address to a joint session of Congress pitching his health care plan, a backbench Republican representative, Joe Wilson of South Carolina, shouted out, "You lie!" in the middle of the speech.

In November, House Democrats muscled through the bill, 220 to 215, just two votes more than a majority. Seven weeks later, on Christmas Eve, Senate Democrats followed suit on their own version, garnering the bare-minimum sixty votes needed to overcome a Republican filibuster. It was not always pretty. The deal with the pharmaceutical industry was followed by deals with individual senators, including an advantage on Medicaid financing for Nebraska to win the vote of Senator Ben Nelson, a sweetener that Republicans branded the "cornhusker kickback."

For another president, that would just be business as usual. But for Obama, who promised to end business as usual, the means cheapened the ends. Suddenly, he no longer looked like the reformer who would slay the dragons of Washington but just another deal-making pol who would cut whatever corners were necessary to get what he wanted. He had not conquered the system. The system had conquered him. "There's a constant tension between the need to get things done within the system as it is and the commitment to change the system," David Axelrod reflected. "Finding that line at any given moment is really, really difficult."

In this case, all the horse-trading had not even finished the matter. The House and Senate versions of the bill were different, meaning they had to be reconciled and voted on again before the program could become law. But after a grueling few months, Obama was satisfied that he was getting to where he wanted to go. As he headed off to spend the holidays in his home state of Hawaii, he had no idea that the whole thing would come unraveled thanks to a former underwear model in a pickup truck.

The unexpected hitch came, of all places, in the deep-blue liberal bastion of Massachusetts, where a special election in January 2010 to fill Kennedy's Senate seat took a surprise turn. Scott Brown, a Republican state senator who once posed semi-nude for *Cosmopolitan* magazine, pulled off an upset after traveling around the state in his GMC Canyon assailing Obama's big-government health care plan. Not only was Brown's triumph seen as the first voter repudiation of Obama since his election, it also cost the Democrats their sixtieth vote in the Senate, depriving them of the unilateral power to break a filibuster and pass legislation at will.

Obama and his staff were in shock. By the end of his first year in office, they had expected not only to have overhauled the health care system but also to have restructured the energy industry to fight climate change, reined in Wall Street with a new regulatory structure, closed the prison at Guantánamo Bay, Cuba, and at least made some progress on liberalizing immigration policy. None of that had happened. Instead, the president's approval ratings had fallen by more than twenty percentage points, unemployment remained higher than even the worst initial White House forecast and Obama's legislative agenda had stalled.

The day after Brown's victory, Obama seemed resigned to retreat. Maybe it was time to return to the "core elements" of the health care plan, he mused publicly. But he quickly stiffened again, authorizing aides to walk back his comments and insist he did not necessarily want a scaled-back program.

A week later, he went before Congress again for his State of the Union address and vowed to press on. "I don't quit," he said. But he pleaded for patience from disappointed supporters. "I campaigned on the promise of change – 'change we can believe in,' the slogan went," he said. "And right now, I know there are many Americans who aren't sure if they still believe we can change – or that I can deliver it. But remember this. I never suggested that change would be easy or that I can do it alone. Democracy in a nation of 300 million people can be noisy and messy and complicated. And when you try to do big things and make big changes, it stirs passions and controversy. That's just how it is."

With Republicans emboldened, Obama felt he had no choice but to lean on his Democratic majorities. In the end, they came up with a bit of legislative legerdemain to push the health care program through. Since Republicans could now filibuster any revised plan in the Senate, Obama convinced House Democrats to simply approve the version already passed by the Senate without changes. That would send it immediately to the president's desk without another vote in the Senate. Then they could pass changes to the program that House Democrats wanted by inserting them into a separate spending bill that under Senate rules could not be filibustered and therefore needed only fifty-one votes instead of sixty.

Republicans cried foul. "The American people are angry," John Boehner declared. The bill was a "fiscal Frankenstein," said Representative Paul Ryan of Wisconsin. Representative Virginia Foxx of North Carolina called it "one of the most offensive pieces of social engineering legislation in the history of the United States."

House Minority Leader John Boehner behind a copy of the Democrats' health care proposal, October 29, 2009.

The path to passage relied on the sort of gamesmanship that candidate Obama might have decried if he were on the other side of the issue but one that President Obama chose to accept.

When the votes were taken that Sunday, March 25, 2010, Obama was gathered in the Roosevelt Room with top aides. Among those on hand to watch on television with him was Hillary Clinton, who had made health care her big push as first lady more than fifteen years earlier. Obama now was finally realizing the dream she had failed to fulfill. After the final tally was called and health care was passed, he rose to his feet and led a standing ovation, then hugged Clinton to celebrate the culmination of their mutual efforts.

With the hour approaching midnight, Obama invited his team for a champagne toast on the Truman Balcony of the White House overlooking the South Lawn and, in the distance, the Washington Monument. The mood was loose and happy. All the hard work, all the ups and downs, the near-death experiences and the comebacks—it had finally paid off.

Obama seemed more relaxed and cheerful than his aides had seen him since the election.

This is better than Election Day, he told them.

Why? someone asked.

Because the whole point of the election was to get to do things like this.

With the health care victory in hand, Obama looked for one more while he still had political capital. The cap-and-trade climate change program had passed the House but was mired in the Senate. No one seemed ready to move on an immigration plan. The biggest opportunity seemed to be new regulations governing the financial institutions that had plunged the country into the Great Recession.

Inside his team, Obama's advisers debated whether to break up the nation's biggest banks, but opted against it. For a time, it looked like Democrats and Republicans might be able to come up with a bipartisan plan. But then, to the chagrin of its own negotiators, the White House decided to turn up the volume and make it a public issue to use against the Republicans. Recoiling, Republicans ratcheted up their opposition.

Flexing the remaining muscles of their majorities, Obama's Democratic allies pushed through a new set of rules named for the two main Democratic sponsors, Senator Christopher Dodd of Connecticut and Representative Barney Frank of Massachusetts. The new Dodd-Frank law expanded federal regulations to more financial institutions and cracked down on derivatives, the complex form of securities that helped trigger the crash of 2008. It also created a new federal consumer protection agency to keep watch on the banks and other financial firms.

Banks and other businesses complained that Dodd-Frank went too far; liberal activists complained it did not go nearly far enough. But Obama took what he could get, with just a few Republican votes. "Because of this law, the American people will never again be asked to foot the bill for Wall Street's mistakes," he said as he signed it into law. "There will be no more taxpayer-funded bailouts. Period."

The Bush era was now over. For better or worse, it was now definitively the Obama era.

Editing a speech on health care before a joint session of Congress, September 9, 2009.

Greeting soldiers at Camp Victory outside Baghdad, April 7, 2009.

CHAPTER II

'Bring Our Troops Home'

An unlikely wartime president faces conflicting choices in trying to remove American forces from Iraq even as he orders more troops to Afghanistan.

On the first Veterans Day he marked as commander in chief, President Obama visited Arlington National Cemetery and wandered among the chalky white tombstones commemorating those who had fallen in the rugged mountains of Central Asia and the scorching deserts of the Middle East. Stern and silent, he kept his thoughts to himself as he stared at the simple markers representing the sacrifices of eight years of war. But he was acutely aware that these would not be the last.

After he was done, Obama headed back to the White House and marched into the Situation Room for the eighth meeting of a long, torturous review in which he was weighing whether to send thousands more young men and women into harm's way. He had come to office determined to end what he called the "dumb war" in Iraq but vowing to make a renewed effort to win the "good war" in Afghanistan. This would be the critical meeting where he shaped the course of his presidency as a wartime commander, essentially settling on a plan to send reinforcements to Afghanistan while setting a limit on how long they would stay.

It was an audacious decision, one that fully pleased neither side in the long-running national debate about security in the wake of the attacks of September 11, 2001. The left objected to doubling down on a guerrilla war with no visible end on the horizon. The right complained that setting a deadline for the additional troops allowed the enemy to simply wait them out. But on Obama's mind were the costs, including those at Arlington and the injured troops he had met at Walter Reed National Military Medical Center in Washington. "I don't want to be going to Walter Reed for another eight years," he had said when visiting wounded soldiers a few weeks earlier.

Obama was an unlikely wartime president, a onetime community organizer whose rise was powered in large part by his opposition to the invasion of Iraq. He was the first president in four decades to inherit a shooting war already raging the day he took office – two, in fact, plus subsidiaries. Along the way, he confronted some of the biggest decisions a president is forced to make, even as he gave every impression of being a reluctant warrior. He demonstrated in the opening period of his presidency that he was willing to use force to advance national interests, tripling forces in Afghanistan, authorizing secret operations in Yemen and Somalia and escalating drone strikes in Pakistan.

But Obama did not see himself as a war president the way his predecessor did. He rarely talked about the wars in public in any extended way, resolving not to let them define his presidency. While George W. Bush

United States troops bound for Afghanistan, April 5, 2010.

saw the conflicts in Iraq and Afghanistan as his central mission as well as opportunities to transform critical regions of the world, Obama saw them as "problems that need managing," as one adviser put it, just some of many, in fact, that needed to be weighed against each other on the scale of national priorities. The result was an uneasy balance between a president wary of endless overseas commitments and a military worried that he was not fully invested in the cause.

"He's got a very full plate of very big issues," said Defense Secretary Robert Gates, the holdover from Bush's Pentagon, "and I think he does not want to create the impression that he's so preoccupied with these two wars that he's not addressing the domestic issues that are uppermost in people's minds."

Obama was an eleven-year-old boy in Hawaii when the last American combat troops left Vietnam, too young to have participated in the polarizing clashes of that era or to have faced the choices the previous two presidents did about serving in the military. "He's really the first generation of recent presidents who didn't live through that," said David Axelrod, his senior adviser. "The whole debate on Vietnam, that was not part of his life experience."

Taking over as president of a country at war, Obama had a steep learning curve. He was taught basics like military ceremonies and titles. He surfed the Internet at night to look into the toll on troops. His campaign recruited retired generals to advise him. He learned how to salute. But it still took time to adjust when he became president. The first time he walked into a room of generals as commander in chief, he was taken back when they stood. "Come on, guys, you don't have to do that," he said, according to an aide.

Perhaps his most important tutor was Gates, the first defense secretary ever kept on by a president of another party. They were an unlikely pair, a forty-seven-year-old Harvard-trained lawyer and a sixty-five-year-old veteran of cold war spy intrigues and Republican administrations. But they were both known for unassuming discipline, and they bonded in the many hours spent around the conference table in the Situation Room.

Obama relied on Gates as his ambassador to the military and deferred to him repeatedly in the opening months of his presidency. When Gates wanted to force out General David McKiernan as commander in Afghanistan in favor of General Stanley McChrystal, Obama signed off. Likewise, cognizant of Bill Clinton's ill-fated effort to end the ban on gay and lesbian soldiers, Obama let Gates set a slow pace in overturning the "don't ask, don't tell" policy that barred them from serving openly, even though he disappointed gay rights advocates by not being more aggressive.

Just as keeping Gates provided political cover against the Democrats' historically weak-on-defense image, Obama surrounded himself with uniformed officers. He kept Bush's war coordinator, Lieutenant General

Douglas Lute, and tapped General James Jones, the former Marine Corps commandant and NATO commander, as his national security adviser, Admiral Dennis Blair as director of national intelligence and Lieutenant General Karl Eikenberry as ambassador to Afghanistan.

It was not an approach that would work out. Oddly passive for a four-star general, Jones was eclipsed by younger aides he scorned as "the water bugs" before being eased out. Blair clashed with White House officials and the C.I.A. director, Leon Panetta, only to find himself fired. Lute never enjoyed the same influence he had in the Bush White House, and Eikenberry ran afoul of his ostensible boss, Secretary of State Hillary Clinton, over the Afghan surge.

An unlikely pair bonds in the White House Situation Room.

Obama had little time to even figure out where the Situation Room was before he was asked to make two huge war-and-peace decisions. Bush left behind a request from General McKiernan to send 30,000 more troops to Afghanistan, deferring to the new president to decide whether to follow through. After a quick review, Obama agreed just four weeks after taking office to send 17,000 troops as reinforcements. Ten days after that, he flew to Camp Lejeune in North Carolina to announce that he would pull out combat forces from Iraq by August 2010 and the rest of American troops by the end of 2011.

The president's priorities were clear in how he announced the two decisions. The Afghan reinforcement was disclosed in a written statement and not treated as a seismic event, generating relatively modest news coverage and little public debate. The Iraq withdrawal, on the other hand, was presented as a historic turning point with television-friendly pictures of the president addressing a crowd of stoic Marines clad in camouflage. "We will complete this transition to Iraqi responsibility, and we will bring our troops home with the honor that they have earned," Obama said.

Although Obama did not acknowledge it, his Iraq withdrawal plan essentially followed the blueprint left behind by Bush. Before he left office, Bush signed a strategic pact with Iraq agreeing to pull American troops out of major cities by June 2009 and leave the country entirely by the end of 2011. Obama retained both of those targets and simply added an intermediate step for combat forces. Even on that, he compromised on the sixteen-month withdrawal of combat troops he had promised on the campaign trail, accepting a nineteen-month time frame instead in deference to Gates and the generals, who wanted more time.

President Obama with Defense Secretary Robert Gates at Cabinet meeting, June 22, 2010.

Special forces carry wounded Afghan National Army soldier, December, 2010.

In announcing the Iraq withdrawal, Obama hailed General David Petraeus, the former Iraq commander, and the military for turning the war around without mentioning the Bush surge of troops and strategy change from 2007 that many credited – and that Obama had opposed as a senator. Nor did he mention that he was about to follow a similar strategy in Afghanistan.

I f Obama thought his quick dispatch of extra forces to Afghanistan in February would buy him time, he soon realized how wrong he was. Within weeks, the military was back, asking for 4,000 more troops. Obama approved the request, bringing the total new forces he had sent to 21,000. But he became wary of mission creep and suspicious of a military hierarchy that he thought was trying to manipulate him. By that summer of 2009, Stanley McChrystal, now installed as commander, was back pressing for even more troops – as many as 40,000 more. If the United States hoped to repeat the counter-insurgency strategy used by Petraeus in Iraq, McChrystal argued, he would need a substantial increase in combat firepower.

Under Bush, the war effort in Afghanistan had always been a small-footprint affair, with just 15,000 to 30,000 American troops at any one time, aided by small numbers of NATO forces in support of a rudimentary Afghan army whose soldiers seemed to run away more than they fought. After the Taliban fell in the months after September 11, 2001, the presumption of victory in Afghanistan led the Bush administration to siphon American resources and attention to Iraq, and the low-grade guerrilla war petered along without resolution until late in his presidency, when it appeared the enemy had taken the upper hand.

With McChrystal now seeking further reinforcements, Obama decided he wanted a more comprehensive assessment than the rushed one he had received in his first weeks in office. The three-month review that followed proved a case study in decision making in the Obama presidency – intense, methodical, rigorous, earnest and at times deeply frustrating for nearly all involved. It was a virtual seminar in Afghanistan and Pakistan, led by a president described by one participant as something "between a college professor and a gentle cross-examiner."

Obama peppered advisers with questions and showed an insatiable appetite for information, taxing analysts who prepared three dozen intelligence reports for him and Pentagon staff members who churned out thousands of pages of documents. He invited competing voices to debate in front of him and guarded his own thoughts until near the end of the process. Obama devoted so much time to the Afghan decision in the fall of his first year – nearly eleven hours on the day after Thanksgiving alone – that he joked, "I've got more deeply in the woods than a president should, and now you guys need to solve this."

The outsize personalities on his team vied for his favor, sometimes

Villager in Marja, Afghanistan, at compound seized by United States Marines, February 13, 2010.

sharply disagreeing as they made their arguments. Gates and Clinton pressed in favor of more troops, while Vice President Joseph Biden, James Jones and Rahm Emanuel, as well as Tom Donilon and Denis McDonough, both deputy national security advisers, were more dubious. Obama came to feel that the military, led by McChrystal, Petraeus and Admiral Mike Mullen, the chairman of the Joint Chiefs of Staff, was trying to game the process – "box in the president," in the parlance used in the White House – by leaking details of the review and exaggerating the impact of not sending more troops. The military and State Department, for their part, suspected Emanuel, McDonough and other White House aides of leaking themselves to undercut the case for more troops.

Prodded by his staff, Obama started the review skeptical of McChrystal's request. Having dinner at Donilon's house one night, Emanuel wandered into the library and asked what he should be reading as they thought about what to do in Afghanistan. Donilon showed him a copy of *Lessons in Disaster*, the Gordon Goldstein book about McGeorge Bundy and the slow, disastrous slide into Vietnam. Emanuel read it and later made sure others in the White House did as well, including Obama. The conclusion they drew from the book was that Presidents John F. Kennedy and Lyndon B. Johnson failed to question the underlying assumptions about monolithic Communism and the domino theory, prompting Obama and his advisers to rethink the nature of Al Qaeda and the Taliban.

Biden encouraged this re-examination, arguing that while Al Qaeda was a threat to the United States, the Taliban really was not. He offered an alternative to a large troop buildup that would focus on counterterrorism and training Afghan forces rather than the broader mission of population protection and nation building envisioned by the McChrystal request.

Fueling the skepticism of a large troop buildup was the economic cost. The Office of Management and Budget predicted that a surge of 40,000 troops on top of existing forces plus commitments to nation-building projects like electricity and schools would push the expense of the American venture in Afghanistan to $1 trillion over the following ten years. Obama found himself in sticker shock, watching his domestic agenda vanish in front of him.

Adding to his worries was the mercurial leadership of Afghan President Hamid Karzai, who often seemed overtly hostile to his American allies and flirted with Taliban leaders. In the midst of the White House review, Karzai prevailed in a re-election campaign marred by widespread corruption, only reminding Obama what a problematic partner he was investing in. David Petraeus described the Karzai government as "a crime syndicate." Karl Eikenberry, in a classified cable, said that Karzai "is not an adequate strategic partner" and "continues to shun responsibility for any sovereign burden."

But McChrystal had the most important advocate in the Situation

Hamid Karzai in Kabul, July 25, 2016.

Room in Gates. A seasoned hand at such reviews, Gates had served eight presidents and cycled in and out of the Situation Room since the days when it was served by a battery of fax machines. His low-wattage exterior masked a wily inside player, and he knew enough to keep his counsel early in the process to let it play out. He had a strong ally in Clinton, who if anything seemed even more hawkish than Gates did.

'What I'm looking for is a surge. This has to be a surge.'

Recognizing that it would be politically difficult for Obama to agree to the entire request for 40,000 troops, Gates developed an option that would send 30,000 instead, reasoning that NATO could make up most of the difference. Warned that anything less would risk the success of the project, Obama was inclined to accept the compromise, but he was frustrated that the Pentagon was projecting a long timetable for the deployment. He wanted the extra troops to arrive within six months, just as they had for Bush's Iraq buildup. "What I'm looking for is a surge," he told advisers. "This has to be a surge."

Obama gathered his team at 8:15 p.m. three days before Thanksgiving in a Situation Room strewn with coffee cups and soda cans. The late hour added to the momentous feeling. Obama presented a revised version of Gates's plan titled "Max Leverage" calling for 30,000 more troops to arrive by mid-2010. When combined with earlier troop increases, he would be tripling the total force in Afghanistan. But unlike Bush, he was not making an open-ended commitment. He wanted to start withdrawing the surge troops by July 2011 – two years after the arrival of the first reinforcements he dispatched shortly after taking office. His theory was that if the effort was not working after two years, it probably was not going to work at all.

A few days later, he told his advisers that he was ready to approve such a plan. He went around the room one last time to let anyone voice dissent.

"I'm not asking you to change what you believe," he said. "But if you do not agree with me, say so now."

No one said anything.

"Tell me now," Obama repeated.

The advisers fell in line.

"Fully support, sir," Mike Mullen said.

"Ditto," added David Petraeus.

With the decision made, Obama wanted to announce it at an appropriate setting. Flying to West Point in New York on December 1, 2009, Obama addressed 4,000 cadets at the United States Military Academy, at least some

United States soldier during helicopter raid, Alam Khel, Afghanistan, 2011.

DOUG MILLS/NEW YORK TIMES

of whom could be sent into harm's way by the new plan. "If I did not think that the security of the United States and the safety of the American people were at stake in Afghanistan, I would gladly order every single one of our troops home tomorrow," he told them in a prime-time address televised to the nation. "So no, I do not make this decision lightly." But he argued that the comparison to Vietnam was "a false reading of history."

After setting a course for the troops, a surprise honor.

"Let me be clear: None of this will be easy," he added. "The struggle against violent extremism will not be finished quickly, and it extends well beyond Afghanistan and Pakistan. It will be an enduring test of our free society and our leadership in the world."

But he also sent a signal that his commitment was not unlimited. He instructed his speechwriters to include a quote from President Dwight Eisenhower, the hero of World War II, to make the point that the Afghanistan operation would have to compete with other priorities, presumably like health care and economic stimulus – a balancing that only he, as president, could make. "I must weigh all of the challenges that our nation faces," Obama said. "I don't have the luxury of committing to just one. Indeed, I'm mindful of the words of President Eisenhower, who, in discussing our national security, said, 'Each proposal must be weighed in the light of a broader consideration, the need to maintain balance in and among national programs.'"

General Stanley A. McChrystal reviews troops at his retirement ceremony, Fort McNair in Washington, July 23, 2010.

Barely a week later, Obama boarded Air Force One again, this time to deliver a speech in a very different setting. On an overnight flight to Oslo, the president who had just escalated his nation's eight-year-old war in Afghanistan scratched out what he wanted to say when he collected the Nobel Peace Prize.

The juxtaposition could hardly have been more powerful or perplexing. While he did not like to think of himself this way, Obama was in fact a wartime president and while he had set course to pull troops out of Iraq he was sending more to Afghanistan. He had also ordered a dramatic surge of unmanned drones over the skies of Pakistan to launch missiles at presumed terrorist targets and had retained some other controversial national security policies of his predecessor.

As Obama was greeted by trumpets and presented to the king and queen of Norway for the honor, his challenge was squaring the circle, explaining how a commander in chief could be a champion of peace, how a

General David H. Petraeus, second from left, walks behind President Obama with Vice President Biden and Admiral Michael Mullen following the announcement that Petraeus would replace General Stanley A. McChrystal, June 23, 2010.

of whom could be sent into harm's way by the new plan. "If I did not think that the security of the United States and the safety of the American people were at stake in Afghanistan, I would gladly order every single one of our troops home tomorrow," he told them in a prime-time address televised to the nation. "So no, I do not make this decision lightly." But he argued that the comparison to Vietnam was "a false reading of history."

After setting a course for the troops, a surprise honor.

"Let me be clear: None of this will be easy," he added. "The struggle against violent extremism will not be finished quickly, and it extends well beyond Afghanistan and Pakistan. It will be an enduring test of our free society and our leadership in the world."

But he also sent a signal that his commitment was not unlimited. He instructed his speechwriters to include a quote from President Dwight Eisenhower, the hero of World War II, to make the point that the Afghanistan operation would have to compete with other priorities, presumably like health care and economic stimulus – a balancing that only he, as president, could make. "I must weigh all of the challenges that our nation faces," Obama said. "I don't have the luxury of committing to just one. Indeed, I'm mindful of the words of President Eisenhower, who, in discussing our national security, said, 'Each proposal must be weighed in the light of a broader consideration, the need to maintain balance in and among national programs.'"

General Stanley A. McChrystal reviews troops at his retirement ceremony, Fort McNair in Washington, July 23, 2010.

Barely a week later, Obama boarded Air Force One again, this time to deliver a speech in a very different setting. On an overnight flight to Oslo, the president who had just escalated his nation's eight-year-old war in Afghanistan scratched out what he wanted to say when he collected the Nobel Peace Prize.

The juxtaposition could hardly have been more powerful or perplexing. While he did not like to think of himself this way, Obama was in fact a wartime president and while he had set course to pull troops out of Iraq he was sending more to Afghanistan. He had also ordered a dramatic surge of unmanned drones over the skies of Pakistan to launch missiles at presumed terrorist targets and had retained some other controversial national security policies of his predecessor.

As Obama was greeted by trumpets and presented to the king and queen of Norway for the honor, his challenge was squaring the circle, explaining how a commander in chief could be a champion of peace, how a

General David H. Petraeus, second from left, walks behind President Obama with Vice President Biden and Admiral Michael Mullen following the announcement that Petraeus would replace General Stanley A. McChrystal, June 23, 2010.

president prosecuting war could practice diplomacy, how a man who signed deployment orders for soldiers could follow in the footsteps of the Rev. Dr. Martin Luther King and Mohandas Gandhi. For Obama, it was a chance to explore the concept of a "just war" as debated through the ages.

"As someone who stands here as a direct consequence of Dr. King's life work, I am living testimony to the moral force of non-violence," Obama said. "I know there's nothing weak, nothing passive, nothing naïve in the creed and lives of Gandhi and King. But as a head of state sworn to protect and defend my nation, I cannot be guided by their examples alone. I face the world as it is, and cannot stand idle in the face of threats to the American people. For make no mistake, evil does exist in the world. A non-violent movement could not have halted Hitler's armies. Negotiations cannot convince Al Qaeda's leaders to lay down their arms. To say that force may sometimes be necessary is not a call to cynicism – it is a recognition of history, the imperfections of man and the limits of reason."

Obama was only the third sitting president awarded the Nobel Peace Prize, after Theodore Roosevelt, who won for brokering an end to the Russo-Japanese War, and Woodrow Wilson, who won for negotiating the Versailles Treaty after World War I. The difference was that Obama's prize was more of a promissory note than a reward for past service. The committee gave him the prize for "extraordinary efforts to strengthen international diplomacy and cooperation between peoples," but even Obama did not think he had done enough to merit it in just the first few months of his presidency.

"To be honest," he said in the Rose Garden on the day the committee made its announcement, "I do not feel that I deserve to be in the company of so many of the transformative figures who have been honored by this prize, men and women who've inspired me and inspired the entire world through their courageous pursuit of peace."

If anything, the prize was a reminder of the gap between the ambitious promise of his words and his actual accomplishments to that point. It drew attention to the fact that while much of the world was celebrating him as the anti-Bush, he had not broken as fully as he had once implied he would from the previous administration's national security policies. And it set off another round of mocking criticism from opponents who chafed at what they saw as Obama's charmed and entitled rise.

"The real question Americans are asking is, 'What has President Obama actually accomplished?'" Michael Steele, the chairman of the Republican National Committee, said after the announcement.

No one at the White House had prepared for the prize. Word of it arrived at the White House in the form of an e-mail message from the Situation Room at 5:09 a.m., Friday, October 9, 2009, with the subject line, "item of interest."

Shortly before 6 a.m., Robert Gibbs, the White House press secretary, telephoned Obama, awakening him with the news.

The White House had no idea how to handle what was a decidedly mixed burden. Some thought Obama should turn it down in recognition that he had not yet earned it. Others thought that would be rude and inappropriate, that the prize could be a spur to achieving what it set out to honor. "I'd like to believe that winning the Nobel Peace Prize is not a political liability," David Axelrod said shortly after the announcement. "But this isn't something I gave a moment of thought to until today."

In the end, on that October day, Obama chose to present it as an honor to America more than him. But it was lost on no one that he ended the day closeted with his national security team talking about escalating the war in Afghanistan.

PHOTO COURTESY OF JO-IN TERRY

Obama's three-month Afghan review became a case study, in effect, for a new commander in chief coming to grips with the office. For Obama, like most of his predecessors, the presidency was learned one day at a time. The complexities of policy, the nuances of politics, the clashing interests of competing factions, the trade-offs of any decision — all that took time to master. As he settled into the job, Obama developed his own style and rhythm, yet there were unconscious parallels to those who had occupied the office before him.

In some ways, he seemed like a cross between his two most immediate predecessors. Like Bill Clinton, he enjoyed digging into the details of policy, consumed long memos and books on issues confronting him and solicited views from around the table, as he did during the Afghan review. He had little patience when briefers recited what had already been presented to him on paper. "I've already read that," he would snap. He zeroed in on the one aide sitting in the back of the room who had remained quiet during a discussion, insisting that he or she give a view. Yet like Clinton, he could also be slow to make decisions as he wrestled with the complexities and nuances of a given issue, sometimes to the point of aggravating aides.

Like George W. Bush, Obama preferred a disciplined operation and prized punctuality. He occasionally even started a meeting early, although the longer his presidency went on the more his fidelity to finishing on time seemed to slip. While he sometimes took his time to decide, Obama was like Bush in that once a decision was made, he rarely looked back. He did not revisit policies after they were set, wondering whether he had made the right call, and he did not invite appeals from the losing side of any internal debate. He was a linear thinker, unlike Clinton, whose mind ranged widely and creatively, often seeing connections that others did not. And like Bush, Obama relied mainly on a close-knit team of advisers he trusted, like Valerie Jarrett, David Axelrod, David Plouffe, Denis McDonough and Benjamin Rhodes; he was not one to make midnight calls around Washington seeking input from a variety of outside figures as Clinton would do.

Lieutenant Commander John Terry, an amputee, does lunges with President Obama at the Walter Reed National Military Medical Center in Bethesda, Maryland.

Members of Company K rest at an airfield in Helmand Province, Afghanistan, hours before an attack on suspected Taliban positions in Marja, February 12, 2010.

TYLER HICKS/NEW YORK TIMES

OLIVIER MORIN/AGENCE FRANCE-PRESSE/GETTY IMAGES

President Obama receiving the Nobel Peace Prize medal from Thorbjorn Jagland,
chairman of the Nobel committee, in Oslo, December 10, 2009.

If the people around him learned a lot about Obama from the Afghan review, the president took away his own lessons that would shape the rest of his time in office. In the end, he gave the military most of what it wanted but it left a bitter taste in the Oval Office. Already convinced that Bush had given the military too much latitude, Obama came away from his first year in office believing that the generals were playing politics with him. Robert Gates reassured Obama that the various leaks and public comments that had stirred the president's ire were happenstance with no ulterior motive. But Gates understood the suspicions. "My position was this is not a deliberate attempt to jam the president," he said later. "It's indiscipline."

Rolling Stone *drops a bombshell that angers the White House.*

Still, Gates bristled at what he thought were untoward efforts by White House officials to dictate to commanders. He resented it when Obama dispatched Denis McDonough to Haiti after a 2010 earthquake to monitor military rescue efforts. "That was a degree of micromanagement I found intolerable," Gates said later. Gates grew so annoyed at White House officials bypassing him to call combatant commanders directly that he ordered a dedicated line at military headquarters in Afghanistan pulled out. He instructed commanders to refer presidential aides to him. "And by the way, they were to say go to hell," Gates said.

It was against this backdrop that Obama's press secretary, Robert Gibbs, walked over to the private quarters of the White House one evening in June 2010. He had with him a copy of an article by Michael Hastings in *Rolling Stone* magazine profiling General McChrystal. "Stanley McChrystal, Obama's top commander in Afghanistan, has seized control of the war by never taking his eye off the real enemy: the wimps in the White House," read the magazine's summary of the article. The text quoted McChrystal aides disparaging Obama, Biden, James Jones and others. McChrystal himself was, by and large, not the author of the offensive statements, but he clearly had assembled a team that openly showed disrespect to the commander in chief.

The article set off anger in the White House. McChrystal tried to head off the furor by calling Biden on Air Force Two and, in a brief and confusing conversation over a scratchy connection, warned the vice president that there would be an article coming out that he might not like. Biden was baffled until his staff managed to find a copy. Aides to the president began talking about how the general should be fired. Obama, inclined to agree, ordered McChrystal to fly back from Afghanistan to explain himself.

While McChrystal made the fourteen-hour flight home, a series of meetings at the White House sealed his fate. Gates appealed to Obama to spare McChrystal, afraid that sacking the Afghan war commander at this stage of the surge operation would undercut the mission. But when Obama suggested that he might replace McChrystal with David Petraeus, Gates accepted the decision.

McChrystal arrived at the White House on June 23 with a resignation letter in hand. During a twenty-minute conversation with Obama, he apologized. But the president accepted the letter. Then he summoned Petraeus, who happened to be in the building for a separate meeting anyway, and offered him the job. Petraeus took it without taking time out to call his wife first.

Not since President Harry S. Truman fired General Douglas MacArthur during the Korean War had a commander in chief cashiered a top general for insubordinate behavior. The dramatic clash set the tone for Obama's relationship with the military for years to come.

"I welcome debate," he said, "but I won't tolerate division."

Calling on former Presidents Bush and Clinton to help with the devastating earthquake in Haiti.

Port-au-Prince neighborhood virtually leveled after a 7.0 magnitude earthquake in January, 2010.

DAMON WINTER/NEW YORK TIMES

CHAPTER III

'Time to Turn the Page'

A near-miss domestic airplane bombing provides a chilling wake-up call to re-examine the nation's security.

P resident Obama was singing Christmas carols with his family at a lavish rental house in Hawaii, celebrating the end of his first year in office, when a military aide arrived with head-snapping news. Someone had just tried to blow up a plane over Detroit, the aide reported. Breaking away from his yuletide respite, Obama got on the telephone with his counterterrorism adviser back in Washington, who told him that a twenty-three-year-old Nigerian man aboard Northwest Airlines Flight 253 had attempted to ignite chemicals hidden in his underwear, only to have passengers and crew members jump him before the improvised bomb could go off.

If not for the quick thinking and instinctive courage of a group of civilians, America would have endured another devastating airborne terrorist attack in the opening year of another presidency. Beyond the nearly 300 people on board, hundreds more on the ground could easily have been killed by the wreckage of a demolished airliner plummeting into a big city. More than eight years, two overseas wars, millions of airport pat-downs and hundreds of billions of dollars after the crucible of September 11, the near-miss in the skies over Michigan brought home the grim reality that Islamic radicals determined to wage holy war on America and its allies not only had not been defeated but were branching out in dangerous and unpredictable ways.

The initial public response by Obama and his team was less than sure-footed. While the president conducted regular conference calls with his national security team, it took him three days to emerge from seclusion in his island vacation to address the matter in public and, when he did, he was typically cool and cerebral rather than visceral and reassuring. Obama deemed Umar Farouk Abdulmutallab, the Nigerian by then universally called the underwear bomber, an "isolated extremist," and Janet Napolitano, his secretary of homeland security, declared that "the system worked." Neither assertion was true. Abdulmutallab was affiliated with Al Qaeda in the Arabian Peninsula, a branch of the original terror group operating in Yemen, and the young man's own father had warned American officials about him. Worse, after all the post-September 11 reforms, the government possessed conversations intercepted by the National Security Agency that it failed to distribute widely enough to stop him.

In private, Obama was angry at the breakdown. "Let me make this very clear to you," he told advisers on the phone. "While I understand intelligence is hard and I'll never fault anybody for not having full intelligence, what I will fault is when we have full intelligence that's not shared."

After hanging up, aides scrambled to organize a fresh statement to reporters. Denis McDonough, the national security aide, typed out a draft on the president's laptop in Hawaii as an impatient Obama hovered over his shoulder.

"What's the deal?" Obama asked, agitated at the delay.

"I'm just about done," McDonough said.

"Well, just move over," Obama said.

The president sat down and finished it himself. His eventual statement acknowledged a "systemic failure" but it did not quell the political furor that followed and Obama and his team were caught off guard by the intensity of the criticism.

The Christmas bombing attempt proved a searing turning point, forcing Obama to re-examine his assumptions about the nation's security. "The fact that this guy came as close as he did – basically the detonator didn't work – and the fact that we hadn't detected it in advance really came as a shock to them," said John McLaughlin, a former deputy C.I.A. director who later participated in a review of the incident for the administration.

Obama preserves the bulk of his predecessor's counterterrorism strategy.

Obama was the first president to take office in the Age of Terror ushered in by September 11, and he inherited two struggles from George W. Bush – one with Al Qaeda and its ideological allies and another that divided his own country over issues like torture, prosecutions and what it meant to be an American. The first had proved complicated and daunting. The second made the first look easy.

Obama's approach to terrorism had been either a dangerous reversal of the Bush years or a consolidation of them, depending on who was talking. In fact, he adopted the bulk of the counterterrorism strategy that he found on his desk when he arrived in the Oval Office, but it was a strategy that Bush had already moderated from the earliest days after September 11. Obama refined it further, but did not scrap it, managing the unusual trick of angering both former Vice President Dick Cheney and the American Civil Liberties Union at the same time.

Obama was seeking the space where he felt most comfortable, splitting the difference on a tough issue and presenting it as the course of reasoned judgment rather than dogmatic ideology. Where Bush saw black and white, Obama saw gray. Where Bush felt it in his gut, Obama thought about it in his head. Where Bush favored swagger, Obama was searching for a more supple blend of force and intellect. Where Bush saw Islamic extremism as an existential threat akin to Nazism or Communism, Obama believed that overstating the threat had played into terrorists' hands by elevating their stature and allowing them to alter the nature of American society even without another successful attack.

Rather than seeing terrorism as the challenge of his time, Obama rejected the phrase "war on terror" altogether, hoping to recast the struggle

Anwar al-Awlaki at Dar al-Hijrah mosque, where he served as imam, Falls Church, Virginia, 2001.

as only one of a number of vital challenges confronting America. The nation was at war with Al Qaeda, he would say, but not with terrorism, which, after all, was a tactic, not an enemy. Perhaps the biggest change Obama made at first was what one adviser called the "mood music" – the choice of language, outreach to Muslims, rhetorical fidelity to the rule of law and a shift in tone from the with-us-or-against-us days of the Bush administration.

As a matter of emphasis and atmospherics, if not policy, the shift was stark. "You've got almost two extremes," reflected Henry Crumpton, who led the C.I.A.'s operation in Afghanistan after September 11 and later served as the State Department's counterterrorism chief under Bush. "You've got Bush 43 who aspired to have a warrior's ethos. He was driven, I think, by that, and in some ways it hurt us with the lack of rigor and examination of some of the consequences of our actions, Iraq being the most horrible example. Obama comes at it from the other extreme. He comes at it like a lawyer would, someone who may not accept and may even reject this idea of a warrior's ethos. And it is a war. You've got guys out there who want to kill us."

Obama was a state senator in Illinois when the planes smashed into the World Trade Center, the Pentagon and an empty field in Pennsylvania. He was driving to a legislative hearing in Chicago when he heard early reports on the radio. As he arrived, he found that tall buildings in Chicago were being evacuated out of fear of further attacks. "Up and down the streets, people gathered, staring at the sky and at the Sears Tower," he recalled in a memoir.

That day instilled in Bush a sense of unwavering purpose, but Obama's support for the pursuit of Al Qaeda in Afghanistan gave way to doubts about the circumvention of legal structures at home in the name of security. As a Harvard Law School graduate who taught constitutional law and spent part of his childhood growing up in Indonesia, the world's most populous Muslim nation, Obama saw the emerging global campaign through a different lens. By the time he won his Senate seat in Washington and set his sights on the White House, Obama was calling for a new paradigm. "It is time to turn the page," the candidate said.

His own inauguration offered a case study in how hard that would be. In the days before his swearing in, intelligence agencies picked up reports that a group of Somali extremists was planning to cross the border from Canada to detonate explosives on the National Mall in Washington as the new president took the oath of office. With more than a million onlookers on hand and hundreds of millions more watching on television around the world, what could be a more inviting target? Obama's incoming team sat in the Situation Room with Bush's outgoing team as they evaluated the threat and tried to figure out how to prevent it.

As it happened, the threat turned out to be a "poison pen" case, when one group of radicals ratted out another to get the Americans to take out rivals. But for a fledgling president, it was what his adviser David Axelrod called a "welcome-to-the-N.B.A. moment before the first game," not to mention a lesson in the fluid, murky nature of terrorism. The challenge, as the episode made clear, was more than just hunting down bad guys; it was distinguishing between what was real and what was illusion – and determining the balance between acknowledging danger and projecting confidence. For Obama, finding that balance would be a test throughout his presidency.

For a new president, a 'welcome to the N.B.A moment.'

He came in promising to correct what he considered the excesses of his predecessor, signing executive orders drafted by his new White House counsel, Gregory Craig, banning interrogation techniques like waterboarding and ordering the closure of the prison at Guantánamo Bay, Cuba within a year. While Craig and others argued that it was important to send a signal of change from the start, other aides, like John Podesta, the new president's transition chief, worried about taking on such fights at the risk of distracting from larger priorities, like fixing the economy.

To change the dialogue with the Muslim world, Obama made a point of giving an interview to Al Arabiya television network a week after taking office and delivered a much-touted speech in Cairo in June 2009 reaching out to those who believed in Islam. To break with the past and demonstrate transparency, he authorized the release of secret Justice Department memos from the Bush era detailing the use of waterboarding and other techniques that Obama had now banned.

But there were limits. When Craig and others wanted to release photographs of abuses by American interrogators in response to a court challenge, Defense Secretary Robert Gates and the military objected on the grounds that they would inflame radicals and endanger American troops. General Ray Odierno, the top commander in Iraq, made a personal appeal to Obama during a visit to Washington. Obama sided with the commanders and ordered the photos kept secret.

Small wonder that the debate was more vigorous than Obama's liberal supporters might have expected. In addition to Gates and Odierno, Obama was still surrounded by veterans of the Bush era, including Admiral Mike Mullen, the chairman of the Joint Chiefs of Staff; Michael Vickers, the assistant defense secretary for special operations; Stephen Kappes, the deputy C.I.A. director; Michael Leiter, the director of the National Counterterrorism

KIRSTY WIGGLESWORTH/ASSOCIATED PRESS

United States Predator drone over Kandahar Air Field, southern Afghanistan, January 31, 2010.

Detainees in outdoor recreation areas at the prison in Guantánamo Bay, August 20, 2014.

Center; Lieutenant General Douglas Lute, the White House war coordinator; Daniel Fried, an assistant secretary of state under Mr. Bush now tapped to manage the effort to close Guantánamo; Stuart Levey, the under secretary of the Treasury in charge of chasing terrorist financing; Nick Rasmussen, the National Security Council's senior director for combating terrorism at the White House; and General David Petraeus, who started the administration as head of the Middle East regional command before Obama tapped him to replace Stanley McChrystal in Afghanistan.

Perhaps most important was John Brennan, a career C.I.A. official and former station chief in Saudi Arabia known for setting up the National Counterterrorism Center for Bush. Obama had originally eyed Brennan to be C.I.A. director, but his chances were sunk by liberal protests over his ties to the old order, so instead he was made assistant to the president for homeland security and counterterrorism, a position that did not require Senate confirmation. Solidly built, with a weathered face and close-cropped, retreating hair, Brennan looked the part of a terrorist fighter. And he soon became one of Obama's most trusted advisers, hoping to correct what he saw as the mistakes of the Bush administration while defending his agency against what he considered an overreaction by his critics.

He and Obama were helped in this by none other than Bush, who had pulled back some of the more radical tactics used in the terror war before leaving office. Long before Obama showed up at the White House, Bush had halted waterboarding, emptied the secret C.I.A. black site prisons where terror suspects had been held incommunicado overseas, and secured bipartisan congressional approval for restructured versions of his warrantless surveillance program and military commission system. Bush had even declared that he wanted to close Guantánamo and, while he did not succeed, his team released or transferred about 500 detainees in pursuing that goal.

Obama built on those changes without overturning the whole security apparatus he inherited. He left the surveillance program intact, embraced the Patriot Act, retained authority to use renditions to spirit suspected terrorists out of other countries and embraced some of Bush's claims to state secrets. Obama preserved the military commissions and national security letters he criticized during the campaign, albeit with more due-process safeguards. While he once decried the indefinite detention of terror suspects without charge, now he felt compelled to approve the continued and essentially permanent imprisonment of about fifty Guantánamo inmates deemed most dangerous without ever bringing them to trial. And he dramatically expanded Bush's campaign of unmanned drone strikes against suspected Al Qaeda targets in the tribal areas of Pakistan, authorizing more in his first year in office than his predecessor did in his entire eight-year administration. "The C.I.A. gets what it needs," Obama said during an early meeting in the Situation Room.

In an assessment that Obama the candidate might not have made on the campaign trail, Obama the commander in chief acknowledged that he had inherited from Bush a more measured set of security policies than commonly perceived. "I would distinguish between some of the steps that were taken immediately after 9/11 and where we were by the time I took office," he told *New York Times* reporters on Air Force One. "I think the C.I.A., for example, and some of the controversial programs that have been a focus of a lot of attention, took steps to correct certain policies and procedures after those first couple of years."

To Republicans, the measures are a validation, but some Obama backers are outraged.

The acceptance of elements of the Bush strategy, however, outraged some of Obama's fervent backers on the left who accused him of selling out. At a private meeting with civil libertarians and liberal activists, Obama got an earful. "Look, you're the only politician I've ever believed in," Anthony Romero, the director of the A.C.L.U., told him, according to others in the room. "When I was a gay Puerto Rican growing up in New York, I never thought I could identify with a political leader the way I identify with you. But this stuff really pains me."

To some Republicans and veterans of the Bush administration, Obama's approach was something of a validation after so many years of being criticized by armchair terrorist hunters. "The administration came in determined to undo a lot of the policies of the prior administration," said Senator Susan Collins of Maine, the top Republican on the homeland security committee at the time, "but in fact is finding that many of those policies were better-thought-out than they realized – or that doing away with them is a far more complex task."

Still, others on the right took no solace from Obama's mixed approach, choosing to focus on the change rather than the continuity. No one was more vocal than Cheney, who had quietly fought a rear-guard action against Bush's own moves toward moderation while the two were still in office. Now that he was a private citizen watching a Democratic president taking them further, Cheney felt free to voice his discontent publicly. At one point, he excoriated the new president's policies in a split-screen, near-simultaneous address even as Obama was speaking elsewhere in Washington defending his actions. Cheney was most agitated at Attorney General Eric Holder's decision to re-investigate whether C.I.A. officers violated anti-torture laws in their interrogations of terror suspects, even though a previous investigation had been closed without charges. To Holder, this was a straightforward

President Obama with counterterrorism chief John O. Brennan at the White House, December 14, 2012.

President Obama and Vice President Biden flank Supreme Court nominee Elena Kagan, May 10, 2010.

DOUG MILLS/NEW YORK TIMES

matter of accountability and rule of law. To Cheney, it was selling out loyal soldiers who followed orders in the interest of protecting the country at a perilous time.

Objections grew even louder when Obama planned to bring Guantánamo inmates to an American prison in Illinois so that the island facility could finally be closed. Even a preliminary move provoked a furor underscoring the difficulty facing Obama. Gregory Craig, the White House counsel, and others decided to try a test case involving several Chinese Uighurs who were not affiliated with Al Qaeda or the Taliban and had been swept up by mistake, but could not be sent home to China where they might be persecuted. When Craig proposed resettling them in the United States, congressional Republicans revolted and, with Democratic support, voted in May 2009 to ban the administration from transferring prisoners from Guantánamo to American shores.

Shock at Fort Hood: soldiers shot by a fellow soldier with extreme Muslim beliefs.

A year came and went and still Guantánamo had not been closed as promised; indeed, a plan by Holder to bring Khalid Sheikh Mohammed, the mastermind of the September 11 attacks, to New York for trial eventually collapsed amid vociferous complaints about security and precedent. Obama's failure to shutter Guantánamo and resolve the cases of its inmates became a sore point not only for him but for many liberals who blamed him for lack of commitment to the values he ostensibly advocated. By the end of the year, Craig, their favorite champion inside the White House, stepped down in frustration.

The debate over how to handle terrorism came at the same time that the nature of the threat seemed to be evolving. On November 5, 2009, a United States Army officer with extreme Muslim beliefs opened fire at fellow troops at Fort Hood in Texas, gunning down dozens of people in a rampage that left twelve soldiers and a civilian dead. The officer, Major Nidal Malik Hasan, an Army psychiatrist, later told authorities that he was trying to protect Taliban leaders in Afghanistan from American troops before they were sent to the war zone to fight "against the Islamic Empire." It was a shocking turn of events – soldiers mowed down not on a foreign battlefield but on their home post by one of their own.

Obama flew to Texas to lead an outdoor memorial service, standing in front of thirteen sets of boots, rifles, helmets and photographs to symbolize the thirteen victims. One by one, he listed the names of those killed and described their hopes and dreams and the families they left behind. "It may be hard to comprehend the twisted logic that led to this tragedy," he told thousands of soldiers and relatives gathered at the nation's largest Army post. "But this much we do know: No faith justifies these murderous and craven acts. No just and loving God looks upon them with favor. For what he has done, we know that the killer will be met with justice, in this world and the next."

Yet while he linked the massacre to a twisted interpretation of faith, Obama did not use the word terrorism or Islam in his speech, nor did he address the larger questions raised by the tragedy: How did an American soldier become so radicalized in the first place? Did this count as an international terrorist attack? And if so, what could the country do to protect itself against enemies within?

A single link emerges in a series of attacks and failed attacks.

The danger of terrorism seemed more insidious as a new generation of homegrown extremists emerged. During the first year of Obama's presidency, authorities arrested a number of American citizens and legal residents plotting attacks. Among them was Najibullah Zazi, an airport-shuttle driver trained in Pakistan who went to New York near the anniversary of the September 11 attacks intent on mounting what he called a "martyrdom operation" by blowing up himself and others on the subway with a homemade bomb. Authorities also arrested David Coleman Headley, a Pakistani-American who aided terrorist attacks in Mumbai, India; a group of Somali-Americans from Minnesota who wanted to fight in Somalia; and five American Muslims from Virginia who traveled to Pakistan to join the jihad there.

Tying together several of the threats was a single American-born radical cleric named Anwar al-Awlaki, who after September 11 initially preached moderation and then left the United States for Yemen, where he became a leading figure in Al Qaeda in the Arabian Peninsula. Awlaki was an increasingly powerful voice in extremist circles, attracting a large following with audio-taped lectures, a Facebook page and web site, particularly in the English-speaking world, where he was that rare Al Qaeda figure with fluent and even colloquial command of the language. Acolytes made the pilgrimage to Yemen to meet with him. Authorities in the United States, Britain and Canada found Awlaki's calls for violence on the laptops of nearly every suspected terrorist they arrested.

Abdulmutallab, the underwear bomber, told the F.B.I. that his attempted plot was approved and partly directed by Awlaki. Hasan, the Fort Hood shooter, was inspired by the radical cleric and sent him email messages asking his views on the religious justification for killing American soldiers, although Awlaki was noncommittal in his responses. Zazi, the would-be subway suicide bomber, testified that he was radicalized by Awlaki's message, listening to more than 100 hours of taped lectures by the American cleric and another extremist imam. Clearly, Awlaki and his disciples with blue passports or green cards were going to be a recurring threat for Obama's presidency.

Obama was still determined to put that threat in perspective and not let it consume his administration, but he emerged from the string of events acutely aware how serious they were. After the attempted Christmas bombing, his press secretary, Robert Gibbs, consciously or not, used the term war on terror. And Obama made almost as many statements about terrorism in the two weeks following the foiled plot as he had in the eleven months preceding it.

"Our nation is at war," he declared the day after New Year's.

"We are at war," he said again five days later.

As Obama tried to navigate the treacherous politics of national security, he faced other challenges that put his leadership to the test. In January 2010, just a few weeks after the failed airplane bombing, a monster earthquake ravaged Haiti, collapsing buildings and killing as many as 300,000 people in what was already one of the most impoverished nations on the planet.

The killer quake measured 7.0 on the Richter scale, making it the most powerful to hit Haiti since the eighteenth century and leaving in its wake unfathomable scenes of destruction and death. Obama responded as American presidents do, with expressions of grief and promises of aid. He dispatched an aircraft carrier and thousands of American soldiers to help with relief efforts and committed the first of what would become $4 billion for humanitarian relief and longer-term reconstruction.

Although his decision to send his aide, Denis McDonough, aggravated Robert Gates, who saw it as micromanagement, Obama opted to recruit far and wide for help. In keeping with tradition, he tapped two predecessors, George W. Bush and Bill Clinton, to lead a fund-raising drive. The former presidents taped a commercial in the White House Map Room appealing to Americans for help, joined their names in a new web site to organize public efforts and appeared together on five Sunday talk shows. Ultimately, all the public and private American efforts would go a long way toward helping in the short term, but the long-term results would be mixed at best, as Haiti remained mired in corruption, poverty and conflict.

No sooner had Obama put a response in place for Haiti than he faced another seismic event, this one at the intersection of politics and the law. A

A soldier prays a day after the shooting at Fort Hood, Texas, November 6, 2009.

*Fire rages on Deepwater Horizon in
the Gulf of Mexico, April 21, 2010.*

year after Obama appointed Sonia Sotomayor to the Supreme Court, Justice John Paul Stevens announced his retirement, opening a second seat for the president to fill. Stevens, the oldest of the justices and the leader of the liberal wing for many years, gave Obama months of notice to find a replacement, but the president did not have to search far for his candidate. He picked Elena Kagan, his own solicitor general, naming a second woman in a span of two years.

Another Supreme Court nomination, and a disaster in the Gulf of Mexico.

Kagan had never been a judge and would be the first new member of the Supreme Court without prior experience on the bench in nearly forty years, breaking the hold of what some called the judicial monastery on the high court. Many justices in earlier generations had not previously served as judges, but in recent times, experience on the bench had become a virtual requirement. On the other hand, Kagan preserved the Ivy League monopoly on the court. A graduate of Princeton and Harvard, she had worked as a policy aide in Clinton's White House before becoming the first woman to serve as dean of Harvard Law School. She was also the first woman appointed as solicitor general, a position often called the tenth justice because its occupant argues the government's cases before the Supreme Court. The Senate confirmed Kagan after only a modest fight, in part because, like Sotomayor, her appointment effectively replaced a liberal with a liberal and did not shift the balance on the court.

That victory for Obama, though, was overshadowed, at least in the short term, by another disaster on America's southern flank. An explosion on an oil rig in the Gulf of Mexico in April 2010 killed eleven workers and unleashed a gusher of oil and methane gas from an uncapped wellhead a mile beneath the surface. What started as a human tragedy soon transformed into an environmental catastrophe as millions of gallons of oil spread through the area and washed up on the shores of Louisiana and elsewhere along the coast.

For eighty-seven days, the spill at BP's Deepwater Horizon platform seemed to confound Obama, defying his best efforts to stanch the leak and appear in command. As powerful as a president may be, the spill demonstrated that there were limits, and many compared Obama's uncertain response to Bush's handling of Hurricane Katrina. Even the president's eleven-year-old daughter, Malia, seemed baffled by his inability to fix the problem. "Did you plug the hole yet?" she asked him one morning in the bathroom while he was shaving. It would not be until July, nearly three months later, that he would.

Critics in both parties piled on. A web video posted by the National Senatorial Republican Committee spliced Obama's own "never again" words about Katrina together with liberal commentators demanding that he do something about the oil spill. Among them was James Carville, the flamboyant Democratic strategist and television pundit who had a home in Louisiana. "He just looks like he is not involved in this," Carville groused. "Man, you got to get down here and take control of this and put somebody in charge of this thing and get this thing moving. We're about to die down here."

Obama employed most of the tools of his office to respond. He imposed a deep water drilling moratorium, traveled repeatedly to the region to demonstrate solidarity, fired the director of an ineffectual regulatory agency and appointed a commission to study what had happened. He held a news conference to acknowledge responsibility, saying he "was wrong" to assume that oil companies were prepared for the worst as he authorized expanded offshore drilling. He conceded that his administration did not move with "sufficient urgency" to reform regulation of the industry, that in the case of the BP spill it "should have pushed them sooner" to provide images of the leak, and that "it took too long for us" to measure the size of the spill.

Finally, on June 15, nearly two months after the explosion, Obama summoned cameras to make the first prime-time Oval Office address of his presidency, reassuring the nation that he was fully engaged in the crisis and vowing to hold accountable those responsible. He asked for prayers to "guide us through the storm towards a brighter day."

But he knew that if he got through this one, there would be another storm.

"The oil spill," he said, "is not the last crisis America will face."

Nor the last one Obama would.

Aerial view of the BP oil spill.

'Touch It, Dude'

When it came to children, President Obama seemed perfectly comfortable meeting them on their own terms, especially children whose parents were on his staff. That often meant getting closer to the floor, or even on it.

PHOTOS BY PETE SOUZA/WHITE HOUSE

Ella Rhodes, the daughter of Deputy National Security Adviser Ben Rhodes, came to the Oval Office in October 2015 dressed in her Halloween costume, and the president did what anyone does to see an elephant, which is to look up at it.

In May 2009, Jacob Philadelphia, five, had a question for his dad's boss. 'I want to know if my hair is just like yours,' he asked. The president lowered his head and replied: 'Why don't you touch it and see for yourself?' When Jacob hesitated the president urged, 'Touch it, dude!' Jacob did. 'So what do you think?' 'Yes it does feel the same,' was the reply.

CHAPTER IV

'A Shellacking'

Voters in the 2010 midterm elections deliver a
painful repudiation of a leader they had elected
with enthusiasm only two years earlier.

On Election Night in November 2010, President Obama sat in the White House working the telephones as his secretary fed him number after number to call defeated Democrats. There were a lot of calls to make, nearly one hundred in all. He stayed up until 2 in the morning offering condolences and then started again the next day.

One of those he reached was a young freshman Democrat from Virginia named Tom Perriello. There were few stronger supporters of Obama's economic and health care programs than Perriello, despite his conservative-leaning district in the largely rural rolling fields of Virginia, and Obama made a special point of trying to rescue him with a rally the Friday before the election. It did not help. Perriello fell along with dozens of his colleagues.

The midterm elections of 2010 proved to be a painful rejection for Obama, a repudiation by voters of a president they had elected with such enthusiasm just two years earlier. Republicans picked up a whopping sixty-three seats in the House, the biggest swing between parties in a midterm election since 1938, yielding the largest GOP majority since 1948. While Democrats hung onto the Senate, they lost six seats there too, narrowing their ability to control the chamber. Overnight, the gauzy hope of 2009 had faded into the stark reality of divided government. "I'm not recommending for every future president that they take a shellacking like I did last night," Obama said ruefully. "I'm sure there are easier ways to learn these lessons."

The shellacking was particularly painful for Obama because he realized that many of the losing Democrats, like Perriello, went down because of their support for him or his programs. It was his "responsibility," to use the word he repeated six times the day after the vote. "We didn't realize how deep the loss was going to be," Pete Rouse, the president's senior adviser, said later. "The president felt for a number of House Democrats, in particular, who lost in part because of sticking with him on some tough votes, and how many of them, had they voted differently, might have still been there. That was really weighing heavily on him."

The president who muscled through Congress perhaps the most ambitious domestic agenda in a generation now found himself vilified by the right, castigated by the left and abandoned by the middle. He presided over a White House that felt shell-shocked, where aides were busy wondering whether the best days of the Obama presidency were now behind them. Some advisers who had been ready to carve a new spot on Mount Rushmore for their boss two years earlier privately conceded that he would never be another Abraham Lincoln after all. In the toxic environment of Washington, they lamented, the deck may be so stacked against a president that any of them were doomed to be, at best, average. " 'Arrogance' isn't the right word," said one, "but we were overconfident."

Tea Party Support, 2010. Clockwise from top left: Tax Payer March on Washington; 'Honk and wave,' Salt Lake City; Rally in Macon, Missouri; Sarah Palin greets supporters, Reno, Nevada; Pledge of Allegiance, Beverly Hills; Pins with points, Abilene, Texas.

P

ummeled from both sides, Obama is frustrated and, at times, defensive.

As he sorted through the wreckage, Obama mulled the lessons of history and examined his decisions. The easy thing, of course, would be to blame the Republicans for waging a nonstop campaign of obstruction against him, and he certainly subscribed to this view. But even while Obama expressed no regrets about the broad direction of his presidency, he did identify what he called "tactical lessons." He had let himself look too much like "the same old tax-and-spend liberal Democrat," he told *The New York Times*. He realized too late that "there's no such thing as shovel-ready projects" when it comes to public works. Perhaps he should not have proposed tax breaks as part of his stimulus and instead "let the Republicans insist on the tax cuts" so it could be seen as a bipartisan compromise.

Still, Obama ascribed most of his problems to a failure to communicate the merits of his policies, not the policies themselves. "Given how much stuff was coming at us," he said, "we probably spent much more time trying to get the policy right than trying to get the politics right." He and his team took "a perverse pride" in doing what they thought was the right thing even if it was unpopular. "And I think anybody who's occupied this office has to remember that success is determined by an intersection in policy and politics, and that you can't be neglecting of marketing and PR and public opinion."

That presumed that what he had done was the right thing, a matter of considerable debate. At that point, the left thought he had done too little and the right too much. But what was striking about Obama's self-diagnosis in that moment of defeat was that, by his own rendering, the figure of inspiration from 2008 neglected the inspiration after his election. He did not stay connected to the people who put him in office in the first place. Instead, he simultaneously disappointed those who considered him the embodiment of a new progressive movement and those who expected him to reach across the aisle to usher in a postpartisan era. On the campaign trail throughout that fall of 2010, he confronted that disillusionment – the woman who told him she was "exhausted" defending him, the mother whose son campaigned for him but was now looking for hope. Even the artist who made the iconic multi-hued "Hope" poster said he was losing hope.

The policy criticism of Obama, of course, was confusing and deeply contradictory at the same time – he was a liberal zealot, in the view of the right, or a weak accommodater, in the view of the left. He was seen by some as an anti-capitalist socialist and by others as too cozy with Wall Street. He was somehow both a weak-on-defense apologist for America and the validator of George W. Bush's unrelenting anti-terror tactics at the expense of civil liberties.

Pummeled from both sides, Obama was frustrated and, at times, defensive. At a Labor Day event in Milwaukee, he complained that the special interests treated him badly. "They're not always happy with me," he told supporters. "They talk about me like a dog – that's not in my prepared remarks, but it's true."

The friendly fire bothered him the most. "Democrats just congenitally tend to see the glass as half-empty," he groused at a fund-raiser in Greenwich, Connecticut, where he mocked the bellyachers in his party. "If we get an historic health care bill passed – oh, well, the public option wasn't there. If you get the financial reform bill passed – then, well, I don't know about this particular derivatives rule, I'm not sure that I'm satisfied with that. And, gosh, we haven't yet brought about world peace. I thought that was going to happen quicker."

Taking a page or two from Bill Clinton, the Comeback Kid himself.

In some ways, of course, he had no one to blame for inflated expectations but himself. Not only did he benefit from them in 2008, he consciously lifted them, promising grandiloquently to do no less than heal the planet. Now he faced two years in which he had to skillfully lower expectations again so that he could rebound from defeat and win a second term.

For comeback lessons, Obama turned to the so-called Comeback Kid himself, Bill Clinton. The shellacking Obama had taken echoed powerfully the Republican Revolution of 1994 that left Clinton with both houses of Congress in opposition hands. Fitfully at first, deftly after a while, Clinton managed to pivot away from that setback to handily prevail in his re-election bid just two years later.

That Obama was turning to Clinton for advice was remarkable. Just two years earlier, as a candidate, Obama had scorned the forty-second president, deriding his small-ball politics and triangulation maneuvering while comparing him unfavorably to Ronald Reagan. Running against Clinton's wife, Obama had been the anti-Clinton. Now he was hoping to be the second coming of Bill Clinton – because, in the end, it was better than being the second coming of Jimmy Carter.

Within weeks of the election, it looked as if Obama had actually outsourced his presidency to Clinton. He was reading books on Clinton's time in office and cut a Clintonian-style deal with Republicans on tax cuts. Then on a quiet Friday afternoon, he literally turned over the White House lectern to his predecessor. After a private meeting, the two presidents decided spontaneously to head to the briefing room to talk to the assembled reporters. Within a few minutes, Obama excused himself to head to another obligation but left behind Clinton, who happily held forth on the state of politics and answered questions as if it were still a decade earlier and he were still the commander in chief.

Clinton had recovered from his own midterm debacle through a mix of conciliation and confrontation. He tacked to the political center by cutting deals with Newt Gingrich's Republicans on issues like welfare, but he relished fighting with them over the partial government shutdown. Whether Obama could duplicate the feat remained uncertain. He was not as nimble a politician as Clinton, and while he was more of a pragmatist than his critics wanted to admit, he was not instinctively a centrist, as Clinton was.

"There's a lot to learn from what the Clinton White House did in 1994 forward with a similar situation," said Dan Pfeiffer, the White House communications director. "But it's also important to understand we're not in the exact same situation." Indeed, Gingrich's Republicans, while profiting off public discontent with Clinton, came to office with a set of ideas they wanted to advance, some of which happened to coincide with the president's. The Republicans now taking over the House were animated far more deeply by public opposition to Obama than by any particular policy prescriptions. Moreover, Clinton presided over fundamentally better times – unemployment was at 5.6 percent then, compared with 9.8 percent at that point under Obama, and the country was at peace under Clinton, while the wars in Iraq and Afghanistan still consumed the American military in Obama's time.

The first decision Obama had to make after the shellacking was how much political capital to invest in trying to pass leftover legislation in the post-election lame duck session of a Democratic Congress before the House gavel was handed to the Republicans. Obama focused right from the start on an ambitious agenda for the departing Congress, to the point of disregarding the election results, which could have been interpreted as arguing against lame-duck legislating.

"The next day he came into the office and said, 'We got our butts kicked, but we've got a lame-duck session here, and I've got a lot I want to get done,'" David Axelrod recalled. "He recited a lengthy list. And everybody kind of looked at each other and thought, 'What disaster does he not get?'"

The list included restructuring the Bush-era tax cuts, which were due to expire at the end of the year; ending the Clinton-era "don't ask, don't tell" ban on gays and lesbians serving openly in the military; overhauling the immigration system to allow the children of illegal immigrants to stay in the country; and ratifying an arms-control treaty with Russia slashing both sides' nuclear arsenals.

The idea of addressing so many big issues in the lame-duck session seemed fanciful if not defiant – after all, the voters had just served eviction notices on the House Democratic majority. But Obama and his Democratic allies decided to press ahead before surrendering control, realizing that the next two years under Republican rule would be enormously frustrating.

Unlike the other items, the tax cuts required action because of the

President Obama conferring with former President Clinton, New York, June 4, 2012.

T he shooting of Gabrielle Giffords and others by a deranged gunman touches off a divisive debate on gun control.

was first enacted under Bill Clinton as a compromise to his initial promise of repealing the ban altogether. Under the policy, for the previous seventeen years, gay and lesbian troops could serve only if they did not disclose their sexual orientation and they were court-martialed if they did.

Obama had promised since his election to do away with the awkward rule but unlike Clinton, who tried to move immediately after taking office only to run into a buzz-saw of opposition, he took his time, allowing Defense Secretary Robert Gates and Admiral Mike Mullen to conduct a lengthy review that would smooth the way. While activists hammered away at Obama for delaying so long, accusing him of vacillation and irresolution, Gates and Mullen patiently massaged the uniformed leadership to the point that most – although not all – vocal opposition faded inside the ranks by the time Congress acted.

Republicans tried to leverage Obama into dropping the military rule change in exchange for their consent to his New Start arms control treaty, but the president refused to make such a deal and pressed hard for ratification even as he lobbied for the repeal of the military ban. Obama had signed the treaty on April 8, 2010, in Prague alongside President Dmitri Medvedev of Russia in what was supposed to be a basic, relatively modest pact that would set the stage for deeper reductions later in his presidency. But conservatives put up a vigorous fight against the accord, and New Start would turn out to be the end of Obama's arms-control agreements with Moscow, not the beginning.

Under the treaty, both countries were to pare back their nuclear arsenals within seven years to their lowest levels in decades, with no more than 1,550 strategic warheads and 700 deployed launchers each. While those represented relatively small reductions compared to previous treaties, the agreement provided for the resumption of on-site inspections, which had halted when the original Start treaty expired the year before. To secure enough Republican support in the Senate for the two-thirds vote required by the Constitution, Obama promised to spend $85 billion over the next decade modernizing America's aging nuclear complex, a promise that helped win over thirteen Republicans to join his united Democratic caucus in the final 71-to-26 vote.

Obama had less luck with his effort to pass the so-called Dream Act, which would have provided a path to citizenship for college students who were brought to the United States illegally as children. It was meant to be a small but politically attractive down payment on a broader overhaul of the immigration system, but Republican opponents recognized that it was only a first step to what they considered a more objectionable revision of the law allowing millions of illegal immigrants to stay in the country.

While disappointed, Obama was energized by the victories he did achieve – especially coming just weeks after the election drubbing. Of course, this was the last gasp of a Democratic-controlled Congress on the

*Migrants in Mexico head toward the United States aboard "The Beast,"
a train known for accidents and crime, July 2, 2014.*

pending expiration – both sides agreed on that much. Neither Republicans nor Democrats wanted the Bush tax cuts to lapse entirely since that would mean a substantial tax increase for many Americans. Where the two sides differed, as they had since the start of the Obama presidency, was on what to do about the tax cuts for those in the richest American households. Obama wanted to let the tax cuts expire for those in the top two percent of families, while the Republicans wanted to extend all the cuts as they were, regardless of income.

Neither side was ready for a permanent compromise, but they settled on a temporary solution that included victories for both the White House and the Republicans. They agreed to extend the tax cuts unchanged for two more years – including for the wealthy – effectively punting the larger question. As part of the package, Obama won a temporary cut in payroll taxes, which would benefit lower-income workers more than the wealthy, and a thirteen-month extension of jobless benefits for the long-term unemployed, as well as extension of a series of other, smaller tax breaks included in his stimulus program. In addition to preserving all of the Bush tax cuts for the time being, Republicans succeeded in lowering the scheduled tax rate for the largest estates. Neither side came up with spending cuts to offset the tax cuts, so the $858 billion cost of the package would be added to the national debt. But Obama considered the net effect to be like another stimulus to the economy.

Obama announced the deal by himself, not with his Republican partners, a sign that neither side wanted to be seen with the other. Compromises in Washington at that point were to be disdained, not celebrated. When Obama emerged from the Oval Office to defend the agreement, he was clearly in a sour mood. He denounced his erstwhile Republican partners as "hostage takers" because they refused to extend the middle-class tax cuts unless the wealthy kept theirs too. And he lashed out at his critics on the left as "sanctimonious" for piling on him for caving in on the tax cuts for the rich.

"This is the public-option debate all over again," he fumed. "Now, if that's the standard by which we are measuring success or core principles, then, let's face it, we will never get anything done. People will have the satisfaction of having a purist position and no victories for the American people. And we will be able to feel good about ourselves and sanctimonious about how pure our intentions are and how tough we are."

But if Obama accepted a middle-ground resolution on taxes, he opted for all-or-nothing confrontation on his three other lame-duck priorities. In the end, he won two of three – the end of the don't-ask ban and ratification of the nuclear arms treaty with Russia – but lost the third, the immigration overhaul.

The prohibition on gays and lesbians serving openly in the military

T he shooting of Gabrielle Giffords and others by a deranged gunman touches off a divisive debate on gun control.

was first enacted under Bill Clinton as a compromise to his initial promise of repealing the ban altogether. Under the policy, for the previous seventeen years, gay and lesbian troops could serve only if they did not disclose their sexual orientation and they were court-martialed if they did.

Obama had promised since his election to do away with the awkward rule but unlike Clinton, who tried to move immediately after taking office only to run into a buzz-saw of opposition, he took his time, allowing Defense Secretary Robert Gates and Admiral Mike Mullen to conduct a lengthy review that would smooth the way. While activists hammered away at Obama for delaying so long, accusing him of vacillation and irresolution, Gates and Mullen patiently massaged the uniformed leadership to the point that most – although not all – vocal opposition faded inside the ranks by the time Congress acted.

Republicans tried to leverage Obama into dropping the military rule change in exchange for their consent to his New Start arms control treaty, but the president refused to make such a deal and pressed hard for ratification even as he lobbied for the repeal of the military ban. Obama had signed the treaty on April 8, 2010, in Prague alongside President Dmitri Medvedev of Russia in what was supposed to be a basic, relatively modest pact that would set the stage for deeper reductions later in his presidency. But conservatives put up a vigorous fight against the accord, and New Start would turn out to be the end of Obama's arms-control agreements with Moscow, not the beginning.

Under the treaty, both countries were to pare back their nuclear arsenals within seven years to their lowest levels in decades, with no more than 1,550 strategic warheads and 700 deployed launchers each. While those represented relatively small reductions compared to previous treaties, the agreement provided for the resumption of on-site inspections, which had halted when the original Start treaty expired the year before. To secure enough Republican support in the Senate for the two-thirds vote required by the Constitution, Obama promised to spend $85 billion over the next decade modernizing America's aging nuclear complex, a promise that helped win over thirteen Republicans to join his united Democratic caucus in the final 71-to-26 vote.

Obama had less luck with his effort to pass the so-called Dream Act, which would have provided a path to citizenship for college students who were brought to the United States illegally as children. It was meant to be a small but politically attractive down payment on a broader overhaul of the immigration system, but Republican opponents recognized that it was only a first step to what they considered a more objectionable revision of the law allowing millions of illegal immigrants to stay in the country.

While disappointed, Obama was energized by the victories he did achieve – especially coming just weeks after the election drubbing. Of course, this was the last gasp of a Democratic-controlled Congress on the way out of town, not the acquiescence of a new Republican-controlled House. But Obama presented the surprising lame-duck successes as proof of his continued vigor in Washington.

"One thing I hope people have seen during this lame duck – I am persistent," Obama said at a valedictory news conference before heading off for his annual Christmas vacation in Hawaii. "If I believe in something strongly, I stay on it."

With the new year, Obama faced a new era, and he was assembling a new team to do so. Even before the 2010 election, Rahm Emanuel, the hard-charging chief of staff, had stepped down to run for mayor of Chicago. Pete Rouse, the quiet, behind-the-scenes presidential adviser and master political technician, filled in at first, and then the president tapped former Commerce Secretary William Daley to take over. Daley, the brother and son of legendary Chicago mayors, was an outsider to Obama's world, but the president hoped his pro-business, moderate sensibilities would bridge the divide with the newly ascendant Republicans. Robert Gibbs, the public face of the White House and one of Obama's closest advisers, also stepped down as press secretary, replaced by Jay Carney, a former *Time* magazine correspondent who had been working as communications director for Vice President Joseph Biden. David Axelrod and Jim Messina, the president's top political gurus in the West Wing, left to begin building a re-election campaign based in Chicago. David Plouffe, the manager of the first campaign, arrived in Washington and moved into Axelrod's closet-sized office just down the hall from the Oval Office, fulfilling a deal the two Davids had made at the onset of the presidency to each spend two years on the inside. Other aides were brought in or given promotions, including Nancy-Ann De Parle, Alyssa Mastromonaco, Stephanie Cutter and Rob Nabors.

The arrival of a Republican House was always expected to usher in a fresh period of conflict, but the new Congress had barely begun when it was struck by violence. Representative Gabrielle Giffords, an energetic young Democrat from Arizona who was popular with her colleagues on Capitol Hill, was shot in the head on January 8, 2011, while meeting with constituents outside a supermarket in Tucson. Her assailant was a deranged gunman who believed in mind control. The explosion of gunfire killed six other people, including the chief judge of the United States District Court for Arizona and a nine-year-old girl, and wounded thirteen. It also touched off an emotional and divisive national debate about gun control and the rise of incivility and demonization in modern politics.

"At a time when our discourse has become so sharply polarized, at a time when we are far too eager to lay the blame for all that ails the world at the feet of those who think differently than we do, it's important for us to pause for a moment and make sure that we are talking with each other in a way that heals, not a way that wounds," Obama said a few days after the rampage at a memorial service for those who were killed.

But measuring the political temperature on Capitol Hill, Obama made no serious effort to pass new laws restricting access to firearms following the incident and, after bemoaning the tragedy, lawmakers on both sides of the aisle quickly returned to the coarse politics of anger that had dominated Washington in recent years. Aided by her husband, Mark Kelly, an astronaut, Giffords recovered, albeit with permanent damage to her ability to speak, and she went on to become a symbol of courage and a voice for new gun laws.

While Obama managed to push off a permanent resolution of the tax fight, he now faced a Republican House that was eager to rein in spending – and the president at the same time. During Obama's first two years in office, the deficit had shot up to its highest levels as a share of the economy since World War II as the Great Recession sapped tax revenues and the government pumped money into the economy to try to restart its engines. The deficit rose to $459 billion in the fiscal year that ended in the fall of 2008, the last before George W. Bush left office, and then skyrocketed to $1.4 trillion in the fiscal year that included his final three and a half months in office and the first eight and a half months of Obama's presidency. The deficit dipped back down to $1.3 trillion in the 2010 fiscal year, but it still represented 8.7 percent of the gross domestic product. The total national debt had just passed $14 trillion, or roughly 93 percent of the nation's entire economy, as the new Congress arrived in town.

To get control of the situation, Obama had appointed a bipartisan panel led by Erskine Bowles, a former White House chief of staff under Clinton, and Alan Simpson, a Republican former senator from Wyoming. Just before the new Congress took office, the commission came back with a plan of breathtaking ambition – and breathtaking political risk. It proposed to slash $4 trillion in anticipated debt through a mix of painful spending cuts and tax increases, eventually balance the budget by 2035 and cut in half the national debt's share of the economy. Many sectors of society would feel the pain. Homeowners would lose their mortgage deduction. Workers would face a retirement age of sixty-nine instead of sixty-seven. The military would face significant cutbacks. In the end, though, seven of the eighteen members of the commission would not support it, including Representative Paul Ryan, the incoming Republican chairman of the House Budget Committee. And Obama, while praising it in concept, quickly and quietly put it aside, unwilling to embrace its politically explosive provisions. The newly empowered Republicans opted instead to move forward with a deficit plan that only addressed spending, not taxes. During the fall campaign, Ryan, John Boehner, now the incoming speaker, and other Republicans had promised to cut $100 billion in spending in their first year in power. Because Democrats had failed to pass regular, full-year spending bills before the last Congress expired, the government was operating on temporary authority that would expire in the spring, giving the Republicans leverage to exact some spending discipline right away. But they still only controlled one house of Congress, and the president sat on the other end of Pennsylvania Avenue with a veto pen.

In the weeks that followed, the two sides engaged in a game of budget chicken, running up against a deadline that would force the government to shut down all but essential services unless a new spending bill was approved. As midnight approached on April 8, Obama and congressional leaders finally compromised on a plan to cut $38 billion in spending over the next six months and keep the government operating until fall. Lawmakers raced to the floor to vote just before 11 p.m., barely an hour before the cutoff.

Boehner hailed it as the "largest real-dollar spending cut in American history." But it was hardly the sweeping, long-term plan Bowles and Simpson had advocated, nor even as much as the Republicans had promised on the campaign trail. In effect, it was another temporary truce but hardly the end of the battle.

Just days later, Obama headed to George Washington University to deliver a high-profile speech setting the terms of the next round of fighting with his own plan to eliminate $4 trillion in deficits over twelve years, eschewing deep cuts in social entitlement programs and relying in part on tax increases for the wealthiest Americans.

As Obama hovered backstage getting ready to go out, his new chief of staff, Bill Daley, spotted an unexpected guest in the audience – Paul Ryan, the Republican chairman whose budget plan Obama was about to shred. "Try to tell the president!" Daley directed an aide.

It was too late. Obama went on stage and flayed Ryan's plan, declaring that its deep tax cuts and deeper spending reductions would harm students, seniors, the disabled and the nation.

"It's not going to happen as long as I'm president," Obama vowed sternly.

Ryan, who thought he had been invited to hear the president speak about a new collaboration on fiscal matters, fumed in the front row, feeling ambushed as he was singled out for attack in front of a hostile audience. Intentionally or not, the gauntlet had been thrown down.

With the government spending plan now in place, Republicans turned to another deadline to force action on the deficit on their terms: the debt ceiling. Unless Congress voted to raise it, the government would soon be unable to borrow money, which could theoretically put the United States into default. For years, presidents and lawmakers had increased the debt ceiling as a matter of course, sometimes arguing about it, but rarely flirting with the idea of not raising it. But egged on by their most conservative and aggressive members, Republican leaders threatened not to raise the debt

DOUG MILLS/NEW YORK TIMES

Representative Gabrielle Giffords, with her husband, Captain Mark Kelly, waits to testify at a Senate hearing on gun violence, January 30, 2013.

ceiling unless Obama agreed to deeper spending reductions, a prospect that the International Monetary Fund warned would deliver a "severe shock" to the global economy.

Months of laborious negotiations ensued. Obama wanted to craft a "grand bargain" to make sweeping changes rather than simply get through the immediate crisis, and Boehner, by instinct a dealmaker, was open to the idea. They came close at one point, but Obama insisted on more tax increases to match spending cuts, and Boehner was pulled back by Representative Eric Cantor, the Republican majority leader. During a fractious meeting at the White House, Cantor suggested Obama agree to a short-term increase in the debt ceiling to get through the immediate crisis but the president refused. "This could bring my presidency down," Obama said, but "I will not yield on this."

The temporary solution for a budget crisis? A mutual suicide pact.

Finally, the two sides agreed on a makeshift, punt-the-problem-down-the-road compromise. They crafted a measure to raise the debt ceiling by $900 billion and reduce the deficit by roughly the same, mainly through spending cuts. A special joint congressional committee would then be charged with coming up with a more comprehensive plan to rein in the deficit. But if it could not, another $1.2 trillion in spending cuts would automatically take effect across the board, half in domestic agencies and half in national security, a process called sequester. The theory was that neither side wanted cuts that drastic in their favorite programs, and that the threat of an indiscriminate ax coming down on most of what government did would be incentive for both sides to finally put their differences aside and reach a long-term deal. In effect, it was a mutual suicide pact and both sides assumed the other would put down the gun first.

For Obama, the collapse of the grand bargain fundamentally reshaped his attitude toward Washington. "That was a searing experience," said David Plouffe. The lesson: Forget negotiations and use the bully pulpit. Policy was not about applying reason; it was about applying power. "You're never going to convince them by sitting around the table and talk about what's good for the country," John Podesta said. "You had to demonstrate that there's political pain if you don't produce an acceptable outcome."

President Obama with Representative Paul Ryan during a Washington meeting on health insurance reform, February 25, 2010.

Senate Majority Leader Mitch McConnell at the Capitol, November 18, 2014.

Representative John Boehner jokingly raises a box of tissues during his farewell remarks in the House, October 29, 2015.

'The Fever'

To Obama, Republicans were never on the level

The conversation was not going particularly well. President Obama was on the telephone, and John Boehner had grown weary of the long-winded lecturing. Finally, Boehner put the phone down on his desk and lit up a cigarette while the president kept talking. Mitch McConnell had similar conversations with Obama and, while he never put the phone down, he sometimes watched baseball on television while the president went on and on.

To say that Obama and congressional Republicans talked past each other would be an understatement. Hailing from opposite parties, they might never have been friends. But Obama's fractious and often dysfunctional relationships with the leaders of the other party proved a profound challenge during his presidency and contributed to a broader polarization of American politics likely to endure for years.

To Obama, the Republicans were "never on the level," referring to what he considered a strategy of deliberate partisan obstruction. Republicans met the night of his inauguration to plot against him and, even as he headed to Capitol Hill days later to talk about a stimulus package, Boehner preemptively announced that Republicans would oppose it. To Republicans, Obama was making excuses for not genuinely reaching across the aisle. While admittedly not disposed to compromise with him, they bristled at what they considered his high handed intellectual arrogance.

The two most important players in this drama were Boehner and McConnell, the Republican minority leaders until midterm elections elevated them to House speaker and Senate majority leader respectively. Obama considered Boehner likeable but ultimately disappointing. As for McConnell, Obama never found much to like, a feeling that was mutual.

In his memoir, McConnell, an old-school Kentucky conservative, called Obama "condescending" and "annoying," adding that two hours together "would have been more productive had I spent them napping." Obama grated on him. "He's like the kid in your class who exerts a hell of a lot of effort making sure everyone thinks he's the smartest one in the room," McConnell wrote. "He talks down to people, whether in a meeting among colleagues in the White House or addressing the nation."

McConnell famously said in October 2010 that "the single most important thing we want to achieve is for President Obama to be a one-term president." Obama used that line to discredit McConnell, telling audiences that it came at the start of his presidency, although it was actually after nearly two years and in the context of a mid-term election campaign.

But it sealed Obama's view of McConnell as an enemy, a view certainly cemented by the senator's decision not to even consider the Supreme Court nomination of Merrick Garland. Obama scorned the idea that if he simply got along with McConnell, everything would have been better.

"'Why don't you get a drink with Mitch McConnell?' they ask," Obama once joked during a black-tie dinner monologue. "Really? Why don't *you* get a drink with Mitch McConnell?"

Obama was friendlier with Boehner, a merlot-drinking, perpetually tanned son of a bartender from Ohio. While Boehner too found Obama patronizing at times, he was more inclined to negotiation than many in his party and the two shared passions for golf and cigarettes (even if the president had in theory quit). But whenever they came close to a far-reaching agreement, as with the fiscal "grand bargain" in 2011, it fell apart.

Boehner was constrained by rebellious conservatives who considered compromise a dirty word. By his own account, he had to "sneak into the White House" just to talk with Obama. When Obama invited him to play golf, fellow Republicans excoriated Boehner. "You can't believe the grief I got," he recalled. He turned down subsequent invitations.

During his reelection campaign, Obama expressed hope that "the fever may break" afterward. But it never did. Ultimately, Boehner was forced to resign by conservatives who resisted common ground with Obama. The day he announced his decision, Obama called.

"Boehner, man, I'm going to miss you," Obama said.

"Yes, you are, Mr. President," Boehner replied. "Yes, you are."

President Obama, with cabinet members and others from his national security team, are updated on the mission against Osama bin Laden, May 2011. The classified document seen in this photograph was obscured by its source.

PETE SOUZA/WHITE HOUSE

CHAPTER V

'Justice Has Been Done'

As the president and his advisers watch from a small basement room in the White House, a team of Navy Seals storms the compound in Pakistan where Osama bin Laden is hiding and kills America's most sought-after enemy.

Osama bin Laden, Afghanistan, April 1998.

In a cramped, low-ceilinged anteroom off the main Situation Room in the basement of the White House, President Obama stared at a screen and waited for news. He was surrounded by his national security team, all as anxious as he was. The room was eerily quiet that Sunday, May 1, 2011. The president looked stone faced, his eyes intense and narrowed. The vice president fingered his rosary beads. "The minutes passed like days," recalled John Brennan, the White House counterterrorism chief.

From a live hookup across the Potomac River in Langley, Virginia, Obama and his team could hear Leon Panetta, the C.I.A. director, narrating from his agency headquarters what was happening in faraway Pakistan, where it was already Monday morning.

"They've reached the target," he said.

Minutes passed.

"We have a visual on Geronimo," he said.

A few minutes later: "Geronimo EKIA."

Enemy Killed in Action. There was silence in the Situation Room.

Finally, the president spoke.

"We got him."

Geronimo was the code name for Osama bin Laden, author of the most devastating foreign attack on American soil in modern times and the most wanted man in the world. After a decade-long manhunt, C.I.A. operatives had finally tracked him down, and a team of Navy Seals in stealth helicopters slipped into Pakistan on a moonless night in a daring raid to end the chase. America's enemy number one finally met his fate in a sprawling compound at the end of a long dirt road, an American bullet blasting into his skull just above his left eye and at least one more piercing his chest.

"Justice has been done," Obama told the world a few hours later in a hastily arranged televised address from the East Room that Sunday just before midnight. The news touched off an extraordinary outpouring of emotion in the United States as crowds gathered outside the White House, in Times Square and at the ground zero site, people waving American flags, cheering, shouting and laughing. As Obama walked down the Colonnade back to the residence part of the White House, he could hear the chanting: "U.S.A., U.S.A.!" In New York City, crowds burst into "The Star-Spangled Banner." Throughout downtown Washington, drivers honked horns.

That night would prove to be the most unvarnished moment of unity and success in Obama's presidency, the one time Americans of all stripes and ideologies joined together to rejoice. Obama's poll numbers shot up temporarily, his re-election prospects were surely bolstered and at least one triumphant line was etched into his paragraph in the history books. For once, even Obama's most virulent critics gave him credit, if sometimes grudgingly.

The elation, however, led to a fierce debate about whether George W. Bush's program of harsh interrogations had played a role in ultimately hunting bin Laden down, an argument highlighted with the release of a popular Hollywood movie, *Zero Dark Thirty*. Veteran C.I.A. officials asserted that waterboarding essentially led to bin Laden. An exhaustive report by Senate Democrats, however, disputed that, saying the detainee who provided the most important piece of information did so before he was subjected to the techniques widely deemed torture, not after. Panetta later said it was more complicated, that at the very least such interrogations provided a broader understanding of Al Qaeda and its leadership that was critical. What remained unknowable, he said, was whether such information could have been gained even without what he called the damage to American values.

Either way, the dispatch of bin Laden, as emotionally satisfying as it was, would be a fleeting victory in a season of tumult that rocked the greater Middle East and challenged the Obama administration. The geopolitical cross-currents in the region in early 2011, as popular uprisings spread from country to country, would pit Obama's commitment to democracy and internationalism against his instincts for cautious pragmatism and restraint. In Egypt, Libya, Bahrain, Yemen and Syria, Obama would adopt different approaches, often on the fly, with none of them yielding the results he had sought, at least in the medium term. Where he initially hoped that

This image, taken from video released by the United States Department of Defense on May 7, 2011, shows Osama bin Laden wrapped in a blanket while watching television.

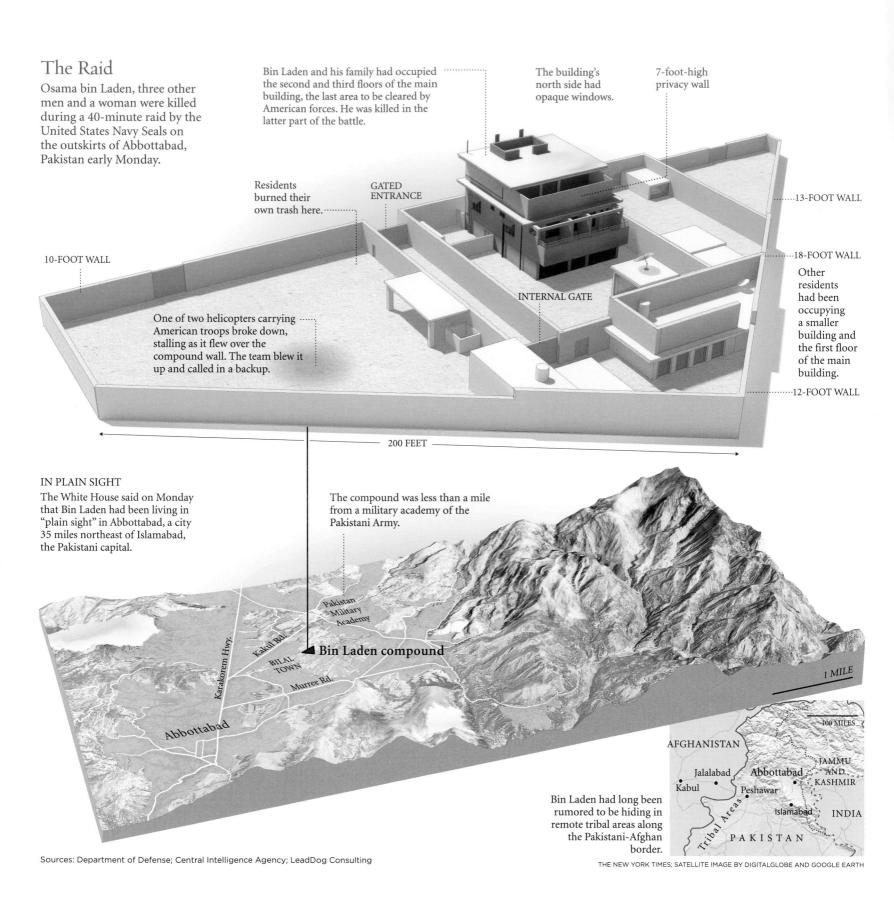

The Raid

Osama bin Laden, three other men and a woman were killed during a 40-minute raid by the United States Navy Seals on the outskirts of Abbottabad, Pakistan early Monday.

Bin Laden and his family had occupied the second and third floors of the main building, the last area to be cleared by American forces. He was killed in the latter part of the battle.

The building's north side had opaque windows.

7-foot-high privacy wall

Residents burned their own trash here.

GATED ENTRANCE

13-FOOT WALL

10-FOOT WALL

INTERNAL GATE

18-FOOT WALL

Other residents had been occupying a smaller building and the first floor of the main building.

One of two helicopters carrying American troops broke down, stalling as it flew over the compound wall. The team blew it up and called in a backup.

12-FOOT WALL

← 200 FEET →

IN PLAIN SIGHT
The White House said on Monday that Bin Laden had been living in "plain sight" in Abbottabad, a city 35 miles northeast of Islamabad, the Pakistani capital.

The compound was less than a mile from a military academy of the Pakistani Army.

Pakistan Military Academy

Karakorem Hwy.

Kakul Rd.

BILAL TOWN

Murree Rd.

▲ Bin Laden compound

Abbottabad

1 MILE

AFGHANISTAN

100 MILES

Kabul

Jalalabad

Peshawar

Abbottabad

JAMMU AND KASHMIR

Islamabad

INDIA

Tribal Areas

PAKISTAN

Bin Laden had long been rumored to be hiding in remote tribal areas along the Pakistani-Afghan border.

Sources: Department of Defense; Central Intelligence Agency; LeadDog Consulting

THE NEW YORK TIMES; SATELLITE IMAGE BY DIGITALGLOBE AND GOOGLE EARTH

an Arab Spring would produce the sort of inspiring peaceful revolution that transformed Eastern Europe after the fall of the Berlin Wall – the ultimate reproach to bin Laden's perversion of Islam – eventually Obama would see the events of that period as a case study in all the ways good intentions could go wrong.

No wonder, then, that he permitted himself to savor that spring night when he announced the final reckoning for bin Laden. It was perhaps the biggest gamble of his presidency to that point, a decision haunted by the ghosts of past botched operations like the failed mission to rescue American hostages in Iran in 1980 and the ambushed effort to capture warlords in Somalia that resulted in the downing of a couple of Black Hawk helicopters and a deadly standoff in 1993. Obama was told that if the Pakistan raid went wrong, it could damage him politically just as the debacle in the Iranian desert hurt Jimmy Carter. He knew that killing civilians by mistake would further inflame the Muslim world. And he realized that even a successful operation conducted without telling Pakistan first could provoke a diplomatic crisis with a key ally in the war with terrorists.

"There were," as Panetta told *The New York Times* later, "a hell of a lot of risks."

The compound in Abbottabad, Pakistan where Osama bin Laden was killed.

Obama learned that the government's bin Laden hunters might have finally cornered their quarry months earlier when Panetta arrived for a meeting with the president and his national security team that was kept so secret that White House officials did not list the topic in their alerts to each other.

Panetta told Obama that day that after years of hearing about a trusted courier for bin Laden, the C.I.A. at last had found him and tracked him to a compound in Abbottabad, a wealthy enclave barely thirty miles north of the Pakistani capital of Islamabad. It was hardly the Spartan cave in the mountains that many had envisioned as his hiding place. Instead, it was a three-story house ringed by twelve-foot-high concrete walls topped with barbed wire and guarded by two security fences. Rather than getting as far away from local authorities as he could, bin Laden had chosen a hideout about a mile from Pakistan's military academy. He was, Brennan said, "hiding in plain sight."

No one was sure, however, that bin Laden was really there. The discovery of the compound led to months of surveillance to determine what the analysts called a pattern of life. They found that the house was unusually cut off from the outside world, with no phone lines or Internet access. Those inside were so concerned about security that they burned their trash rather than putting it on the street for collection. Nearly two dozen people were spotted living there, including family members. Intelligence officers studied the laundry on the clothes line and even set up a fake vaccination program to try to get a first-hand look at the residence and its occupants.

Satellite imagery detected a tall man who regularly emerged for brisk walks around the yard, a man they dubbed The Pacer. "He would go out and he'd walk real fast, like a guy coming out of confinement, you know, in a prison yard," Panetta said. "Kids would walk with him. They'd be all around. It was clear that people there were giving him deference."

Panetta and Vice Admiral William McRaven, commander of the Pentagon's Joint Special Operations Command, developed three options for Obama to consider: a strike with B-2 bombers that would obliterate the compound, a joint raid with Pakistani intelligence operatives who would be told about the mission only hours ahead of time, or a secret helicopter assault using only American commandos penetrating Pakistani territory from a base in Afghanistan.

Telling the Pakistanis was quickly ruled out. No one trusted them. That bin Laden could go undetected in their country for so long fueled long-standing suspicions that at least some Pakistani authorities were aware of his presence and protecting him. A B-2 strike was rejected too because it would leave a giant crater but no body; if they were going to try to kill bin Laden, they wanted to be sure they got him and avoid conspiracy theories that he had somehow survived.

So it came down to the commando raid. Four lawyers were assigned to come up with a legal rationale that would allow the United States to send military forces into the sovereign territory of another nation with which it was not at war, a project so secret that it was kept even from Attorney General Eric Holder. But it was an option that worried many who were in the loop, like Joseph Biden and Robert Gates. Given that some intelligence analysts were saying the chances of it being bin Laden were perhaps fifty-fifty, Biden suggested waiting longer to be sure. Gates, who was preparing to step down, cited the bungled Iran rescue mission. Hillary Clinton offered cautious support for the operation, but Panetta, who was about to replace Gates as secretary of defense, was the only full-throated advocate. "It was a divided room," said Tom Donilon, who had succeeded James Jones as national security adviser.

After a sober discussion that included long stretches of silence, Obama told advisers he would think about it some more and adjourned the meeting. By the next morning, he had made up his mind. He summoned four top aides and, before they could start briefing him, cut them off.

"It's a go," he said.

The timing of the raid was awkward politically. Just days before the Seals were to take off, Obama had been busy trying to once and for all dispatch the false speculation that he was actually born in Kenya, a canard promoted by the likes of Donald Trump, the New York real estate mogul and reality television star who was nursing his own political ambitions. Marching into the White House briefing room, Obama released his long-form birth certificate from Hawaii and expressed hope that it would stop the "silliness" distracting the country from more important matters. He did not say what important matters he might have had in mind.

As it happened, just days later, Obama was scheduled to attend the annual White House Correspondents' Association black-tie dinner, where by tradition he would give a comic speech. Some wondered about launching a raid of this magnitude at the same time as the dinner. "Screw the White House Correspondents' Dinner," Clinton said.

Obama agreed and decided to proceed as if nothing special was going on. Kept in the dark about what was about to happen in Pakistan, the president's political advisers focused on the jokes. But there were clues for those paying attention.

The night before, Obama makes jokes at the White House Correspondents' Dinner.

While the president had lunch with David Axelrod, a national security aide interrupted. "Obviously something was going on," Axelrod said later. "He asked me to step out."

As he waited outside the room, Axelrod overheard someone saying that the national security team did not want Obama playing golf the next day, Saturday, April 30, because they might need him for a meeting.

The biggest hint, though, may have come during a discussion about the lines for his correspondents' dinner speech. One of the draft jokes had the president poking fun at Tim Pawlenty, the former governor of Minnesota positioning himself for a run for the Republican presidential nomination: "Oh, poor Tim Pawlenty," Obama was to say. "He had such promise, but he will never get anywhere with that unfortunate middle name bin Laden."

The president rejected the line. "Oh, bin Laden, that name is so hackneyed," he told the joke writers. "Let's find a different name."

One of the speechwriters suggested "Hosni" instead, referring to Egypt's embattled president Hosni Mubarak.

"Let's do that," Obama agreed.

"It wasn't until the next night that we realized why he had taken bin Laden out of the joke," Axelrod recalled.

Obama spent that Saturday night in his tuxedo on the dais at the Washington Hilton Hotel making fun and chatting with journalists as if it were any other night. Indeed, even though he had edited the bin Laden line out of his presentation, the evening's professional entertainer, Seth Meyers, delivered his own joke about the terrorist leader as part of a riff about how no one watched C-Span.

"All the News That's Fit to Print"

The New York Times

Late Edition
Today, mostly cloudy, a passing afternoon shower, cooler, high 63. **Tonight,** cloudy, low 53. **Tomorrow,** mostly cloudy, a couple of showers, high 69. Weather map, Page D8.

VOL. CLX . . . No. 55,393 + © 2011 The New York Times NEW YORK, MONDAY, MAY 2, 2011 $2.00

BIN LADEN KILLED BY U.S. FORCES IN PAKISTAN, OBAMA SAYS, DECLARING JUSTICE HAS BEEN DONE

AL JAZEERA
As the leader of Al Qaeda, Osama bin Laden, here in video recorded in 2001, waged a terror war against the United States.

Qaeda Leader Reported Dead in 'Targeted Assault'

By PETER BAKER and HELENE COOPER

WASHINGTON — Osama bin Laden, the mastermind of the most devastating attack on American soil in modern times and the most hunted man in the world, was killed in a firefight with United States forces in Pakistan on Sunday, President Obama announced.

In a dramatic late-night appearance in the East Room of the White House, Mr. Obama declared that "justice has been done" as he disclosed that American military and C.I.A. operatives had finally cornered Mr. bin Laden, the Al Qaeda leader who had eluded them for nearly a decade, and shot him to death at a compound in Pakistan.

"For over two decades, bin Laden has been Al Qaeda's leader and symbol," the president said in a statement carried on television around the world. "The death of bin Laden marks the most significant achievement to date in our nation's effort to defeat Al Qaeda. But his death does not mark the end of our effort." He added, "We must and we will remain vigilant at home and abroad."

The death of Mr. bin Laden is a defining moment in the American-led war on terrorism. What remains to be seen is whether the death of the leader of Al Qaeda galvanizes his followers by turning him into a martyr, or whether it serves as a turning of the page in the war in Afghanistan and gives further impetus to the Obama administration to bring American troops home.

PABLO MARTINEZ MONSIVAIS/ASSOCIATED PRESS
President Obama announced that Bin Laden was killed in a firefight earlier Sunday.

The death of Mr. bin Laden came nearly 10 years after Al Qaeda terrorists hijacked three American passenger jets and crashed them into the World Trade Center in New York and the Pentagon outside Washington. A fourth hijacked jet crashed into countryside of Pennsylvania. Late Sunday night, as the president was speaking, cheering crowds gathered outside the gates of the White House shortly before midnight as word of Mr. bin Laden's death began trickling out, waving American flags, shouting in happiness and chanting "U.S.A.! U.S.A.!" In New York City, crowds sang the Star-Spangled Banner.

Continued on Page A12

OSAMA BIN LADEN, 1957-2011

An Emblem of Evil in the U.S., an Icon to the Cause of Terror

By KATE ZERNIKE and MICHAEL T. KAUFMAN

Osama bin Laden, who was killed in Pakistan on Sunday, was a son of the Saudi elite whose radical, violent campaign to recreate a seventh-century Muslim empire redefined the threat of terrorism for the 21st century.

With the attacks on the World Trade Center and the Pentagon on Sept. 11, 2001, Bin Laden was elevated to the realm of evil in the American imagination once reserved for dictators like Hitler and Stalin. He was a new national enemy, his face on wanted posters, gloating on videotape, taunting the United States and Western civilization.

"Do you want bin Laden dead?" a reporter asked President George W. Bush six days after the Sept. 11 attacks.

"I want him — I want justice," the president answered. "And there's an old poster out West, as I recall, that said, 'Wanted: Dead or Alive.'"

It took nearly a decade before that quest finally ended in Pakistan with the death of Bin Laden during a confrontation with American forces who attacked a compound where officials said he had been hiding.

The manhunt was punctuated by a December 2001 battle at an Afghan mountain redoubt called Tora Bora, near the border of Pakistan, where Bin Laden and his allies were hiding. Despite days of pounding by American bombers, Bin Laden escaped. For more than nine years afterward, he remained an elusive, shadowy figure frustratingly beyond the grasp of his pursuers and thought to be hiding somewhere in Pakistan and plotting new attacks.

Long before, he had become a hero in much of the Islamic world, as much a myth as a man — what a longtime officer of the C.I.A. called "the North Star" of global terrorism. He had united disparate militant groups, from Egypt to Chechnya, from Yemen to the Philippines, under the banner of his Al Qaeda organization and his ideal of a borderless brotherhood of radical Islam.

Terrorism before Bin Laden was often state-sponsored, but he was a terrorist who had sponsored a state. For five years, 1996 to 2001, he paid for the protection of the Taliban, then the rulers of Afghanistan. He bought the time and the freedom to make his group, Al Qaeda — which means "the base" — a multinational enterprise to export terror around the globe.

For years after the Sept. 11 attacks, the name of Al Qaeda and the fame of Bin Laden spread like a 21st-century political plague. Groups calling themselves Al Qaeda, or acting in the name of its cause, attacked American troops in Iraq, bombed tourist spots in Bali and blew up passenger trains in Spain.

To this day, the precise reach of his power remains unknown: how many members Al Qaeda could truly count on, how many countries its cells had penetrated, and whether, as Bin Laden boasted, he sought to arm Al Qaeda with chemical, biological and nuclear weapons.

He waged holy war with distinctly modern methods. He sent fatwas — religious decrees — by fax and declared war on Americans in an e-mail beamed by satellite around the world. Al Qaeda members kept bomb-making manuals on CD-ROM and communicated with encrypted memos on laptops, leading one American official to declare that

Continued on Page A10

HENRY RAY/AGENCE FRANCE-PRESSE
The twin towers in Lower Manhattan, a symbol of commerce, were transformed into a symbol of terrorism on Sept. 11, 2001.

NEWS ANALYSIS

President's Vow Fulfilled

By JEFF ZELENY

WASHINGTON — President Obama's late-night announcement from the White House Sunday that Osama bin Laden had been killed delivered not only a long-awaited prize to the United States, but also a significant victory for Mr. Obama, whose foreign policy has been the subject of persistent criticism by his rivals.

In his presidential campaign four years ago, Mr. Obama bluntly declared, "We will kill Bin Laden." But as time passed, Bin Laden's name had gradually fallen from presidential speeches and from political discourse, raising concern from critics that his administration was not sufficiently focused on the war on terror.

In delivering the news from the East Room, as jubilant crowds gathered outside the White House waving American flags and cheering in celebration, Mr. Obama did not address his critics or gloat about his trophy. He instead used the moment to remember the victims of the terrorist attacks on Sept. 11, 2001, and to issue a fresh call to the nation for unity.

"Let us think back to the sense of unity that prevailed on 9/11. I know that it has, at times, frayed," Mr. Obama said. "We are once again reminded that America can do whatever we set our mind to."

The development is almost certainly one of the most significant

Continued on Page A12

Amid Cheers, a Message: 'They Will Be Caught'

By ELIZABETH A. HARRIS

In the midnight darkness, the crowds gathered, chanting and cheering, waving American flags, outside the front gates of the White House. In Times Square, tourists poured out of nearby hotels and into the streets to celebrate with strangers.

In the shadow of the World Trade Center site, as the news of Osama bin Laden's killing by American special forces spread, a police car drove north on Church Street blaring the sound of bagpipes from open windows. Officers raised clenched fists in the air.

"I don't know if it will make us safer, but it definitely sends a message to terrorists worldwide," said Stacey Betsalel, standing in Times Square with her husband, exchanging high fives. "They will be caught and they will have to pay for their actions. You can't mess with the United States for very long and get away with it."

President Obama's stunning announcement Sunday night that the terrorist who had eluded capture for almost 10 years drew an outpouring of emotion from political figures and citizens alike.

"This momentous achievement marks a victory for America, for people who seek peace around the world, and for all those who lost loved ones on September 11, 2001," said former President George W. Bush in a statement. "The fight against terror goes on, but tonight America has sent an unmistakable message: No matter how long it takes, justice will be done."

Mayor Michael R. Bloomberg, whose city bore the brunt of the 9/11 attack, said in a statement: "The killing of Osama bin Laden does not lessen the suffering that New Yorkers and Americans experienced at his hands, but it is a critically important victory for

Continued on Page A12

MANUEL BALCE CENETA/ASSOCIATED PRESS
A crowd outside the White House cheering Sunday night at the killing of Osama bin Laden.

INTERNATIONAL A4-12

Allies Defend Libya Policy
NATO officials defended the aggressive airstrikes in Libya after the Libyan government said one barrage had killed four members of Col. Muammar el-Qaddafi's family. PAGE A4

U.S. Aid to Pakistan Founders
Fears of corruption and incompetence have stymied $7.5 billion in American aid aimed at winning over Pakistanis, officials of both nations said. PAGE A16

Another Side of an Ideal Fish
Farmed tilapia is promoted as good for health and the environment, but researchers say it has drawbacks. PAGE A6

NATIONAL A14-19

New Face of Military Blogging
A gathering of people who blog about the military made clear how much has changed since soldiers began relating their experiences online. For one thing, the military is now on board. PAGE A14

Fight on Deficit Spending
With Congress returning on Monday, Democrats and Republicans generally agree that spending must be controlled, but remain divided on how. PAGE A3

BUSINESS DAY B1-8

Spill Clouds Shell Oil's Plans
The spill in the Gulf of Mexico is complicating Shell Oil's ambitious plans, to be put forth this week, to drill beneath Alaska's Arctic waters. PAGE B1

EDITORIAL, OP-ED A26-27

Paul Krugman PAGE A27

SPORTSMONDAY D1-8

Heat Quickly Leads Celtics
Miami's collection of stars, led by Dwyane Wade and LeBron James, near right, outperformed the Boston Celtics' as the Heat won Game 1 of their N.B.A. conference semifinal, 99-90. The Memphis Grizzlies captured Game 1 on the road for the second consecutive series, beating the Oklahoma City Thunder, 114-101. PAGE D1

ARTS C1-8

Clown Posse Fans Plead Sanity
The followers of Insane Clown Posse are striving to transcend stereotypes and show that they are not the rowdy reprobates depicted in the group's cartoonishly gory lyrics. PAGE C1

NEW YORK A20-22

Seeking a Killer's Online Trail
Suffolk County detectives looking for whoever killed four prostitutes are pursuing leads on the Web. PAGE A20

"People think bin Laden is hiding in the Hindu Kush," Meyers quipped, "but did you know that every day from 4 to 5 he hosts a show on C-Span?"

Obama flashed a huge smile. Gates roared with laughter.

During his own speech, Obama took aim at Donald Trump, mocking him for his "birther" fixation just days after the release of the Hawaii birth certificate. "Now, I know that he's taken some flak lately but no one is happier, no one is prouder to put this birth certificate matter to rest than The Donald," Obama said. "And that's because he can finally get back to the issues that matter – like, did we fake the moon landing, what really happened in Roswell and where are Biggie and Tupac?"

Trump, who was in the audience as a guest of *The Washington Post*, kept a tight, unhappy grimace on his face, evidently simmering at the ridicule.

"All kidding aside," Obama continued, addressing Trump. "Obviously, we all know about your credentials and breadth of experience."

He noted that on a recent episode of *Celebrity Apprentice*, Trump's reality show, a men's cooking team had failed to impress the judges. "You fired Gary Busey," Obama recalled. "And these are the kinds of decisions that would keep me up at night."

The audience loved it, but they would be shocked just twenty-four hours later when they learned what decision really was keeping Obama up that night.

The next day, as the Navy Seals gathered their gear at their base in Jalalabad, Afghanistan, the White House canceled tours lest the unusual flurry of meetings on a Sunday be noticed. Only late in the day were the political aides notified. Dan Pfeiffer, the president's communications director, was at the movies (*Fast and Furious 5*) when he checked his BlackBerry and found a message summoning him to the White House. "As I'm coming in, the cast of *True Blood* is outside the gate trying to figure out why their tour has been canceled," he recalled.

In the Situation Room, national security officials monitored incoming feeds as someone brought provisions from Costco – turkey pita wraps, cold shrimp, potato chips and soda. Eventually, Obama and the others moved to the anteroom to follow the action in real time on a screen.

Suddenly, one of the helicopters approaching the complex in Pakistan stalled and came down hard on the ground. There were no fatalities or serious injuries, but the Seals were unable to get it to take off again, so some of them set about blowing it up to keep sensitive technology from falling into the wrong hands, while the rest of the team raced through the building searching for bin Laden.

When the helicopter went down, "it was kind of a big gulp," recalled Michael Morell, the deputy C.I.A. director.

But Panetta was reassured by Admiral McRaven's cool. "He basically was drinking a Coke and I said, 'Bill, what's going on?'" Panetta recalled. "And he said, 'No problem. We've got the backup helicopter. It's called in.' "

After the fatal shots, the Seals uploaded a photograph of the body to analysts who then fed it into a facial-recognition program, which produced a 95 percent confirmation that it was bin Laden. The Seals wanted to measure the dead man's height to compare it to bin Laden's known dimensions but they had forgotten to bring a tape measure, so one of the commandos lay down next to the corpse for comparison purposes. DNA tests comparing samples with relatives later found a 99.9 percent match, officials said.

The troops loaded the body as well as a trove of documents and computer hard drives onto the remaining helicopters and made their escape even as Pakistani authorities were scrambling to respond to mysterious reports of gunfire and explosions. "This was the longest forty minutes of my life," Obama later told NBC News.

A wave of emotion washes over relatives of 9/11 victims.

The commandos made it out safely. Bin Laden's body was washed and placed in a white sheet in keeping with Muslim tradition. Since no country was willing to take it and a burial site might become a shrine for jihadists, the Americans flew the corpse to the aircraft carrier *USS Carl Vinson*, where it was placed in a weighted bag and eased into the sea, never to be seen again.

Back in Washington, Obama called his predecessor, George W. Bush, who was having dinner at a Dallas restaurant, to let him know that the hunt he had started had finally come to fruition. Panetta called his wife, Sylvia, in California. Four months earlier, his friend, the owner of a Monterey restaurant, had dared him to find bin Laden, vowing to open an 1870 bottle of Château Lafite Rothschild, worth $10,000, if he did. "Call Ted," Panetta told his wife, "and tell him he owes me that bottle of wine."

Pfeiffer and David Plouffe headed over to the East Room to prepare for Obama's televised announcement. "There's just two guys slowly moving chairs," Pfeiffer said. "Plouffe and I are like, We better go get people so we can do this ourselves. We may have killed bin Laden, but we don't have a room to speak in."

The wave of emotion around the country especially washed over relatives of the victims, who had waited nearly ten years for justice. A nation that had spent a decade tormented by its failure to catch the man responsible for nearly 3,000 fiery deaths at long last had its sense of finality.

"It cannot ease our pain or bring back our loved ones," said Gordon Felt, president of Families of Flight 93, a group representing the interests of relatives of the victims. "It does bring a measure of comfort that the mastermind of the September 11th tragedy and the face of global terror can no longer spread his evil."

Like thousands of others, Maureen Hasson, twenty-two, a recent college graduate wearing a fuchsia party dress and flip-flops, raced out into the night and headed to Lafayette Square across from the White House to celebrate. "This is full circle for our generation," she said. "Just look around at the average age here. We were all in middle school when the terrorists struck. We all vividly remember 9/11, and this is the close of that chapter."

Other chapters, however, were just opening. At the same time Obama was huddling with intelligence officers studying satellite images and trying to decide whether The Pacer was really a terrorist, the rest of the Middle East was convulsing with change that would test the president in fresh ways and force him to rethink his views about American power and America's role in the world.

In a rural town in Tunisia in December 2010, an unlicensed fruit seller

DOUG MILLS/NEW YORK TIMES

Outside the White House, crowds cheer the news of Osama bin Laden's death, May 2, 2011.

ordered to turn over his wooden cart and slapped by a female police officer protested his humiliation by setting himself on fire. In that instant, a far greater blaze was ignited across the region. Moved by his desperation, Tunisians mobilized protests. Clashes with authorities broke out, killing dozens. Under pressure from the streets, the government fell in January 2011, and President Zine el-Abidine Ben Ali fled to Saudi Arabia after twenty-three years in power, the first time popular demonstrations had forced out an Arab leader.

As young Egyptians fight for freedom, Obama feels drawn to their cause.

Inspired by the events in Tunisia, dissenters began agitating around the region, in places like Bahrain, Libya, Syria and most notably Egypt, the historic center of the Arab world. Hundreds, then thousands, then hundreds of thousands of protesters crowded onto Tahrir Square in Cairo demanding that President Hosni Mubarak step down. Mubarak, a powerfully built former air force commander, had ruled Egypt with a firm hand for thirty years since the assassination of President Anwar Sadat and had become the epitome of a Middle East autocrat. But he was also a stalwart friend of the United States as well as a reliable guarantor of the peace treaty between Egypt and Israel born out of Jimmy Carter's Camp David summit.

Watching from Washington, Obama felt torn. He had scorned Bush's "freedom agenda" promoting democracy around the world, seeing it as messianic, hypocritical and at times counterproductive. He focused instead on promoting mutual respect and understanding. In his Cairo speech just a few months after taking office, he had tempered his words of support for democratic aspirations by noting that "there is no straight line to realize this promise." When Iranians upset at elections they deemed rigged took to the streets that same summer in what was dubbed the Green Revolution, Obama remained mostly quiet, reasoning that American support would only discredit the homegrown opposition.

But he had come to regret the silence, and two years later, as he watched young Egyptians fighting for their freedom in the streets and on Twitter and Facebook, he felt increasingly drawn into their struggle. Joseph Biden, Hillary Clinton, Robert Gates and other, more seasoned figures cautioned him against throwing Mubarak overboard, but younger, more idealistic advisers like Benjamin Rhodes, his national security speechwriter, urged the president to be on the right side of history, as they put it. Obama agreed. If this really was a repeat of the popular uprisings in Eastern Europe, he wanted to be remembered as a champion of freedom.

Libyan opposition fighters push on as a natural gas facility burns, March 9, 2011.

V. 'JUSTICE HAS BEEN DONE'   113

A short-lived and ill-conceived diplomatic mission by a special envoy, Frank Wisner, to try to ease out Mubarak did little good. Anger on the street continued to grow. Obama's national security team was thirty minutes into a meeting on what to do when the president suddenly came through the door to join the conversation. The question on the table: Should he call for Mubarak to step down?

Amid the discussion, the door opened and an aide handed a note to Tom Donilon. "Mubarak is on," Donilon announced.

The Situation Room screens were tuned into Al Jazeera as Mubarak addressed his nation. The Egyptian leader was defiant and imperious. He agreed not to run for another term but would not step down right away. "This is my country," he declared. "I will die on its soil."

The American officials watched in grim silence. Finally, Obama spoke up. "That's not going to cut it," he said.

Obama made a telephone call to Mubarak to tell him he had not gone far enough. The line crackled with tension.

"I know the last thing you want to see is Egypt collapse into chaos," Obama told him. "How can you help manage the change?"

Mubarak did not even wait for Obama's words to be translated. "You don't understand my people," he scolded. "I do understand my people."

After they hung up, Obama resolved to publicly push Mubarak to do what he was refusing to do. He already had a statement drafted declaring that a "transition must begin now."

Biden, Clinton and Gates objected, urging him either to not make a statement or at least to take out the "must begin now" line.

Obama refused. "If 'now' is not in my remarks," he replied, "there's no point in me going out there and talking."

"Now" stayed in and ten days later Mubarak was driven from power. Suddenly, the whole Middle East appeared to be heading in a new direction. It was heady and powerful. How influential Obama's push was in sealing Mubarak's fate could be debated. Americans tend to give great weight to their own ability to shape events in far-off countries that in many cases are determined by their own internal dynamics and politics. But if Mubarak was to go anyway, Obama at the very least had put himself and the United States on the side of change. What he did not fully anticipate was how much other allies in the region like Saudi Arabia, the United Arab Emirates and Kuwait would see that as a betrayal. If the American president was willing to cut loose a longtime friend as loyal as Mubarak, they concluded, he could not be relied on to back them in moments of crisis.

So when protests broke out days later in the Persian Gulf island state of Bahrain, where the United States Navy based its Fifth Fleet, the Saudis and Emiratis decided to take matters into their own hands. Shiite protesters were standing up to a Sunni monarchy, a situation that did not sit well with the neighbors. Without telling the Americans, Saudi Arabia sent a column of tanks, artillery and troops across the sixteen-mile King Fahd Causeway into Bahrain to help the government clear out Pearl Square in the capital of Manama by force. The Emiratis also sent troops.

Obama stewed at the intervention and violent suppression of demonstrations but Saudi Arabia was different than Egypt. Not only did the conservative Saudi royal family play an outsized role in the world economy through its oil fields, it held a much firmer grip over its people. It saw the Shiite uprising next door as a threat that could embolden Iran and encourage Shiites in its own country to follow suit. And in effect, the Saudi sheiks were challenging Obama even as they turned guns and tear gas on peaceful protesters.

This time, Obama turned away. There were limits to how far he was willing to go to nurture change in a volatile region.

While Obama relied on strong arm diplomacy in Egypt, he was drawn into using real arms next door in Libya. The same popular wave sweeping through the rest of the region led many in the North Africa pariah state to finally rise up against Colonel Muammar el-Qaddafi, who with his wild hair, beady eyes and trademark sunglasses had become one of the world's most recognizable tyrants during forty-two years in power.

The first protests began in the seafront city of Benghazi in February just four days after Mubarak's ouster. Qaddafi had watched Mubarak's end and had no intention of sharing his fate. Rather than go down peacefully, he ordered his army to move against those rebelling against his rule. In a typically defiant tirade, he went on television to denounce his opponents as "rats" and "cockroaches" and called on his supporters to "attack them in their dens."

Worried about a slaughter, France and Britain pushed the United Nations Security Council to approve a resolution authorizing foreign powers to establish a no-fly zone over Libya. Never enamored of Qaddafi, the Arab League pushed for intervention as well. With American troops still fighting in Afghanistan and in the process of withdrawing from Iraq, though, Obama and his team had little interest in getting involved. Susan Rice, the president's ambassador to the United Nations, called her French counterpart and warned him against Western military interference. She feared that if the Europeans went in themselves, the United States would feel obliged to follow. "You are not going to drag us into your shitty war," Rice told the French ambassador.

Indeed, there was fierce resistance in the Situation Room to any American military action. "Can I finish the two wars I'm already in before you guys go looking for a third one?" Robert Gates asked. Joseph Biden and Tom Donilon agreed with him. But some of the same right-side-of-history advisers argued that Obama could not sit idly by while Qaddafi massacred

DREW ANGERER/NEW YORK TIMES

Meeting with Egyptian President Hosni Mubarak at the White House, September 1, 2010.

civilians. This time, Hillary Clinton was on their side, having met with Libyan opposition leaders who impressed her. Her advice may have been decisive. Obama later told Gates privately in the Oval Office that the Libya operation was a "51-49" decision – and Gates was convinced Clinton was the one who put it over the top.

In March, a month after protests began, the United Nations Security Council authorized "all necessary means" to protect Libyan civilians. Russia's President Dmitri Medvedev, who had forged a constructive working relationship with Obama and had been given considerable leeway in international affairs by his country's paramount leader, Prime Minister Vladimir Putin, agreed not to block the resolution and ordered his ambassador to abstain.

Rebels storm Qaddafi's compound, ending his reign once and for all.

But Obama was going along on one condition: The Europeans, for once, would have to take the lead. Libya was their problem, just 300 miles from their southern borders. The Americans would use their overwhelming airpower to stop the feared massacre, but after the first ten days it would be up to London and Paris to take over the operation and figure out what came next.

In effect, exhausted from its own international exertions of the past decade, the world's last superpower was subcontracting out the latest crisis. One aide told *The New Yorker* that Obama was "leading from behind," an infelicitous phrase that would be used against him for the rest of his presidency as a metaphor for passivity.

Within a month, the airstrikes succeeded in stopping the advance of Qaddafi's forces, saving the civilians of Benghazi. Obama went on national television to declare victory. "When people were being brutalized in Bosnia in the 1990s, it took the international community more than a year to intervene with air power to protect civilians," he boasted. "It took us thirty-one days."

Emboldened, Obama in August injected himself into yet another roiling Arab crisis, calling for the resignation of President Bashar al-Assad of Syria, who was beginning a bloody crackdown on protesters. Momentum seemed on the side of change. Just days afterward, Libyan rebels stormed Qaddafi's compound in Tripoli, ending his reign once and for all.

Two months later, they found Qaddafi himself in a sewer pipe, dragged him out, beat him to a pulp and sodomized him with a bayonet. He was soon dead. Grisly and unseemly as his demise was, Washington celebrated

Volunteers clean up Tahrir Square in Cairo on the day after President Hosni Mubarak resigned, February 12, 2011.

V. 'JUSTICE HAS BEEN DONE' 117

Colonel Muammar el-Qaddafi leaves a hotel in Tripoli after addressing the Libyan People's Congress, March 2, 2011.

the elimination of a man who had been an irritant or worse for four decades. "We came, we saw, he died!" Clinton exulted privately.

Around the same time, another enemy of America, this one from a newer generation, met a similar fate. Anwar al-Awlaki, the American-born propagandist and recruiter for Al Qaeda who had inspired and helped orchestrate a host of attacks, including the Fort Hood shootings and the attempted Christmas airline bombing, was killed by a C.I.A. drone strike in Yemen.

At forty years old, Awlaki was one of the most hunted terrorist figures after Osama bin Laden and few mourned his death, but the missile that delivered retribution to him in the desert sparked a different kind of debate back in the United States. Unlike bin Laden or other Al Qaeda figures targeted by drones, Awlaki was a United States citizen, born in New Mexico, and for the first time in the war on terror a president had authorized the killing of an American without trial. Also killed in the strike was Samir Khan, another American who was with Awlaki at the time but was not an intended target.

In issuing the kill order, Obama had gone where even George W. Bush had not. American law banned the killing of Americans abroad, but Obama's Justice Department argued that wartime provided an exception. Even though there was no armed conflict in Yemen, the administration lawyers concluded that the United States could still target its enemies there, given Al Qaeda's activities in the country. Civil libertarians and other critics decried the decision, saying it gave the government too much power to kill its own citizens.

Obama acknowledged the tricky issues and said such actions should be reserved for only the most dire circumstances, comparing Awlaki to a sniper shooting down on a crowd and taken out by a police SWAT team. "I would have detained and prosecuted Awlaki if we captured him before he carried out a plot, but we couldn't," Obama said later. "And as president, I would have been derelict in my duty had I not authorized the strike that took him out."

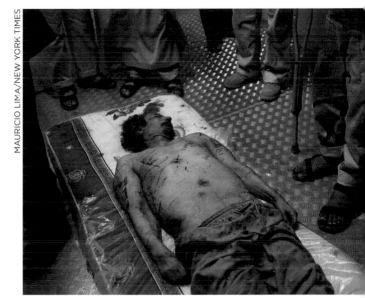

Qaddafi's body lies at a market in Misurata, Libya, October 21, 2011.

For Obama, this was an invigorating period. Osama bin Laden, Muammar el-Qaddafi and Anwar al-Awlaki were all dead. The president asserted that Al Qaeda was on the ropes. And now he was about to end the war in Iraq, or at least the American involvement in it.

Under the agreement Bush had left behind and that Obama embraced, American troops were to leave Iraq by the end of 2011. The situation on the ground seemed calm and Obama and his team were ready to claim victory and go home. Still, both sides had originally imagined they might negotiate a follow-up deal to keep a small American detachment behind as a force for stability, and Obama now confronted the question about whether and how to do that.

General Lloyd Austin, the commander on the ground, developed proposals for keeping as many as 24,000 troops after 2011, but he ran into instant resistance at the White House. To Obama's aides, it looked like a permanent South Korea-style presence, with the military still trying to do everything it was doing before, just with fewer troops. The White House said no. Austin and the Pentagon refined the proposal, developing options for leaving behind 19,000 troops, 16,000 troops and 10,000 troops. The general preferred the highest number and deemed the lowest unwise. Tom Donilon asked Gates if he could live with 10,000. Gates said he could. But even that would not last. The plan was later reduced to 5,000 troops.

If Obama seemed ambivalent about any troops staying behind, so was Iraq's prime minister, Nuri Kamal al-Maliki. Even while the debate over numbers raged, Washington and Baghdad became mired in a dispute over legal protections for American troops. The Pentagon wanted a liability shield approved by the Iraqi parliament, continuing the same protections it had had over the past eight years, but while Maliki agreed to submit it, no one thought it would pass. Maliki suggested that the United States depend on his own authority to approve such a measure, but Pentagon lawyers insisted it have the sanction of Iraq's querulous lawmakers. At loggerheads, the two sides quit the negotiations altogether. There would be no residual force. But the failure to resolve the liability issue in some ways provided the public rationale for an outcome that did not trouble either Obama or Maliki. "We really didn't want to be there, and he really didn't want us there," a top aide to Obama at the time said privately. "It was almost a mutual decision, not said directly to each other, but in reality that's what it became. And you had a president who was going to be running for re-election, and getting out of Iraq was going to be a big statement."

In December, Obama sent Biden to officially end the mission in an emotional ceremony at Al Faw Palace in Baghdad. Afterward, Biden called Obama back in Washington.

"Thank you for giving me the chance to end this goddamn war," Biden said.

"Joe," Obama responded, "I'm glad you got to do it."

In a public statement, Obama declared the withdrawal "a moment of success," one he had promised in his original campaign. "We're leaving behind a sovereign, stable and self-reliant Iraq, with a representative government," he said.

But for how long?

Opposition forces in Ras Lanyuf, Libya, March 9, 2011.

TYLER HICKS/NEW YORK TIMES

President Obama and Vice President Biden in Chicago on election night, November 6, 2012.

'My Brother'

At first distant, Barack and Joe forge an unlikely bond

They were as unlikely a pair as could be imagined – the cool, diffident, fortysomething African-American community organizer and the voluble, backslapping Irish-American career politician nearly two decades older. And to be sure, it was a partnership that did not start off all that strongly. But by their second term together, President Obama and Vice President Joseph Biden had forged a real bond. "Joe," an uncharacteristically emotional Obama once told his number two, "you are my brother."

Like many brothers, Biden did not always follow directions and his influence waxed and waned over the years. He was often the go-to negotiator when tensions flared with Capitol Hill and he was given some of the highest profile assignments of Obama's presidency, including overseeing the economic recovery spending package and the withdrawal of American troops from Iraq. But he lost internal fights over foreign policy, got crosswise with the president over gay rights and failed to deliver the gun control package Obama asked him to push through Congress.

In some ways, Biden became the human face of an administration led by a president known for robotic stoicism. Where Obama rarely revealed any inner life, Biden rarely disguised his. Anger, joy, frustration, eagerness – if he felt it, he expressed it. When his son, Beau, died of brain cancer at forty-six in 2015, Biden's raw grief was on display for all to see, generating waves of sympathy across party lines. As he weighed whether to run for president in 2016, Biden talked repeatedly about his son's death, almost as if engaging in public therapy. "Sometimes it just sort of overwhelms you," he told the talk show host Stephen Colbert.

Biden grew up in a middle-class Catholic family in Scranton, Pennsylvania, and Wilmington, Delaware, drawing modest grades before earning a law degree at Syracuse. He was elected to the Senate from Delaware in 1972, served for thirty six years and ran for president twice before accepting Obama's invitation to join his ticket in 2008. He played the seasoned mentor, helping a young and inexperienced president navigate the treacherous politics of the capital.

Obama did not initially warm to Biden, put off by the vice president's loquacious, gaffe-prone style. When Biden said there was a 30 percent chance that Obama's economic recovery program would fail, the president dismissed it publicly. Annoyed and unwilling to be presented as the Uncle Joe of the administration, Biden complained to Obama during a private lunch and the president resolved to avoid diminishing his partner in public.

Biden was the in-house skeptic on the use of force, arguing against a troop surge to Afghanistan, military intervention in Libya and the special forces raid into Pakistan that killed Osama bin Laden. That put him at odds with more hawkish members of the team, like Robert Gates, the defense secretary held over from President George W. Bush's administration, who later called Biden "wrong on nearly every major foreign policy and national security issue over the past four decades."

Obama did not see it that way. He came to appreciate his vice president, brushing off aides who floated the idea of replacing him on the re-election ticket in 2012 and embracing Biden's contrary voice.

"Joe, in that sense, can help stir the pot," he told *The New York Times*. And Biden, who at first bristled at the idea of serving as junior partner to a newcomer nineteen years his junior, came to appreciate Obama's place at the top of their partnership. "It's the right order," he said.

By the time they left office, there was much chatter about what Obama jokingly called "our bromance." Just days before the end of their tenure, Obama surprised Biden by bestowing on him the Presidential Medal of Freedom, with the additional honor of "with distinction," the only time he did so in his presidency.

Biden was overcome with emotion and turned away from the audience to wipe away tears with a handkerchief. As the medal was presented, he stared up in an effort to keep control, his eyes watery and cheeks wet.

Obama called him "the best vice president America has ever had." Biden returned the compliment, calling Obama "a remarkable man who did remarkable things."

CHAPTER VI

'Fought Our Way Back'

Despite a lackluster debate performance and a terrorist attack in Libya, the president turns back Mitt Romney's challenge to win re-election and claim four more years to transform America.

President Obama and the First Lady with Sasha and Malia in Chicago, November 7, 2012.

By the time President Obama took the stage at the Fox Theater in Redwood City, California, that spring evening in 2012, he was in the eighteenth hour of a nineteen-hour day. His tie was still knotted all the way to the top as he launched into his stump speech, attacking his opponent's record and defending his own. "I still believe in you," he told the audience, "and I hope you still believe in me."

That was a proposition Obama was about to test four years after the political winds converged behind his original, improbable journey to the White House. In marathon trips across the nation, he tried to justify the faith supporters had invested in him. He was running against himself as much as the Republicans, or rather, two versions of himself – one, the radical ruining the country that conservatives saw and the other, the savior of the country that he had struggled to live up to.

Obama had pulled the nation back from the edge of the economic abyss, saved the auto industry and imposed new regulations on Wall Street, but unemployment still topped 8 percent, millions of Americans who did have jobs were stuck with low pay and the national debt had skyrocketed. American troops had come home from Iraq, but the war in Afghanistan raged on inconclusively, and the situation in Libya was beginning to unravel amid factions battling each other for power. Obama had taken out Osama bin Laden, signed a nuclear arms treaty with Russia and put two liberal justices on the Supreme Court, but he had failed to close the prison at Guantánamo Bay, overhaul immigration rules, pass climate-change legislation or usher in a new era of bipartisanship. His biggest legislative accomplishment, his health care program, was a double-edged sword. It expanded coverage to millions who were vulnerable but alienated many Americans who resented government interference in their lives, while still leaving some in his liberal base disgruntled that he did not go further.

The protesters waiting outside a campaign fund-raiser in Denver one day in May were probably never supporters to begin with, but some of their signs cut close to the bone for a president who had built his career on inspiration.

"Out of Hope, Ready for Change," one read.

"Obama's Blvd. of Broken Promises," said another.

Indeed, this was a president who had yet to realize the lofty expectations that had propelled him from obscurity to the Oval Office. This was a proud yet humbled president, a confident yet scarred president, a dreamer mugged by reality, a pragmatist confounded by ideology, a revolutionary to

President Obama and Governor Mitt Romney make points at their Hofstra University debate, New York, October 16, 2012.

some, a sellout to others. He would "never be a perfect president," he conceded at one campaign stop after another. Long after the messiah jokes had vanished, the oh-so-mortal Barack Hussein Obama was left to make the case that while progress was slow, he was taking America to a better place – and that he would be a better president over the next four years.

Against Romney, Obama positions himself as a champion of the middle class.

Still, Obama started out the 2012 election year in relatively strong shape. While his approval rating had slid from its highs after the bin Laden raid, it was still hovering around 50 percent. And he could summarize his argument in a pithy bumper sticker slogan that Joseph Biden would later use at the Democratic National Convention: "Osama bin Laden is dead and General Motors is alive." Obama had two other advantages. The first was a clear path to the nomination for a second term. The only incumbent presidents to be defeated at the polls or driven from the race in the previous eighty years all had primary challenges within their own parties. The second was a Republican opposition driven by rural, anti-elite Tea Party populism but represented by a moderate, wealthy New England investor who enacted a precursor to Obama's health care program in his own state. Mitt Romney, the former governor of Massachusetts soon to be nominated by the Republicans, once favored abortion rights and "full equality" for gay and lesbian Americans, but now was trying to lead a far more conservative party in its bid for the White House, a challenge even after his selection of Representative Paul Ryan of Wisconsin, a favorite of the right, as his running mate.

If Obama's own accomplishments were not impressive enough for some, then he aimed to make sure the public saw the Republicans as even worse. Obama planned to paint the Republicans as obstructionists bent only on stopping him. Romney would be presented to the public as a rapacious capitalist whose firm, Bain Capital, snatched up distressed companies and laid off workers to squeeze out profits for itself. With his privileged lifestyle and multiple houses, including one with a car elevator, Romney played into the image of a manicured plutocrat.

Obama planned to position himself as a champion of the middle class in a time of widening income inequality, denouncing the "breathtaking greed" of those at the top of the economic ladder. Starting with a speech in Osawatomie, Kansas, on December 6, 2011, Obama was trying to coopt the arguments of the left wing of his party that had staged Occupy Wall Street sit-ins to protest the super-wealthy. He even adopted their formulation by

The Republican Presidential Forum at Fox News, New York, December 3, 2011.

complaining that the top one percent of Americans were benefiting at the expense of the other 99 percent.

"This is a make-or-break moment for the middle class and all those who are fighting to get into the middle class," Obama told an auditorium of supporters in Osawatomie, a hardscrabble town of 4,500 chosen because it was the place where Theodore Roosevelt laid out his own progressive platform called the New Nationalism a century earlier. "At stake is whether this will be a country where working people can earn enough to raise a family, build a modest savings, own a home and secure their retirement."

At times, though, Obama undercut his own argument. At a news conference in June, he said "the private sector is doing fine." He was comparing it to the public sector, where teachers and firefighters were being laid off. A month later, during a campaign stop in Virginia, he told an audience, "If you've got a business, you didn't build that." His point was that government played an important role in creating the environment for business to thrive. But his attempts at intellectualized arguments only made him seem out of touch about the depth of the economic pain in the country and outright disdainful of American entrepreneurship. And they handed Republicans useful ammunition when they presented Obama as an enemy of capitalism who had failed to rebuild the economy after the crisis of 2008.

As he headed toward the fall contest, Obama had one more issue to confront to consolidate his own base. While much of the rest of the country had moved steadily toward favoring a right to marriage for same-sex couples, Obama had been left behind in opposition. For years, he had officially supported civil unions, but not marriage, for gays and lesbians.

He had been a friend to them in other ways. He had pushed through legislation finally allowing them to serve openly in the military, and his Justice Department had refused to defend in court the Defense of Marriage Act, the 1990s law barring federal recognition for same-sex weddings. But his position against same-sex marriage remained a sore point to many liberals. To be sure, he had tried to fudge in recent years, saying that his thinking was "evolving," but with more states adopting laws and polls showing growing support, especially among key young voters, Obama found himself at odds with his own supporters.

Any plans for an elegant, carefully scripted reversal, though, were abruptly upended one spring Sunday, when Biden unexpectedly came out publicly for same-sex marriage. Interviewed by David Gregory for NBC's *Meet the Press* on May 6, Biden, a Catholic who like Obama had opposed same-sex marriage until then, was asked if he was comfortable with it now. Caught off guard, the habitually outspoken vice president chose to say what he thought.

"I am absolutely comfortable," Biden said, "with the fact that men marrying men, women marrying women and heterosexual men and women marrying one another are entitled to the same exact rights, all the civil rights, all the civil liberties, and quite frankly I don't see much distinction beyond that."

Aides watching the taping recognized that the vice president had just put his boss in a box. They highlighted a transcript of the interview with yellow pen and sent it to the president's advisers as a warning before it aired. Obama's advisers were livid. Now it was untenable for the president to maintain his position or wait to announce a new one. "There was a little apoplexy around here," Biden admitted later to *The New York Times*. But the vice president was unapologetic. "I was going to sit there and not say what I believe at this point in my career? They can have the goddamn job."

At the White House briefing the day after *Meet the Press* aired, Jay Carney, the press secretary, was pummeled with questions from skeptical reporters about Obama's stance. How could he continue to oppose same-sex marriage when his own vice president supported it?

From the vice president, an unscripted endorsement of same-sex marriage.

The next morning, as Obama was about to leave the White House for an event in Albany, New York, several aides intercepted him in the Oval Office and told him he had to change his position promptly. He agreed. The next day, he sat down with ABC's Robin Roberts to complete his "evolution." "At a certain point," Obama told her, "I've just concluded that for me personally it is important for me to go ahead and affirm that I think same-sex couples should be able to get married."

Obama's shift was not without risk, coming just a day after voters in North Carolina, site of the upcoming Democratic National Convention and a key battleground state in the fall election, approved a ban on same-sex marriage. But he moved only after polls showed dramatic changes in attitudes nationally. Where just 27 percent of Americans supported same-sex marriage in 1996, when Bill Clinton signed the Defense of Marriage Act, fully 50 percent now thought it should be legal. Among Democrats, support reached 65 percent, making it almost unsustainable for a Democratic president to remain in opposition when nearly two-thirds of his party was on the other side. In this case, Obama was a follower more than a leader.

But on another issue important to his base, he took the initiative just weeks later. With Congress balking at immigration reform, Obama relied on his own executive authority to allow as many as 800,000 young people brought into the country illegally as children to stay without fear

Scott Van Duzer hugs the president at a campaign stop in Van Duzer's pizza shop, Fort Pierce, Florida, September 9, 2011.

of deportation, to work legally and obtain driver's licenses and other documents.

In effect, Obama was asserting that he had the power to do what Congress had specifically rejected when it defeated the Dream Act nearly two years earlier. Liberal advocates applauded the move while pressing Obama to help not just the "dreamers," as they were called, but their parents and others too. The president, however, said that was as far as he could go; he did not have the power to go further. At least that was his position for the moment.

Heading into the campaign season, much of Obama's record hinged on the health care program that now effectively bore his name. It had been dubbed Obamacare by scornful opponents in a bit of mockery, but the president decided to embrace the name by arguing that it showed that Obama did in fact care.

The question was whether Obamacare would survive until the election. On June 28, 2012, the president was standing outside the Oval Office watching cable television when two networks, CNN and Fox, announced that the Supreme Court had just struck down his health care program.

For a few moments, Obama absorbed the news that his signature domestic achievement, the program he thought would help define his place in history, was no more. But just then, Kathryn Ruemmler, his White House counsel, rushed into the room and flashed two thumbs up. The networks were wrong – the court had in fact upheld the program.

While a conservative majority had indeed determined that the government could not force individuals to buy health insurance under the commerce clause of the Constitution, as the Obama administration had argued that it could, a majority consisting of the four liberal justices joined by Chief Justice John Roberts found that it could do so using the taxing power. The reasoning may have been different, but the bottom line was the program was constitutional. It would go forward.

Obama hugged Ruemmler and called Solicitor General Donald Verrilli, who had argued the case before the court, to congratulate him.

Still, there was a pretty big asterisk. The court also ruled that Washington could not force states to expand Medicaid by threatening them with the loss of existing federal payments. That was a key element of the program expanding coverage for poor Americans. Now states would get to choose whether to participate, and many with Republican governors quickly made clear they would not.

Obama chose to interpret the split verdict as a victory and declare vindication. Mitt Romney, hoping to mobilize conservatives behind him, vowed to overturn the law if he were elected, never mind its similarities to his own program in Massachusetts.

It was a mark of Obama's presidency that the program remained so

President Obama at the Democratic National Convention, Charlotte, North Carolina, September 6, 2012.

controversial two years after its passage. Aides had once predicted that when the fury of the partisan battle surrounding its passage faded, Americans would accept and even welcome the program. But in the weeks leading up to the Supreme Court decision, just 34 percent of Americans told pollsters that they supported it, essentially unchanged from the 32 percent who favored it when it passed in 2010.

Opponents spend more time talking about Obamacare than Obama does.

The president's advisers argued that social programs often were unpopular when first enacted, only to build support once they were put in place and Americans came to rely on them. But history suggested otherwise. Social Security was popular from the start, supported by 73 percent of Americans in early 1937 and by 78 percent a year later. Medicare had the approval of 62 percent in early 1965 and 82 percent by the end of that year.

In the face of relentless conservative opposition, the White House had never made a sustained effort to win over an unenthusiastic public. The strategist hired to design public outreach for the program was soon given other projects as well. Attempts to educate voters about the program were

President Obama in the Oval Office, October 18, 2013.

sporadic and underfunded. From the time of its passage to the Supreme Court decision, opponents had spent $235 million on ads attacking the program, compared with the $69 million that was spent on those supporting it.

In essence, Obama's team had concluded that the issue was a political loser in the short term and decided to focus energy elsewhere. When the president delivered his State of the Union address in 2012, heading into his re-election campaign, he devoted just two sentences to the program that he had once hoped would be his main argument for a second term – forty-four words out of more than seven thousand. Instead, he and his advisers decided to emphasize jobs.

As it turned out, his opponents would spend more time talking about his health care program in the fall than he would.

If Obama was hoping the rest of the world would cooperate with his bid to win another term, the harsh reality was on display that summer. Europe seemed unable to contain its rolling economic crisis. Flare-ups of violence in Baghdad recalled the worst of the Iraq war. Vladimir Putin had reclaimed the presidency in Russia and was cracking down at home and rattling sabers abroad.

The Arab Spring that had started out with so much hope was taking a sinister turn as well. Egypt's popular revolution had elevated the Muslim Brotherhood to power and was at risk of being reversed by the military. Libya was falling into a miasma of revenge killings as rival militias and Islamists competed for power. And in Syria, where President Bashar al-Assad had casually defied Obama's call for him to step down, a full-blown civil war was raging with government forces shelling civilian neighborhoods while insurgent groups begged for help from Arab states and the West.

Obama wanted no part in their war but over one weekend in August, the White House received alarming intelligence reports. American spy agencies had detected signs that the Assad government was moving part of its huge stockpile of chemicals weapons out of storage, and the Syrian military was mixing chemicals, a possible indication that they were being prepared for use. As Obama's national security team rushed back for weekend consultations, the president decided to try to intimidate Assad into not employing the poisonous weapons on his own people, sending secret messages through Russia, Iran and other governments.

Obama went public with his message the next day when asked about Syria at a news conference. Moving or using large quantities of chemical weapons, he declared, would cross a "red line" and "change my calculus" about American involvement in the conflict.

The advisers who had attended meetings on Syria over the weekend listened with surprise, wondering where the "red line" came from. With such an evocative yet off-the-cuff phrase, the president had defined his policy in a way some advisers soon wished they could take back.

The New York Times

Late Edition

Today, plenty of sunshine, low humidity, high 80. **Tonight,** mostly clear, low 64. **Tomorrow,** sunny for the most part, a warm afternoon, high 80. Weather map, Page B12.

VOL. CLXI .. No. 55,893   © 2012 The New York Times   NEW YORK, THURSDAY, SEPTEMBER 13, 2012 $2.50

Obama Grows More Reliant On Big-Money Contributors

Change in Emphasis From '08 Grass-Roots Effort

By NICHOLAS CONFESSORE

Kirk Wagar, a Florida lawyer who has raised more than $1 million for President Obama's re-election bid, had his choice of rooms for the Democratic convention at Charlotte's Ritz-Carlton or Westin hotels and nightly access to hospitality suites off the convention floor.

Jay Snyder, a New York financier who has raised at least $560,000 for Mr. Obama, was entitled to get his picture taken on the podium at the Time Warner Cable Arena.

And Azita Raji, a retired investment banker who has raised over $3 million for Mr. Obama — more than almost anyone else during the last two years — could get pretty much anything that she wanted last week in Charlotte: briefings with senior Obama officials, invitations to post-speech parties, along with "priority booking" at the city's finest hotels.

In the race for cash, Mr. Obama often praises his millions of grass-roots donors, those diehards whose $3 or $10 or $75 contributions are as much a symbol of the president's political identity as they are a source of ready cash. But his campaign's big-dollar fund-raising has become more dependent than it was four years ago on a smaller number of large-dollar donors and fund-raisers.

All told, Mr. Obama's top "bundlers" — people who gather checks from friends and business associates — raised or gave at least $200 million for Mr. Obama's re-election bid and the Democratic National Committee through the end of May, close to half of the total up to that point, according to internal campaign documents obtained by The New

Continued on Page A19

23 Years After Soccer Tragedy, An Apology and a Shift in Blame

By JOHN F. BURNS

LONDON — Nearly a quarter of a century after 96 Liverpool soccer fans were crushed to death in one of the worst stadium disasters in history, Prime Minister David Cameron formally apologized on Wednesday to the victims' families, saying their "appalling deaths" were compounded by an attempt by the police, investigators and the news media to depict the victims as hooligans and to blame them for the disaster.

Before a hushed House of Commons, Mr. Cameron said the families had suffered "a double injustice" in the failures of the police, fire officials and other authorities to anticipate the disaster or to contain its scale once it occurred, and in the efforts that followed to

cover up police failings by altering witness statements, and to pin responsibility on the victims for their own deaths.

The prime minister's apology, and the findings of a new inquiry panel on which it was based, marked a stunning reversal in a saga that has been an open wound in Britain since April 15, 1989, when 3,000 Liverpool supporters sought to crowd into standing-room terraces approved for barely half that many at Hillsborough Stadium in Sheffield, 150 miles north of London. All but one of the victims perished that day, many of them within minutes. The last victim remained in a coma until he died in 1993.

It has become known simply as

Continued on Page A3

Decades Later, a Vision Survives

President Obama and Secretary of State Hillary Rodham Clinton in the courtyard of the State Department on Wednesday.

PAUL J. RICHARDS/AGENCE FRANCE-PRESSE — GETTY IMAGES

ROBERT WRIGHT FOR THE NEW YORK TIMES

Louis Kahn's design comes to fruition at Four Freedoms Park.

The park — a memorial to Franklin Delano Roosevelt — was conceived four decades ago. The visionary architect who designed it died in 1974. The site, a landfill along one of the more dramatic stretches of waterfront in New York City, remained a rubble heap while the project was left for dead.

But in a city proud of its own impatience, perseverance sometimes pays off. Next month, on that triangular plot on the southern end of Roosevelt Island, the four-acre Franklin D. Roosevelt

MICHAEL KIMMELMAN

ARCHITECTURE REVIEW

Four Freedoms Park will open, a belated and monumental triumph for New York and for everyone who cares about architecture and public space.

Louis Kahn is the architect. He completed drawings for the park just before he died suddenly, in Pennsylvania Station, at 73. That Kahn's plan survived periodic calls to privatize the government-owned property and build a hotel and fancy town houses, among other commercial proposals, proves the benefit of resisting short-term financial imperatives. In the end the value of the project

Continued on Page A4

ATTACK ON U.S. SITE IN LIBYA KILLS ENVOY; A FLASH POINT FOR OBAMA AND ROMNEY

A Challenger's Criticism Is Furiously Returned

By PETER BAKER and ASHLEY PARKER

WASHINGTON — The deadly attack on an American diplomatic post in Libya propelled foreign policy to the forefront of an otherwise inward-looking presidential campaign and presented an unexpected test not only to the incumbent, who must manage an international crisis, but also to the challenger, whose response quickly came under fire.

While President Obama dealt with the killings of an ambassador and three other Americans and deflected questions about his handling of the Arab world, Mitt Romney, the Republican seeking his job, wasted little time going on the attack, accusing the president of apologizing for American values and appeasing Islamic extremists.

"They clearly sent mixed messages to the world," Mr. Romney told reporters during a campaign swing through Florida.

But Mr. Romney came under withering criticism for distorting

A BIGGER CONCERN THAN LIBYA

Egypt, where unrest continued, may pose a long-term problem for the White House. Page A14.

the chain of events overseas and appearing to seek political advantage from an attack that claimed American lives. A statement he personally approved characterized an appeal for reli-

gious tolerance issued by the American Embassy in Cairo as sympathy for the attackers even though the violence did not occur until hours after the embassy statement. Mr. Romney on Wednesday said the embassy statement, which was disavowed by the administration, was "akin to apology, and I think was a severe miscalculation."

Mr. Obama fired back later in

Continued on Page A13

ESAM OMRAN AL-FETORI/REUTERS

The American diplomatic mission in Benghazi, Libya, after an attack by Islamists using antiaircraft weapons and grenades.

Video That Stoked Violence Has Murky History

By ADAM NAGOURNEY

LOS ANGELES — The film that set off violence across North Africa was made in obscurity somewhere in the sprawl of Southern California, and promoted by a network of right-wing Christians with a history of animosity directed toward Muslims. When a 14-minute trailer of it — all that may actually exist — was posted on YouTube in June, it was barely noticed.

But when the video, with its al-

most comically amateurish production values, was translated into Arabic and reposted twice on YouTube in the days before Sept. 11, and promoted by leaders of the Coptic diaspora in the United States, it drew nearly one million views and set off bloody demonstrations.

The history of the film — who financed it; how it was made; and perhaps most important, how it was translated into Arabic and posted on YouTube to Muslim viewers — was shrouded

Wednesday in tales of a secret Hollywood screening; a director who may or may not exist, and used a false name if he did; and actors who appeared, thanks to computer technology, to be traipsing through Middle Eastern cities. One of its main producers, Steve Klein, a Vietnam veteran whose son was severely wounded in Iraq, is notorious across California for his involvement with anti-Muslim actions, from the courts to schoolyards to

Continued on Page A14

A Wave of Unrest Shows a Region Still Volatile

By DAVID D. KIRKPATRICK and STEVEN LEE MYERS

CAIRO — Islamist militants armed with antiaircraft weapons and rocket-propelled grenades stormed a lightly defended United States diplomatic mission in Benghazi, Libya, late Tuesday, killing the American ambassador and three members of his staff and raising questions about the radicalization of countries swept up in the Arab Spring.

The ambassador, J. Christopher Stevens, was missing almost immediately after the start of an intense, four-hour firefight for control of the mission, and his body was not located until Wednesday morning at dawn, when he was found dead at a Benghazi hospital, American and Libyan officials said. It was the first time since 1979 that an American ambassador had died in a violent assault.

American and European officials said that while many details about the attack remained unclear, the assailants seemed organized, well trained and heavily armed, and they appeared to have at least some level of advance planning. But the officials cautioned that it was too soon to tell whether the attack was related to the anniversary of the Sept. 11 attacks.

Fighters involved in the assault, which was spearheaded by a Islamist brigade formed during last year's uprising against Col. Muammar el-Qaddafi, said in interviews during the battle that they were moved to attack the mission by anger over a 14-

Continued on Page A12

INTERNATIONAL A6-17

Bailout Upheld in Germany

In a victory for Chancellor Angela Merkel, the Federal Constitutional Court allowed Germany to contribute to a bailout fund for euro countries. **PAGE A6**

NEW YORK A24-29

Regulating Circumcision Ritual

A city proposal would require parents to acknowledge the risks of an ancient part of a circumcision method common in some Jewish communities. **PAGE A24**

BUSINESS DAY B1-11

Finally, the New iPhone

After weeks of anticipation, Apple introduced the iPhone 5, which is lighter, thinner and faster than its predecessor and provides a bigger screen. **PAGE B1**

ONLINE

Calling All Baby Boomers

Starting today, Booming, a new blog, offers news and commentary about the way baby boomers live now.

nytimes.com/booming

EDITORIAL, OP-ED A30-31

Gail Collins   PAGE A31

While Syria occupied the front burner in the Situation Room, Libya was "farmed out to the working level," as Dennis Ross, a top Middle East adviser to the president, put it. Now that the Libyan civilians were saved and Muammar el-Qaddafi was gone, Obama and his team were intent on avoiding getting entangled in the sort of nation-building in North Africa that dragged down the Bush administration in Afghanistan and Iraq.

The United States would now help Libya with its emergence from tyranny only if three conditions were met: First, it had to be a situation where America had unique capability that Europe or others did not. Second, Libya had to explicitly ask. And third, Libya would have to pay for the help with its oil revenue. By setting the bar so high, the White House effectively ensured that it would stay on the sidelines. Even when Hillary Clinton proposed sending a hospital ship to treat wounded fighters, the White House rejected the idea.

Christopher Stevens, handpicked by Clinton as ambassador to the new Libya, sent warning flares to Washington about a "security vacuum" in Benghazi. In a memo he titled "The Guns of August," after Barbara Tuchman's iconic history of the epic miscalculations that led to World War I, Stevens said Benghazi was moving "from trepidation to euphoria and back as a series of violent incidents has dominated the political landscape."

At age fifty-two, Stevens was a longtime foreign service officer with deep experience in the Arab world and an equally deep commitment to making Libya work. He was willing to take risks others might not. As dangerous as he knew Benghazi was, Stevens was back there on September 11. He spent the day in meetings and then retired for the evening at an American diplomatic post. Suddenly, though, a diplomatic visit turned tragic. Libyan gunmen stormed the compound, firing into the main building and setting it on fire. Over the course of the next few hours, Stevens was killed along with three other Americans: Sean Smith, an information officer with the State Department, and Tyrone Woods and Glen Doherty, two former Navy Seals working as security contractors for the C.I.A. It was the worst attack on an American diplomatic facility in more than a decade, coming on the anniversary of the day hijacked planes slammed into the World Trade Center and Pentagon.

Back at the White House, confusion reigned about what was going on. The attack in Benghazi happened on the same day demonstrations got out of control at the American embassy in Egypt, where protesters angry about an anti-Islam video made by a Florida pastor expressed their rage and, in a few cases, scaled the fence. Some in Washington thought the Benghazi attack must have stemmed from similar anger at the video. But the State Department's operations center sent an email to the White House, Pentagon, F.B.I. and other agencies reporting that Ansar al-Sharia, a terrorist group, had claimed credit for the Libya assault on Facebook and Twitter. In an email to her daughter, Chelsea, later that night, Clinton made clear she

A protester is silhouetted as flames engulf the United States diplomatic facility in Benghazi, September 11, 2012.

considered the episode a terrorist attack. "Two of our officers were killed in Benghazi by an al Qaeda-like group," she wrote.

In public, though, the White House and State Department cited the video as if the attack were simply a protest that got out of control. Addressing reporters in the Rose Garden the next day, Obama did use the word terror when he said, "No acts of terror will ever shake the resolve of this great nation." Yet he also focused on the video. "We reject all efforts to denigrate the religious beliefs of others," he said. "But there is absolutely no justification to this type of senseless violence. None."

During an interview later in the day, Obama agreed when Steve Kroft of CBS News noted that he had shied away from using the word terrorism. Kroft asked if he believed it was a terrorist attack.

"Well, it's too early to know exactly how this came about, what group was involved," Obama replied. "But obviously it was an attack on Americans, and we are going to be working with the Libyan government to make sure that we bring these folks to justice one way or the other."

By the weekend, the administration was sticking to the narrative of a video-inspired retaliation. After Clinton begged off weekend television appearances, Susan Rice, the ambassador to the United Nations, was sent onto five Sunday talk shows and – relying on talking points that had been scrubbed in prickly negotiations between the White House, State Department and C.I.A. – she repeated the suggestion that the assault in Benghazi was a protest taken over by extremists, not a premeditated terrorist operation. It would not be until eight days after the incident that a high-ranking American government official – Matt Olsen, director of the National Counterterrorism Center – would call it a "terrorist attack." Even then, Obama continued to avoid the term over the next few days.

Republicans quickly accused the president of trying to play down what happened in Benghazi because it would undermine his election-year claim to have crippled Al Qaeda. Democrats accused the Republicans of exploiting a tragedy for partisan advantage. What started as a calamity and foreign policy nightmare became a political football. Legitimate questions about the security of American installations overseas and the larger Obama approach to Libya were lost in the cross-fire of political figures more eager to defend or denigrate than to undertake a sober examination of what went wrong and why.

Either way, it left Obama on the defensive just weeks before voters were to go to the polls to render their verdict on his presidency. "Instead of Obama being the successful guy that got bin Laden, we're talking about Obama as the second coming of Jimmy Carter," said Michael Rubin, a Middle East scholar and former Bush administration official. "And that's not something the campaign wants to see."

J ust a few days after the attack in Benghazi, Obama paid tribute to the four slain Americans at a somber ceremony at Andrews Air Force Base outside Washington as their bodies were returned. The president put his arm around Clinton as she fought back tears watching four flag-draped caskets being loaded into four hearses. After he was done, Obama headed to Democratic party headquarters to practice for his upcoming election debate.

The juxtaposition of the two obligations that September day, one deeply profound, the other acutely political, underscored the challenges for an incumbent president seeking re-election. While a challenger could schedule time as he or she saw fit, a president had to juggle the nation's duties with campaign commitments. Aides noticed that Obama seemed distracted that day after the Benghazi ceremony as he tried to bone up for his confrontation with Mitt Romney. He never cared much for debates to begin with, much less debate preparations. They were, he said, "a drag."

Obama had been warned that incumbent presidents tended to lose their opening debate during re-election campaigns. Not only do they have competing demands on their time and mental energy, they are often rusty, while their challengers are fresh off a primary season and at their most practiced at the verbal jousting that comes during a debate. After nearly four years in office, a president can grow unaccustomed to being challenged so frontally and can grow cocky. A challenger is elevated in stature simply by sharing a stage with the incumbent. Obama shrugged off the worries of his advisers. "I'll be there on game day," he assured them. "I'm a game day player."

After a bad first debate, the president laces up the gloves in the second.

But forewarned is not always forearmed. Obama proved no exception to the incumbent's curse at his first debate in Denver on October 3, with 67 million Americans watching. In private, Obama scorned Romney and did not think him worthy, an impression he had a hard time masking in public. When he appeared opposite his challenger at the University of Denver, the president was flat, long-winded and pedantic. He kept looking down and did not use the cutting lines advisers had given him to assail Romney, who kept the president off guard with a forceful indictment of his leadership. Obama did not mention Bain Capital, the centerpiece of his campaign case against Romney. Obama did not even pursue the most potent line of attack he had available – a videotape secretly made at a closed-door fundraiser showing Romney dismissing 47 percent of the nation as people who were "dependent upon government, who believe that they are victims, who believe the government has a responsibility to care for them." Democrats had pounced on the tape, using it to paint Romney as an out-of-touch elitist. But not Obama, who never mentioned it on stage.

Obama aides watching in a back room groaned their way through the debate and did not even wait for it to end to convene a damage-control conference call. Top Colorado Democrats left the debate hall practically despondent, convinced that the president's poor performance had put their state back in play for Republicans. Suddenly, for Obama, a race that seemed well in hand appeared up for grabs.

The president himself walked off stage thinking he had done well. "That was a terrific debate," he said in its closing minutes. Only after he began reading early reviews on his iPad did he realize how badly it had gone. He called his adviser, David Axelrod, on the way back to his hotel room.

"I guess the consensus is that we didn't have a very good night," Obama said.

"That is the consensus," Axelrod said.

After watching a videotape of his performance, Obama understood better and began calling panicky donors and supporters to reassure them. "This is on me," he told them, vowing to do better the next time.

Obama "faced his own political mortality," as his aide, Dan Pfeiffer, put it later. In attempting a course correction, Obama concluded that he had been "too polite" in the first debate and dispensed with any fears he harbored of alienating swing voters by coming on too strong. "If I give up a couple of points of likability and come across as snarky," he told advisers, "so be it."

Thirteen days after he took presidential decorum to a Xanax extreme, Obama tucked away a dinner of steak and potatoes and went on stage at Hofstra University in Long Island with plenty of red meat for anxious supporters watching his second debate. He waited all of forty-five seconds into the encounter before making clear that he came not just ready for a fight but ready to pick one.

He talked right over Romney, who tried to talk over him back. The president who had waited patiently for his turn the last time around forced his way into Romney's answers this time. At one point, Obama squared off

A painting of Syrian President Bashar al-Assad in the Mujtahid Hospital, Damascus, March 28, 2013.

ANDREA BRUCE/NEW YORK TIMES

Hurricane Sandy's wake in Long Beach, New York, November 2012.

with Romney face to face, almost chest to chest, in the middle of the stage, as if they were roosters in a ring.

"What Governor Romney said just isn't true."

"Not true, Governor Romney, not true."

"What you're saying is just not true."

Obama painted Romney as a tool of big oil who was soft on China, hard on immigrants, politically crass on Libya and two-faced on guns and energy. He deployed many of the attack lines that went unused in Denver, going after Romney's business record, income taxes and the 47 percent remark. A front-page *New York Times* analysis the next morning summed it up in a concise three-word headline: "Punch, Punch, Punch."

From that point on, Obama was back in command of the race. The third debate in Boca Raton, Florida, did nothing to change that, nor did the last-minute surprise of Hurricane Sandy in October, which ravaged New York, New Jersey and other parts of the east. Suspending his campaign briefly, Obama appeared beside Governor Chris Christie of New Jersey, a leading Republican, to collaborate on storm relief – a bipartisan show of solidarity that made him seem above the trivial politics of the moment.

Wrapping up the campaign, Obama very rarely confronted the nearly half of America that polls said did not support him, those who blamed

New Jersey Governor Chris Christie and President Obama visit with victims of Hurricane Sandy.

President Obama and the First Lady wave to the crowd on Pennsylvania Avenue during his inaugural parade, January 21, 2013.

half of America that polls said did not support him, those who blamed him for the economic troubles still afflicting the country. He seemed taken aback at Cleveland's West Side Market when he asked a chicken vendor how business was going.

"Terrible since you got here," the man said.

The vendor meant only that the presidential visit with its extensive entourage had interfered with business that day, but he inadvertently voiced the frustration of many Americans.

For Obama, the question as the sun rose on November 6 was whether those critics reflected a majority of voters who would go to the polls. For a few hours, it looked like they did. "There was this moment where you think you might actually lose," Dan Pfeiffer said. The first report Obama's team got on election day, he said, "showed in some states a very jacked-up Republican turnout relative to what we thought it would be – and youth and African-American and Latino turnout down from what we thought it would be. It was a 'holy crap' moment."

That first report was wrong, as so many had been in recent elections, but as Obama watched the returns come in on television that evening, he was primed for bad news. When MSNBC called the race for him, Obama remained cautious.

"Let's wait and see when Fox calls it," he told excited aides.

A few minutes later, Fox called it for Obama too. It was time to celebrate.

Obama garnered 51 percent of the vote to Romney's 47 percent, not a landslide but a clear and convincing victory in an evenly divided country. He was the first president since Ronald Reagan to win a majority of the popular vote twice, and he secured a decisive Electoral College majority as well, with 332 votes to 206 for Romney. But he lost two states he had won four years earlier – Indiana and North Carolina – and his share of the popular vote was down two percentage points, making him the first president since Andrew Jackson in 1832 to win a second consecutive term with less popular support than his first.

Nonetheless, Obama relished the moment. For the forty-fourth president, there would be four more years, a chance to preserve what he had accomplished and finish what he had not. He would have an opportunity to secure a legacy as a president who made a mark not simply by virtue of his original barrier-breaking election but by transforming America in his image – for the better, he hoped; for the worse, his critics feared.

"He said this one was sweeter in a lot of ways," said David Axelrod, "because it was harder, because of the road we had to travel, because just two years earlier we had encountered this disaster and a year earlier, people were writing him off."

Instead of being written off, Obama now could write another few sentences for his paragraph.

Chief Justice John Roberts.

'A Little Too Monastic'

John Roberts's Supreme Court gives Obama fits and reprieves

Barack Obama never knew John Roberts at Harvard Law School. Roberts had graduated nearly a decade before Obama arrived. But they both excelled at the nation's most prestigious legal academy, graduating magna cum laude. Cerebral, charming and ambitious, each of them vaulted to the highest offices in the land after just short stints at the next level down. And each was seen initially as a conciliator, only to lead eventually on the strength of his own majority.

Many years after their campus days, Obama and Roberts emerged as the intellectual gladiators in a great struggle over the role of government in American society. In a moment of churning uncertainty and ideological ferment, it was a struggle that defined Obama's presidency – and perhaps surprisingly few other figures outside the White House ultimately played as critical a role as Roberts did in shaping Obama's legacy.

During his two terms in the White House, Roberts's Supreme Court gave Obama fits and gave him reprieves. Roberts and his colleagues slapped down what they characterized as Obama's executive overreach, but the chief justice also saved the president's signature domestic initiative. Overall, by one measure, Obama enjoyed less success before the court than any president since Harry S. Truman; heading into the last full term of his tenure, Obama's administration had won just 47 percent of the cases it was a party to.

Obama would attribute that record to an ideological, partisan court. His critics would attribute that to Obama's abuse of power. Either way, it made for an antagonistic eight years. "It's fair to say he's had a more contentious relationship with the court than any president I can remember, at least since Nixon," said Curt Levey, executive director of the FreedomWorks Foundation, a conservative advocacy group.

Obama and Roberts got off to a bad start. As a senator, Obama opposed Roberts's confirmation and later became the first president sworn in by a chief justice he had voted against. To make matters worse, Roberts fumbled the words of the oath of office during the 2009 inauguration, forcing a do-over the next day.

But it was the Citizens United case, in which Roberts's court ruled that corporations have First Amendment rights to spend money in election campaigns, that exposed the real tension. Obama criticized the decision repeatedly, including during a State of the Union address with Roberts and other justices in the chamber. Roberts later called the political atmosphere of the event "very troubling."

In the years to come, the court ruled that Obama exceeded his power to make recess appointments and overstepped by trying to force family businesses to pay for insurance coverage of contraceptives despite their religious beliefs. The court also overturned part of the Voting Rights Act over Obama's objections and blocked his attempt to use executive authority to protect five million illegal immigrants from deportation.

Yet when it came to the most important idea of Obama's presidency, it was Roberts who came to his rescue. While other conservative justices wanted to declare Obama's health care program unconstitutional, Roberts found a different legal justification to uphold it. Conservatives howled in protest, but Roberts said he would not use the power of the bench to undo an election. "It is not our job," he wrote, "to protect the people from the consequences of their political choices."

Obama appointed Sonia Sotomayor and Elena Kagan, but as liberals replacing liberals, they did not change the balance of power. Only in his last year, after Antonin Scalia passed away, did Obama have a chance to truly reshape the court, but Senate Republicans refused to even consider his nomination of Merrick Garland.

Some supporters of Obama imagined a way for him to take on Roberts even after his presidency: Appoint him to the court.

Obama laughed off such talk.

"Being a justice is a little bit too monastic for me," he said. After eight years in the presidential bubble, he added, "I think I need to get outside a little bit more."

DOUG MILLS/NEW YORK TIMES

CHAPTER VII

'Governing by Crisis'

A horrific mass shooting at a Connecticut elementary school, a hostile Congress and a gaffe-filled start to the health care plan all take their toll on the president.

President Obama was fighting back the tears. It was just a month after his re-election and he had been feeling optimistic about the path ahead when aides suddenly brought him chilling news: A young man armed with a Bushmaster XM-15 semi-automatic rifle had rampaged through an elementary school in Newtown, Connecticut, killing twenty children, all six or seven years old, as well as six adult staff members. Never before in American history had anyone shot and killed so many children in a schoolhouse.

Obama the president prepared to make a statement. But Obama the father of two girls was struggling to hold it together. His speechwriter, Jon Favreau, came into the Oval Office to help with editing and was stunned to find the usually stoic president wracked with emotion. "I had never seen him like that as long as I've known him," Favreau said later. "He was sitting at his desk and he was looking down at the statement and he was making some edits and he was barely looking up at us and his voice was the most somber and the most halted that I had ever heard it." At that moment, Favreau said, "everything kind of weighed on him."

Obama got up and steeled himself to go to the White House briefing room to face the cameras. Joseph Biden came down to the Oval Office to see if the president wanted him to join him but one of Obama's aides waved him off, saying the president was too emotional and would only be more so if Biden were with him. "He was having real trouble," Biden recalled.

Standing at the lectern moments later, Obama could not mask his feelings from reporters either. His face was ashen and his eyes were ringed with grief. He noted that the dead were just children, then wiped a tear from his eye. He paused, staring down, trying to regain his composure. Twelve long seconds passed in silence before he spoke again, an eternity in the life of a televised presidential statement. "They had their entire lives ahead of them," he finally said, "birthdays, graduations, weddings, kids of their own."

He paused again, unable to speak for another seven seconds before mourning the adults who were killed as well. He wiped away another tear. "Our hearts are broken today," the president at last continued. "This evening, Michelle and I will do what I know every parent in America will do, which is hug our children a little tighter, and we'll tell them that we love

Police lead children from the Sandy Hook Elementary School in Newtown, Connecticut, after a shooting at the school, December 14, 2012.

them and we'll remind each other how deeply we love one another. But there are families in Connecticut that cannot do that tonight."

Obama would later call that day, Friday, December 14, 2012, the worst of his presidency. He had delivered similar statements after a series of mass shootings over his first term – at Fort Hood, in Tucson and in Aurora, Colorado. Each time, he lamented the deaths, made a perfunctory call for more gun control and then moved on. He knew that the politics of gun rights made legislation difficult if not impossible to pass, and he always had other priorities to focus his limited energy on. This time was different. As he flew to Connecticut a few days later for a memorial service, he sat in his cabin on Air Force One scratching out what he would say, his aides not at all certain how far he would go. As they would soon discover, to their own surprise, this time his grief would be channeled into a cause.

"No single law, no set of laws, can eliminate evil from the world or prevent every senseless act of violence in our society," Obama told a gathering of 1,700 in the small New England town, including children clutching stuffed puppies handed out by the Red Cross. "But that can't be an excuse for inaction." He added that "in the coming weeks I'll use whatever power this office holds" in an effort "aimed at preventing more tragedies like this. Because what choice do we have? We can't accept events like this as routine. Are we really prepared to say that we're powerless in the face of such carnage? That the politics are too hard?"

The massacre at Sandy Hook Elementary School would reframe the start of Obama's second term before it even began. While he had plenty of other issues on his priority list, suddenly gun control vaulted to the top. He assigned Biden to assemble a plan and began revising his strategy to use whatever honeymoon he had earned from his re-election. "I will put everything I've got into this," Obama said at one point, "and so will Joe."

But before he could get started, Obama had to clear out the underbrush remaining from his first four years. Thanks to the collective failure in Washington to find a resolution to the economic issues plaguing the country, a series of tax cuts from both the Bush and Obama eras were due to expire while the deep, automatic, across-the-board spending cuts known as the sequester were scheduled to be enacted at the end of the year – a massive cumulative hit on the economy that Ben Bernanke, the chairman of the Federal Reserve, had dubbed the "fiscal cliff." Unless Obama and the Republicans came together to put the brakes on, the country might easily tumble over the edge into another recession.

Burned by past negotiations and emboldened after his re-election, Obama this time refused to budge until Republicans allowed the expiration of the part of George W. Bush's tax cuts that went to the richest Americans. At last, he won on that point, but not without compromise. Instead of raising rates back to their pre-Bush levels for those earning $250,000 a year, they went up only for those making at least $400,000. In addition, Obama

President Obama joins Newtown family members following the failed gun control vote on Capitol Hill, April 17, 2013.

succeeded in increasing estate and capital gains taxes and renewed his own tax credits for child care, college tuition and renewable energy production. He also managed to extend unemployment benefits for two million jobless Americans. Yet the two sides could not agree on spending and so once again punted the issue down the road by simply extending current levels. Liberals groused that Obama had given away too much, but he felt satisfied that he had finally put the Bush tax cut debate behind him, largely on his terms.

Obama formally opened his second term a few days later with an assertive Inaugural Address that offered a robust articulation of modern liberalism in America. Dispensing with the post-partisan appeals of four years earlier, a more hardened president instead laid out a forceful vision of advancing gay rights, easing the lives of illegal immigrants, preserving the social welfare safety net and acting to stop climate change. Instead of declaring the end of "petty grievances," as he did the first time he took the oath, he challenged Republicans to step back from their staunch opposition to his agenda.

"Progress does not compel us to settle centuries-old debates about the role of government for all time – but it does require us to act in our time," he said in the eighteen-minute address from the West Front of the Capitol, delivered a day after his official swearing in because January 20, 2013, fell on a Sunday. "For now, decisions are upon us and we cannot afford delay," he went on. "We cannot mistake absolutism for principle or substitute spectacle for politics or treat name-calling as reasoned debate. We must act."

Absolutism and spectacle, however, were hardly going away in Obama's Washington. And those who had invested such hopes and dreams in him the last time were a little more subdued. For the ceremony, hundreds of thousands of people gathered on a brisk but bright day, a huge crowd by any measure but far less than the record turnout of four years earlier. If the day felt restrained compared with the historic mood the last time, it reflected a more restrained moment in the life of the country. The expectations that loomed so large with Obama's arrival in office, even amid economic crisis, had long since faded into a starker sense of the limits of his presidency.

Now fifty-one years old and noticeably grayer, Obama appeared alternately upbeat and reflective. When he re-entered the Capitol at the conclusion of the ceremony, he stopped his entourage to turn back toward the cheering crowds on the National Mall and soak it in.

"I want to take a look, one more time," he said. "I'm not going to see this again."

His daughters, Malia, now fourteen, and Sasha, eleven, were in a playful mood. Malia at one point sneaked up behind her father and cried out, "Boo!" Sasha used a smartphone to take a picture of her parents kissing in the reviewing stand outside the White House, then made them do it again.

Obama once again used Abraham Lincoln's Bible to take his oath, but also added a second Bible once owned by the Rev. Dr. Martin Luther King Jr. He became the first president ever to mention the word "gay" in an Inaugural Address, linking the struggle for gay rights to past movements for women and African-Americans. "Our journey is not complete until our gay brothers and sisters are treated like anyone else under the law," he said.

But scarred by four years of battles, the president felt little need to reach out to the opposition, and some Republicans took his message as inappropriately partisan for an inaugural ceremony that historically tended to emphasize more unifying themes. "I would have liked to see a little more on outreach and working together," said Senator John McCain, his vanquished opponent from 2008. "There was not, as I've seen in other inaugural speeches, 'I want to work with my colleagues.'"

'I want to take a look, one more time. I'm not going to see this again.'

As he recharged his presidency, Obama reshuffled his Cabinet and White House staff. Hillary Clinton, Leon Panetta, Timothy Geithner and others departed as the president assembled a second-term team to confront the challenges ahead. For secretary of state, he tapped Senator John Kerry, who first propelled Obama to national fame by assigning him the keynote address at the Democratic National Convention in 2004. For secretary of defense, Obama tapped former Senator Chuck Hagel, a Republican maverick who had been a sharp critic of George W. Bush. For treasury secretary, Obama appointed Jack Lew, who had succeeded William Daley as White House chief of staff. And to replace Lew as chief of staff, he promoted Denis McDonough, the national security aide who had been with him from the beginning.

Obama devoted little of his Inaugural Address to foreign policy because he wanted to focus his energies on domestic affairs, like gun control. But he was hoping to straighten out his international agenda to clear the way. In his initial overseas trip after his re-election, he became the first sitting president to travel to Burma, also called Myanmar, to encourage its emergence from decades of isolation and repression, making a personal pilgrimage to the home of opposition leader Daw Aung San Suu Kyi, where she was held under house arrest for nearly two decades. In his State of the Union address, Obama announced he would withdraw 34,000 more troops from Afghanistan over the next year, or more than half the remaining force, in hopes of winding down the war by the time he left office. And he paid his first visit as president to Israel to try to smooth over longstanding friction with its conservative prime minister, Benjamin Netanyahu.

Showing support for Maricopa County Sheriff Joe Arpao in Surprise, Arizona, October 16, 2009.

For a brief moment, Obama could begin to think about the mark he would leave in history. He traveled to Dallas in April to join all the other living presidents for the opening of the George W. Bush Presidential Library and Museum. Obama recalled that the last time all the presidents had assembled in one place was right before he had taken office. He had learned something since then, he said.

"No matter how much you think you're ready to assume the office of president," he told the audience, "it's impossible to truly understand the nature of the job until it's yours."

The nature of the job was unrelenting, and by spring Obama had found his post-inaugural optimism soured by a cloud of partisanship and scandal. Despite his vision of an activist government as a force for good in American society, the first months of his second term seemed to reinforce fears of an overreaching government while calling into question Obama's ability to master his own presidency.

His drive to enact new gun-control measures proved to be the first casualty. Painfully aware of the power of gun-rights advocates led by the National Rifle Association, Obama put forward a package of relatively modest initiatives. He called on Congress to reinstate a ban on assault rifles that had been on the books for a decade before expiring, and he pressed to outlaw armor-piercing bullets and magazines with more than ten rounds, like those used in Newtown and other mass shootings. He also proposed closing a longstanding loophole that allowed buyers to avoid criminal background checks by purchasing weapons from unlicensed sellers at gun shows or through private sales. The vast majority of Americans supported such ideas, according to polls.

But as the shock of Newtown faded, so did the momentum for change. "Nothing the president is proposing would have stopped the massacre at Sandy Hook," said Senator Marco Rubio, a Republican rising star from Florida. "President Obama is targeting the Second Amendment rights of law-abiding citizens instead of seriously addressing the real underlying causes of such violence."

The N.R.A., which once supported background checks, now lobbied furiously against expanding them to gun shows. Instead, the organization argued that more people should own guns to stop crazed killers like the one in Newtown. "The only thing that stops a bad guy with a gun," said Wayne LaPierre, the N.R.A.'s executive vice president, "is a good guy with a gun."

By April, Obama's push for gun control, the effort he made the opening bid of his second term, was effectively over. While Senators Pat Toomey, a conservative Republican from Pennsylvania, and Joe Manchin III, a conservative Democrat from West Virginia, put together a bipartisan package of new restrictions, they failed to garner the sixty votes necessary to cut off a filibuster in the Senate. Three other Republicans joined Toomey in supporting it, but four Democrats from states that Obama lost in 2012 refused to go along. Sitting in the Senate gallery, the mother of a woman killed in the 2007 mass shooting at Virginia Tech and a survivor of the shooting in Tucson that injured Gabrielle Giffords shouted in unison, "Shame on you!"

For Obama, it was a devastating blow. He had promised to put "everything I've got" behind the gun-control legislation, and it had not been enough. A second-term president coming off re-election has one chance to use the mandate that comes with victory, and Obama had nothing to show for it. His enemies now knew they could beat him, even in a Democratic-controlled Senate and even though his proposals had the strong support of voters. In effect, he repeated Bush's experience when he started his second term with a proposal to restructure Social Security and allow some payroll taxes to be invested in the stock market, only to watch it die in Congress.

In a chilling attack, bombs explode at the Boston Marathon.

Further frustrating Obama were several flaps that left him on the defensive. The revelation that the Justice Department had seized telephone records of reporters for The Associated Press as part of a national security leak investigation undercut Obama's promises of transparency and raised questions about his commitment to freedom of the press. A mushrooming congressional investigation into the terrorist attack in Benghazi, Libya, was highlighting the administration's failure to guard its diplomats and its manipulation of talking points. And news that the Internal Revenue Service had singled out nonprofit applicants using the terms "Tea Party" or "patriots" in their titles roiled the president's opponents and fueled impressions of abuse of power even though there was no evidence tying the practices to the White House.

On top of those troubles came a chilling new terrorist attack on American soil, this time a pair of pressure-cooker bombs set off twelve seconds apart at the Boston Marathon on April 13, 2013. Three people were killed and about 240 others seriously injured amid the chaos and confusion, with seventeen people losing at least one leg. During a subsequent manhunt, the bombers, a pair of Chechen brothers named Dzhokhar and Tamerlan Tsarnaev, killed a Massachusetts Institute of Technology police officer and carjacked a sports utility vehicle. They wound up in a blazing firefight that wounded another pair of officers. Tamerlan, twenty-six, died after Dzhokhar, nineteen, ran over him with a car attempting to escape. Dzhokhar was later apprehended and would eventually be convicted and

Police scramble after the second explosion near the finish line of the Boston Marathon, April 15, 2013.

JOHN TLUMACKI/BOSTON GLOBE VIA ASSOCIATED PRESS

sentenced to death. The brothers were inspired by Anwar al-Awlaki, the radical cleric killed in a 2011 drone strike.

In that spring of his discontent, Obama grew exasperated at his inability to shape events. He felt trapped in a system in which he could not even speak forthrightly. In private, he talked longingly of "going Bulworth," a reference to the offbeat 1998 Warren Beatty movie about a senator who risked it all to say what he really thought. While Beatty's character had neither the power nor the platform of a president, the metaphor highlighted Obama's desire to be liberated from what he saw as the political constraints holding him back.

He bristled at a column by Maureen Dowd in *The New York Times* that compared him unfavorably with Michael Douglas's title character in *The American President*, written by Aaron Sorkin. At the White House Correspondents' Association dinner in April, Obama turned to Douglas, who was in the audience. "Michael, what's your secret, man?" Obama asked, in a tone that probably sounded more bitter than he intended. "Could it be that you were an actor in an Aaron Sorkin liberal fantasy?"

He grew ever more scornful a few days later when a reporter skeptically asked about the prospects for further legislation given his setbacks. "As Mark Twain said," Obama responded, "rumors of my demise may be a little exaggerated at this point."

In June came a challenge of a different sort. *The Washington Post* and Britain's *Guardian* newspaper began publishing a series of explosive reports about secret American surveillance programs with vaster reach than previously known. The government, they reported, had forced telecommunications firms to hand over telephone records for millions of Americans in the name of hunting terrorists.

The National Security Agency, the electronic spy organization, used the records to search the so-called metadata – information such as which phones called which other phones, when they were in contact and how long the calls lasted. Warrants were still required to actually listen in on Americans' phone calls. But the scope of the net was breathtaking and set off a new furor over the sacrifice of civil liberties for national security. More disclosures followed. It turned out that the N.S.A. had been eavesdropping on the phone calls of foreign leaders, including allies like Chancellor Angela Merkel of Germany. Not surprisingly, Merkel was furious.

Soon, the source of the leaks revealed himself publicly, a former N.S.A. contractor named Edward Snowden, who proclaimed himself disturbed by what he saw as the government's unjustified intrusions into privacy. Snowden had fled the United States before going public, winding up at an airport in Moscow, where Russian authorities decided to give him temporary asylum while crowing about his disclosures. Irked by the Kremlin's decision, and already dubious about further dealings with President

Vladimir Putin, Obama decided to cancel a stop in Moscow for a one-on-one summit, the first time a meeting of the top Russian and American leaders had been scrapped out of anger in more than half a century.

The Snowden revelations not only disrupted Obama's relations with Merkel and Putin but tarnished his image as a reformer. As a candidate, he had vowed to rein in what he described as a surveillance state run amok. "That means no more illegal wiretapping of American citizens," he declared in 2007. Like other presidents before him, though, the idealistic candidate wary of government power found that the tricky trade-offs of national security issues looked different to the person receiving intelligence briefings every morning detailing the threats to public safety. "When you get the package every morning, it puts steel in your spine," said David Plouffe, his senior adviser. "There are people out there every day who are plotting."

Obama orders the N.S.A. to stop surveillance on close allies.

Still, the public disclosure of the surveillance seemed discordant with Obama's own effort to pivot away from the limitless war on terrorism. Just a couple of weeks earlier, in a much-touted speech at the National Defense University, Obama had forecast the eventual end of the struggle, saying that while America still needed to work to dismantle terrorist groups, "this war, like all wars, must end."

Obama privately viewed Snowden as a self-important narcissist who had not thought through the consequences of his actions, but aides said the president too was surprised to learn just how far the surveillance had gone. "Things seem to have grown at the N.S.A.," Plouffe said, citing specifically the tapping of foreign leaders' telephones. "I think it was disturbing to most people and I think he found it disturbing." Obama ordered the N.S.A. to stop tapping Merkel and other close allies and appointed a task force to reconsider the programs.

He found himself under fire not just from his usual opponents but from within his own party as liberals protested what they saw as big-brother policies. Democrats were also busy undercutting their president on another front, mounting a public campaign against Obama's leading candidate for Federal Reserve chairman, Lawrence Summers. Objections from the left forced Obama to abandon the controversial Summers, choosing instead Janet Yellen, making her the first woman ever to head the central bank. The rupture inside his own party was a sign of political weakness. But he would need his fellow Democrats for the fight ahead.

Because Congress had not passed the appropriate legislation, the

Edward Snowden on a webcast at the Forbidden Research conference of the Massachusetts Institute of Technology Media Lab, July 21, 2016.

federal government would run out of money to operate on October 1 and would reach its debt ceiling and therefore default on its obligations a couple of weeks later. Republicans were determined to use the deadlines to force concessions from Obama on health care and other issues, but he resolved to stand firm.

Ever since Bill Clinton emerged victorious from a budget fight in 1995 and 1996, it had been an article of faith for more experienced Republicans that shutting down the government in fiscal disputes was bad politics. But the newer generation of conservatives, elected on the strength of the Tea Party movement in the Obama era, did not see it that way and they were itching for a fight.

An uneasy calm descends in the Capitol, as the money runs out.

Their attempts to either repeal or gut Obama's health care program had become a mission, and they were willing to take any risk. Obama was never going to sign a bill that meant doing away with his signature domestic achievement, even at the cost of letting much of the government close temporarily. At 12:01 a.m. on October 1, an uneasy calm descended in the halls of the Capitol as the money officially ran out. By morning's light, tourists were barred from entering the building and government offices across Washington and the country remained locked. While essential services continued, the military service academies suspended intercollegiate sports competitions, the Food and Drug Administration halted routine establishment inspections, the Consumer Product Safety Commission stopped recalling products that did not present an imminent threat and the National Zoo's online "Panda Cam" showing images of the latest panda bear cub was turned off. National attractions from the Statue of Liberty in New York to Alcatraz prison in San Francisco Bay were closed. Angry veterans from World War II and Vietnam pushed past barricades at a closed memorial in Washington. Some 800,000 federal workers were told to stay home.

Appropriately enough, the start of the shutdown coincided with the first real day of Obama's health care program. Obama brought to the Rose Garden several uninsured Americans who would benefit from expanded coverage to illustrate the consequences and bullhorn his defiance of his Republican critics. "As long as I am president, I will not give in to reckless demands by some in the Republican Party to deny affordable health insurance to millions of hard-working Americans," he said. Gesturing toward his guests, he said, "I want Republicans in Congress to know – these are the Americans you'd hurt if you were allowed to dismantle this law."

For sixteen days, the two sides remained at loggerheads while Republicans watched their poll numbers sink and their options narrow. On the eve of the debt ceiling deadline, they finally gave in. A partially shuttered government was one thing, but a national default was too much. Senate Republicans, never as enthusiastic about the game of fiscal chicken as their House counterparts, cut a deal with Democrats to reopen the government and increase the debt ceiling. Eighty-seven House Republicans broke ranks to support the agreement and end the impasse.

"We fought the good fight," House Speaker John Boehner said afterward. "We just didn't win."

Conservatives were not convinced their leaders really had their hearts in it. "Unfortunately," Senator Ted Cruz said, "the Washington establishment is failing to listen to the American people."

Obama, though, bemoaned the scorched-earth confrontation that led to the deal. "We've got to get out of the habit of governing by crisis," he said.

A few days before his health care system was supposed to debut, Obama previewed it for the public. "This is real simple," he said in a speech in Maryland. "It's a web site where you can compare and purchase affordable health insurance plans side by side the same way you shop for a plane ticket on Kayak, same way you shop for a TV on Amazon. You just go on and you start looking and here are all the options."

Real simple. Except it wasn't. On October 1, 2013, the same day much of the government shut down, the health care web site went live. Unlike Amazon's web page, though, it was a disaster. Millions of Americans tried going to the site on its first day and many came away unable to navigate it. The site would not allow many to create accounts, shop for plans or fully enroll. While Obama and sympathetic celebrities like Lady Gaga tweeted to followers to #GetCovered, many could not.

"An unknown error has occurred," they saw on their screens.

What Obama and his team hoped was a temporary problem soon extended into days and then weeks. The president chewed out aides in private, demanding to know how this could go so wrong. But his White House had no one to blame but itself, since it had assigned political officials with no background in major software systems to manage the creation of a web site for a nationwide insurance marketplace.

Evoking Bush's troop surge to turn around the Iraq war in his second term, Obama launched a "tech surge" to bring what the administration called "the best and the brightest from both inside and outside government" to fix the web site. But the problems defied quick resolution and provided endless fodder for late-night television comedians.

"Today, there were more problems with the web site," Jay Leno joked on *The Tonight Show* on NBC. "It seems when you type in your age, it's

For 16 days in the fall of 2013, the government is partly shut down. The halls of Congress are quiet, while legislators debate a budget deal to avert debt default.

CLOCKWISE FROM BOTTOM LEFT: DOUG MILLS/NEW YORK TIMES, GABRIELLA DEMCZUK/NEW YORK TIMES, GABRIELLA DEMCZUK/NEW YORK TIMES, DOUG MILLS/NEW YORK TIMES

CLOCKWISE FROM BOTTOM LEFT: STEPHEN CROWLEY/NEW YORK TIMES, STEPHEN CROWLEY/NEW YORK TIMES, DOUG MILLS/NEW YORK TIMES, GABRIELLA DEMCZUK/NEW YORK TIMES

confusing because it's not clear if they want the age you are right now or the age you'll be when you finally log in."

Stephen Colbert, on the Comedy Channel, attempted to sign up for Obamacare on camera. When he pressed the button, the screen said, "The webpage cannot be found." Colbert, in his faux conservative persona, cheered. "Whoo! Obamacare's a train wreck! Whoo!"

As it happened, truth was imitating comedy with stunning precision. After weeks of efforts to fix the problem, Kathleen Sebelius, Obama's secretary of health and human services, visited a Miami medical center to talk with local residents trying to sign up for coverage, only to watch haplessly as the web site failed while television news cameras recorded the moment for maximum public embarrassment.

"Sorry, our system is down," the screen told the husband and wife who were attempting to enroll in front of her.

"Uh oh," Sebelius said.

The health care web site becomes fodder for late-night comedians.

Just as bad, insurance companies were kicking many customers off their old plans even though Obama had promised they would not. It was one of the most explicit and categorical assurances he had offered when the health care law was being written back in 2009: "No matter how we reform health care, we will keep this promise to the American people: If you like your doctor you will be able to keep your doctor, period. If you like your health-care plan, you'll be able to keep your health-care plan, period. No one will take it away, no matter what."

But in fact, whenever an insurance company changed an existing plan, it was no longer grandfathered under the law and therefore had to be upgraded to meet the higher standards of the Obama program. That meant many Americans were being sent cancellation notices and told they had to replace their plans with other, more comprehensive versions that conformed to the new law – and cost more money. Glenn Kessler, the fact-checker for *The Washington Post*, gave the president four Pinocchios for a false statement. PolitiFact, another journalistic effort to truth-squad politicians, rated the "you can keep it" promise the "Lie of the Year." Obama apologized and tried to temporarily extend existing plans for many of those affected. But the damage was done.

The botched kickoff of the health care web site proved a short-term blow to the system, since it depended greatly on drawing in younger, healthier workers whose premiums in the aggregate would subsidize medical services for less healthy older customers. The troubles with enrolling alienated many of those younger workers. They also proved a balm for Republicans emerging from the government shutdown. Instead of enduring the backlash from a public turned off by their tactics, they could change the subject by focusing attention on Obama's failed web site. And the president, instead of turning his victory over the Republicans in the budget standoff into fresh momentum for other initiatives, found himself on the ropes as many of his own supporters wondered whether he and his team were up to the task.

"No one is madder than me," Obama declared at one point. With plenty of reason.

Department of Health and Human Services Secretary Kathleen Sebelius appears before the committee to review implementation of the Affordable Care Act, October 30, 2013.

DOUG MILLS/NEW YORK TIMES

'Normal Kids'

Sasha and Malia grow up in front of the public, and humanize their dad

They arrived at the White House as little girls, smiling, nervous, shy and precocious. They left eight years later as young women, tall and dignified, still quiet in public but occasionally rolling their eyes at dad or making a face recognizable to parents of mortified teenagers anywhere. In between, they lived a life of contrasts – forced to eat their vegetables and make their beds one minute, introduced to the pope or given a private tour of the Kremlin the next.

Malia and Sasha Obama grew up in front of America's eyes, but they remained an enigma amid the klieg lights. More seen than heard, they made it through those awkward years without really making themselves known to the public. Unlike other presidential offspring, they stayed out of trouble, at least the kind that would land them in gossip columns. But in political terms, they humanized their father, reinforcing the image of a loving family man with a stable home life.

"I want them to be normal kids, just like you guys, polite and respectful and kind," Michelle Obama once told a group of students.

By all accounts, they seemed to be. They loved iPhones and laptops, hung out with friends, played tennis and basketball. They watched *Modern Family* even if their own was anything but typical.

If the unparalleled opportunities of living in the White House or the unique stresses of having a Secret Service detail in the seventh grade had warped their upbringing, they were adept at hiding it.

Malia was ten when her father took office and Sasha seven. Obama, who grew up without a father and had been an absentee dad himself while in the Senate and on the campaign trail, made a point of leaving the Oval Office early enough each day to have dinner with them even if he worked later in the evening. He made most parent-teacher conferences and showed up to watch sports outings at their exclusive Sidwell Friends School, one of Washington's premier academies.

The girls were taken to the Grand Canyon and Carlsbad Caverns, toured the Eiffel Tower and the slave port in Ghana, strolled down the streets of Havana and boated on Lake Nahuel Huapi in Argentina. There were few celebrities they did not get to meet, including their favorite Jonas Brothers – though not without a tongue-in-cheek warning from the father in chief. "Sasha and Malia are huge fans," he said. "But boys, don't get any ideas. I have two words for you: Predator drones. You will never see it coming."

Michelle laid down the rules: Television only on weekends. Bedtimes initially at 8 p.m. Write reports about trips they took. Take up two sports, one of their choosing and one selected by their mother. "I want them to understand what it feels like to do something you don't like and to improve," she explained.

The girls were shielded. When a toymaker began selling Marvelous Malia and Sweet Sasha dolls, the parents expressed displeasure and the company pulled them. When a Republican congressional aide berated the girls on Facebook for appearing antsy at the annual Thanksgiving turkey pardon – "try showing a little class" – a backlash forced her to apologize and resign.

The girls were not identical, though. "We have one who generally stays here," the first lady told an interviewer, indicating an even keel. "And then we have one we call our grumpy cat, our salty biscuit. You just never know what you're going to get from that one." Which was which? "I'm not saying – they could be watching."

As their White House days ended, Malia, by now eighteen, planned to take a year off before attending Harvard. Sasha, fifteen, had two more years of high school, so Obama decided to stay in Washington after his tenure ended, renting a house until she could graduate.

Still, even as he planned his new life to maximize time with his girls, he knew it would never be the same. "They don't always want to go with us," he lamented. "They're teenagers now."

President Obama jokes with daughters Sasha, left, and Malia during the holiday tree lighting, Washington, December 1, 2011.

Barack and Michelle Obama, with daughters Sasha and Malia,
wait for the results of his Senate bid on election night, 2004.

The Obamas pose for a family portrait with Bo and Sunny
in the Rose Garden on Easter Sunday, April 5, 2015.

'You Think I'm Joking'

For Obama, humor is a means to an end

President Obama was not a natural wit. Dry and discursive, he did not keep them laughing at news conferences or spontaneously throw out one-liners in interviews. He was not one for waggish banter or a roguish double entendre. His picture would not be found in the dictionary next to rollicking.

But when the moment demanded it, he had pitch-perfect comedic timing and could deliver jokes scripted for him with a wry tone that brought down the house. For a stoic man, he appreciated humor. He had a way of telling a joke from a teleprompter at a black-tie Washington dinner and then stopping to chuckle at his own cleverness.

He was also a good sport and played along with his generation's new brand of comedy, bringing a younger, rawer, edgier sensibility drawn from pop culture. He traded insults with Jake Galifianakis on *Between Two Ferns*, slow-jammed the news with Jimmy Fallon on *The Tonight Show*, read mean tweets on *Jimmy Kimmel Live!* and filled in for Stephen Colbert on *The Colbert Report*. He drove around the White House compound with Jerry Seinfeld and shot a cheerfully goofy video for BuzzFeed with a selfie stick. If some traditionalists thought it was a little unseemly at times, others celebrated it. *Vanity Fair* called him "America's Cool Guy in Chief." *The Washington Post* dubbed him "the first alt-comedy president."

For Obama, though, humor was a means to an end. He methodically cultivated it as a major tool of his presidency. It was a way of connecting to his base among younger American and an opportunity to get across a serious policy point or two that would otherwise go unnoticed in the era of 500 channels and streaming video. Obama had never seen Galifianakis's show when his aides pitched the idea of going on it but his teenage daughter, Malia, had watched every episode. He used the appearance to urge uninsured young people to sign up for coverage under his health care program and the federal web site saw a 40 percent increase in traffic afterward.

He also used humor as a way to vent his frustrations with what he saw as the absurdity of Washington. At one White House Correspondents' Association dinner, he teamed up with Keegan-Michael Key of *Key & Peele*, who served as Luther, Obama's "anger translator." Obama would mouth a typical presidential platitude and Key would "translate" his inner thoughts.

Obama: "Despite our differences, we count on the press to shed light on the most important issues of the day."

Luther: "And we can count on Fox News to terrify old white people with some nonsense. Sharia law is coming to Cleveland! Run for the damn hills!"

Unlike some other presidents, Obama did not favor self-deprecation in his humor so much as mockery of others. His most common pokes at himself focused on his graying hair, his supposed Muslim past and his mythical birth in Kenya. Even there, he was really making fun of others who criticized him.

Possibly the most memorable, and consequential, example came at the 2011 correspondents dinner when he ridiculed Donald J. Trump for promoting the false conspiracy theory about Obama's birth. The president sarcastically expressed admiration for Trump's experience and decisiveness, citing an episode of his reality television show *The Celebrity Apprentice* when contestants failed to adequately cook steaks.

"You fired Gary Busey," Obama said, addressing Trump. "These are the kinds of decisions that would keep me up at night. Well handled, sir! Well handled."

Trump happened to be in the audience and did not look amused. He would try to exact his revenge five years later. On Election Day 2016, Trump got the last laugh.

President Obama at the White House Correspondents' Dinner, April 28, 2012.

2009:

❝ I've cut the tension by bringing a new friend to the White House. He's warm, he's cuddly, loyal, enthusiastic. You just have to keep him on a tight leash. Every once in a while he goes charging off in the wrong direction and gets himself into trouble. But enough about Joe Biden. ❞

2010:

❝ The Jonas Brothers are here. They're out there somewhere. Sasha and Malia are huge fans. But boys, don't get any ideas. I have two words for you: Predator drones. You will never see it coming. ❞

2011:

❝ Now I know that he's taken some flak lately but no one is prouder to put this birth certificate matter to rest than The Donald. And that's because he can finally get back to focusing on the issues that matter, like, did we fake the moon landing? What really happened in Roswell? And where are Biggie and Tupac? ❞

2012:

❝ It's great to be here this evening in the vast, magnificent Hilton ballroom – or what Mitt Romney would call a little fixer-upper. ❞

❝ I want to especially thank all the members [of Congress] who took a break from their exhausting schedule of not passing any laws to be here tonight. ❞

2013:

❝ The problem is that the media landscape is changing so rapidly you can't keep up with it. I mean I remember when BuzzFeed was just something I did in college around 2 a.m. ❞

❝ Sheldon [Adelson] would have been better off offering me $100 million to drop out of the race. I probably wouldn't have taken it, but I would have thought about it. Michelle would have taken it. You think I'm joking. ❞

2014:

❝ In 2008, my slogan was 'Yes, we can.' In 2013, my slogan was 'control-alt-delete.' ❞

2015:

❝ I am determined to make the most of every moment I have left. After the midterm elections, my advisers asked me, 'Mr. President, do you have a bucket list?' I said, 'Well, I have something that rhymes with bucket list.' Take executive action on immigration? Bucket. New climate regulations? Bucket. ❞

❝ I look so old John Boehner's already invited Netanyahu to speak at my funeral. ❞

2016:

❝ If this material works well, I'm going to use it at Goldman Sachs next year. Earn me some serious Tubmans. ❞

CHAPTER VIII

'Red Line'

After staunchly resisting involvement in
the bloody civil war raging in Syria, Obama
is confronted with new evidence that the
country's embattled leader has used chemical
weapons on his own people.

They circled the oval pathway on the South Lawn once, twice, three times and kept going. As President Obama paced outside the White House that late-summer evening, he wrestled out loud with his chief of staff, Denis McDonough, over one of the most profound decisions any commander in chief makes: Whether to go to war. For forty-five minutes, he walked and talked, weighing the consequences of action and inaction, before coming to his conclusion. He and McDonough then headed back into the Oval Office to reveal his decision to the rest of his team.

For Obama, that day at the end of August 2013 would prove a turning point in his approach to the world – and its approach to him. After publicly drawing a "red line" warning Syria not to use chemical weapons against its own people, he now confronted compelling evidence that the government of President Bashar al-Assad had done just that. Intelligence agencies from America and its European allies had confirmed that a sarin gas attack killed an estimated 1,400 men, women and children in Ghouta outside the Syrian capital of Damascus ten days earlier, and Western analysts had little doubt that the government was responsible.

The Syrian civil war had raged for two and a half years by that point, with ruinous results. Unlike in other Arab countries where popular uprisings had either resulted in quick and relatively non-violent change or been quickly suppressed, the anti-government movement in Syria had evolved from peaceful protests into a full-blown armed rebellion exploited by outside Islamist extremists and met with brutal and unrelenting violence by Assad's forces. Tens of thousands of people on both sides of the war had been killed, and many times more than that had been injured or displaced from their homes. Obama's call on Assad to step down had been ignored with impunity. Now the question was whether his "red line" would be as well.

Obama had steadfastly resisted pressure to get involved in Syria's civil war. After nearly five years in office, he had come to see unforgiving lessons about the limits of America's ability to influence the course of events abroad

President Obama and Chief of Staff Denis McDonough on the South Lawn of the White House, June 3, 2013.

through the use of military force. His surge of troops to Afghanistan had not yielded a clear-cut victory and he was now busy pulling forces out. His intervention in Libya had toppled Muammar el-Qaddafi but otherwise left behind a broken state and a stew of factionalism and radicalism that led to the attack that killed an American ambassador and three other Americans in Benghazi. Even Obama's prolific use of drone strikes to take out key terrorists on his "kill list" was proving less satisfying, and the president had promised to begin reining in their use by shifting more of them from the C.I.A. to the Pentagon.

Obama is devastated by images of the sarin gas attacks in Syria.

When it came to Syria, Obama had rejected advice from around the table in the Situation Room to become more involved. He dismissed the idea of setting up a no-fly zone over parts of Syria to protect civilians from Assad's air force, convinced that it would not work without American troops on the ground. And while the C.I.A. was arming select rebels, the president had rebuffed a plan advanced in his first term by Hillary Clinton, Leon Panetta and David Petraeus for a broader training program by the United States military to create a Syrian rebel force capable of taking out Assad. To Obama, the chance that American arms could end up in the wrong hands on a battlefield that increasingly attracted sympathizers of Al Qaeda outweighed any possible benefit of the program. Greater American involvement, he concluded, would simply lead to greater chaos.

So when Obama heard about the Ghouta attack, he felt he was in a bind. Three days after the massacre, he gathered his national security team in the Situation Room and told them that he was devastated by the images of women and children convulsing from the effects of the sarin gas. "I haven't made a decision yet on military action," he told his aides. "But when I was talking about chemical weapons, this is what I was talking about."

In the days that followed, Obama seemed to be clearly moving toward a decision to attack Assad's government in retaliation. Any attack would last just a day or two with missiles and bombs, not troops, a "pinprick strike" designed to make a point, not to genuinely shift the dynamics of the war. But Obama and his team made clear that the slaughter of innocents using chemical weapons in contravention of international standards demanded a military response. American destroyers armed with Tomahawk missiles sailed into position in the eastern Mediterranean Sea. Secretary of State John Kerry, who had been privately urging a more robust

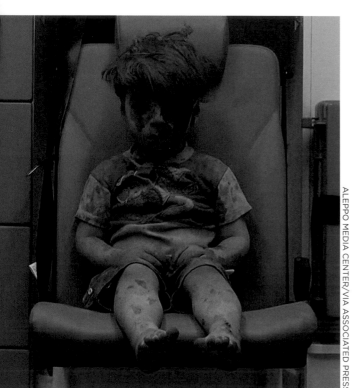

Five-year-old Omran Daqneesh in an ambulance after being pulled from the rubble of an airstrike in Aleppo, Syria, August 17, 2016.

Syrian men carry babies through the debris after a reported air strike on the rebel-held Salihin neighborhood of Aleppo, September 11, 2016.

approach to Syria, led the public charge, declaring that "history would judge us all extraordinarily harshly if we turned a blind eye to a dictator's wanton use of weapons of mass destruction against all warnings."

All the same, Obama's own ambivalence was plain to see. Where Kerry was fiery, Obama was restrained. Where Kerry described a moral imperative to act, Obama was stressing the "limited, tailored" nature of what he had in mind. "We don't have good options, great options, for the region," the president told an interviewer from PBS.

To attack or not, Obama's ambivalence is obvious.

His uncertainty seemed to reflect public attitudes. Even though he was only talking about a quick airstrike, much like those ordered by previous presidents without much public opposition, many Americans reacted this time as if he were contemplating a new Iraq-style land war. Overseas, Obama had no hope of support from the United Nations with Russia holding a veto on the Security Council, and even America's closest ally, Britain, backed out of any military operation after its Parliament voted against authorizing action.

Suddenly, Obama looked – and felt – all alone. On the early evening of Friday, August 30, when he decided to go for a walk with Denis McDonough on the South Lawn, the president was stewing about the right course. He thought Britain's Prime Minister David Cameron had mishandled the matter in London. But if Cameron had submitted the question to lawmakers, Obama said, maybe he should too. After all, Americans were no less war weary than the British. And authorizing a strike all on his own, Obama reasoned, would flout his own statements about moving away from a permanent war footing and unilateral executive action. He found a sympathetic ear in McDonough, who had been one of the leading voices against the troop surge to Afghanistan in 2009 and other military entanglements since then.

Heading back into the Oval Office shortly before 7 p.m., Obama gathered some of his other top aides, including Susan Rice, now his national security adviser; her deputies, Antony Blinken and Benjamin Rhodes; the deputy chief of staff, Rob Nabors; Dan Pfeiffer, now a senior advisor, and others. Notably absent were Kerry and Defense Secretary Chuck Hagel.

"I have a pretty big idea I want to test with you guys," Obama told them as he tried to couch his change of heart.

If he was testing the idea, it did not earn high grades. Obama's aides were aghast at the idea of letting Congress decide whether to launch the strike. During all the discussions over the past week, this option had not come up except in passing, and it reeked of desperation.

Among other things, presidents had long reserved the power to initiate quick, limited military actions without requiring congressional approval, and Obama would be setting a precedent that could tie not only his hands but those of his successors. Moreover, international opposition might only grow while he waited for Capitol Hill to consider the idea. What was worse, they told him, he very likely could lose the vote, a debilitating defeat that would weaken him on foreign policy for the rest of his presidency.

For two hours, the president and his team debated the merits and drawbacks of his idea, but he was not moved by the opposition of his advisers. Only then, after he had made up his mind, did Obama call Kerry and

President Obama with Russian President Vladimir Putin at the United Nations, September 28, 2015.

DOUG MILLS/NEW YORK TIMES

Hagel to tell them of his decision, essentially cutting his top diplomat and top military adviser out of any real role in the deliberations.

The next morning, Saturday, August 31, the White House summoned reporters and cameras to the Rose Garden for an unusual weekend announcement. Nearly everyone in Washington assumed he was about to announce that the expected airstrike was underway. Television news channels aired wall-to-wall coverage waiting for the president's statement as journalists and analysts speculated on the impact of a military operation.

Instead, Obama shocked the world by saying he would defer to Congress. "I'm prepared to give that order," the president said. "But having made my decision as commander in chief based on what I am convinced is our national security interests, I'm also mindful that I'm the president of the world's oldest constitutional democracy."

If Obama is going to take a chance, he wants Congress to take it with him.

The reaction was instant and visceral. As Obama's aides predicted, lawmakers still feeling the hangover of Iraq were not at all enthusiastic about helping him get the United States into another ugly war in the Middle East. On this issue, at least, he had no reliable base of support on Capitol Hill. Liberals were instinctively anti-war and conservatives were instinctively anti-Obama. "Obama hasn't got a chance to win this vote if he can't win the majority of his own party, and I doubt he can," Representative Tom Cole, a Republican from Oklahoma, pointed out within hours of the president's announcement. "He is a war president without a war party."

While the Constitution gave Congress the power to declare war, lawmakers had not formally done so since World War II, essentially ceding that authority to the president. In modern times, presidents have used military force with and without congressional approval. George H. W. Bush and George W. Bush both sought and won authorization votes from Congress before going to war with Iraq, while Ronald Reagan and Bill Clinton took action in Grenada, Libya, Bosnia, Afghanistan, Sudan, Iraq and Kosovo without securing explicit permission ahead of time from Capitol Hill. As a candidate, Obama had said a president has no power to launch a military attack except to stop "an actual or imminent threat to the nation." But he acted unilaterally in Libya in 2011 without any clear threat to the United States.

The real difference here was the treacherous politics. If Obama was going to take the chance, he wanted Congress to take it with him. But if he assumed he could persuade lawmakers to go along on the theory that Congress traditionally supports a commander in chief in times of conflict, he badly misjudged the political environment. And failing to secure the authorizing votes he now sought would leave him in an untenable position. If he went ahead with a strike anyway, he would surely provoke a scathing backlash – and, his aides worried, even an impeachment effort – for ignoring Congress and public will. If he backed off his threat because Congress would not go along, he would look weak in the eyes of the world and, aides argued, would basically be deprived of any credible threat of military action for the rest of his presidency, no matter what the circumstances. Why would Iran, for example, worry anymore that the United States might use force to stop it from obtaining a nuclear weapon when Obama would not use force to punish Syria for using chemical weapons? Even if war with Iran was a horrific possibility, making Iran fear that America might resort to it certainly had some value as deterrent.

'He is a war president without a war party,' says one lawmaker.

Amid the furor that followed his Rose Garden speech, Obama flew to St. Petersburg, Russia, for the annual summit meeting of the Group of 20 nations, called the G-20, hosted by Vladimir Putin. Strongly opposed to any attack on Syria, an old client state of Russia's, Putin had used the threat of a veto at the United Nations to block any Security Council action. During a long, late-night discussion about Syria in St. Petersburg, the two presidents effectively competed for the support of the other leaders, each man arguing his position and soliciting peers as if they were voters. "I don't agree with his arguments," Putin said later, "and he doesn't agree with mine."

At the end, Putin boasted that most of the big powers present joined him in opposing an American military strike on Syria, including China, India, Germany, Italy and Brazil. The only ones that backed it, such as France and Saudi Arabia, were already on Obama's side before he arrived. In other words, he won no converts. Obama pivoted quickly back to the domestic debate as he raced home on Air Force One. From the air, he phoned lawmakers from both parties in hopes of winning them over. He also ordered aides at home to fan out with speeches, briefings, telephone calls and television appearances, and he announced that he would deliver a prime-time televised address to the nation from the White House to lay out his case to the American people.

But before he left St. Petersburg, there was an intriguing moment. Just as the summit was breaking up, Putin approached Obama and began chatting casually. Breaking the ice of their dispute over Edward Snowden, Obama suggested the two leaders sit down, and they pulled chairs into a corner of the room. As they talked, Putin brought up an idea. What if Syria voluntarily surrendered its stockpiles of poison gas to the international community? Would that be an acceptable alternative to military action? Obama was cautious but interested and suggested they have their top diplomats explore it further.

A couple days later, while in London, Kerry seemed to open the door to such an idea publicly when he was asked by a reporter if there was anything Syria's Assad could do to avert a strike.

"Sure," Kerry said. "He could turn over every bit of his weapons to the international community within the next week, without delay." Then, perhaps realizing that he had opened the door too widely in public, Kerry quickly added: "But he isn't about to do it."

Aides later downplayed his comments as a hypothetical discussion prompted by a reporter's question, but as Kerry flew home, he talked from his plane with his Russian counterpart, Sergey Lavrov, who cited the secretary of state's comments and said Russia would make a public proposal that Syria give up its weapons and allow in international monitors.

It was an idea that, even before St. Petersburg, Obama and Putin had discussed in very theoretical terms. Several others had floated it too, including Israel's prime minister and Poland's foreign minister. But suddenly, it seemed like a lifeline to Obama, who clutched it as a way out of his no-win scenario. When he went on television for his prime-time address, instead of pressing Congress to vote for war, Obama announced that he would try Russia's plan first – hitting the pause button on his airstrikes for the second time in two weeks. Rarely had a commander in chief been seen thinking out loud and changing his mind on the fly quite so publicly.

In the end, Obama's fits-and-starts handling of the matter largely worked in terms of substance and failed in terms of politics and perception. Over the coming months, Syria did give up its chemical weapons, or at least nearly all of them, which Obama argued was a far better result than just blowing up a few buildings in Damascus and leaving the munitions in Assad's hands. But Obama's painfully public vacillation was taken by many in the region as a sign of irresolution, especially by America's Arab allies. For years to come, Obama's decision to call off the Syria strike would be cited as evidence that he had grown so allergic to military entanglement in the Middle East that he would not back up his own "red line" threats.

"There's absolutely no question he's very uncomfortable being commander in chief," said Senator Bob Corker, a Republican from Tennessee who was working with the White House to rally support for a strike until it was called off. "It's like he wants to slip the noose. It's like watching a person who's caged, who's in a trap and trying to figure a way out."

If Obama truly was trying to find a way out, there would be no easy escape. No matter how much he tried to focus on other priorities, he kept finding himself drawn back to crisis after crisis in the Middle East. At the same time he was struggling with what to do about Syria, he was struggling with what to do about Egypt.

The traditional anchor of the Arab world, Egypt had yet to find its way in the two years since mass demonstrations pushed out President Hosni

Demonstrators hurl stones at supporters of ousted Egyptian President Mohamed Morsi, Cairo, July 15, 2013.

NARCISO CONTRERAS/NEW YORK TIMES

Mubarak with Obama's support. Democratic elections after Mubarak's ouster installed Mohamed Morsi, leader of the Muslim Brotherhood, as the new president, and for a time Obama thought he had found a partner he could work with. When fighting erupted in Gaza in late 2012, Obama teamed up with Morsi to quell the violence.

The ouster of Morsi in Egypt leaves Obama in a lose-lose position.

But Morsi failed to broaden his base of support at home beyond Islamists and Obama became increasingly worried that the Egyptian's approach was destabilizing his country. Morsi had a habit of demonizing his critics, accusing them of a treasonous conspiracy, an approach that, combined with a dire economic situation, fired up opposition. This time, the tens of thousands of demonstrators in Tahrir Square were pressing Morsi to step down. The military and intelligence services, a bulwark of Mubarak's Egypt, had always despised the Muslim Brotherhood, and now saw that Morsi had made the group more vulnerable than at any time in its eight decades underground. In July, the military moved in, arresting Morsi and rounding up scores of his allies.

Obama reacted with restraint, making no public comments, opting instead for tempered written statements. Since 1979, Egypt had been the top recipient of American foreign aid behind only Israel, slated to receive $1.5 billion in the next year. But under law, Obama was required to cut off assistance in the case of a military coup. That led to all sorts of definitional gymnastics in Washington over whether Morsi's ouster qualified. Egypt's new authorities argued that it was not technically a military coup, but a popular uprising, and that the military only stepped in to preserve order. To almost everyone who did not have a stake in the matter, it seemed a fairly obvious dictionary version of a military coup, given that the generals locked up the democratically elected president and sent soldiers into the streets.

In the Situation Room, the State Department's top lawyer, Mary McLeod, said it was a clear-cut example of a coup. While other advisers to the president were looking for ways out of following the law as written, she gave no ground. Eventually, Obama and his team decided to resolve the dispute by not resolving it. They would not formally judge whether the transfer of power was a coup or not. If they did not characterize it one way or the other, they reasoned, the aid cutoff would not be triggered. It was a semantic game to skirt the law, they knew, but one they concluded was in the nation's best interest to maintain an alliance that had been critical to the United States for generations.

In Cairo, the generals made a cold-eyed calculation that Obama would not suspend assistance – and that even if he did, they could replace it from Saudi Arabia or other Gulf states that bitterly opposed the Muslim Brotherhood and were happy to see the military back in power in Cairo. Unconstrained by the Americans, Egyptian forces opened a ferocious assault on protesters in the streets, killing sixty Morsi supporters at a sit-in a few days after the ouster, eighty more at a subsequent demonstration and eventually more than 1,000 others. The crackdown left Obama in a lose-lose position: Risk a partnership that had been the bedrock of Middle East peace for thirty-five years or stand by while longtime allies held onto power by mowing down opponents. From one side, the Israelis, Saudis and other Arabs lobbied him to go easy on the generals in the interest of thwarting what they saw as the larger and more insidious Islamist threat. From the other, an unusual mix of American conservatives and liberals urged him to stand more forcefully against the sort of autocracy that had been a staple of Egyptian life for decades.

Ultimately, Obama decided the relationship with Egypt's military was more important than a stand on democracy. He suspended just a part of the aid, about $260 million, and temporarily withheld the delivery of several big-ticket weapons systems, including Apache attack helicopters, Harpoon missiles, M1-A1 tank parts and F-16 warplanes. "The administration is trying to have it both ways," complained Senator Patrick Leahy, a Vermont Democrat and chairman of the subcommittee that oversaw aid to Egypt. "By doing that, the message is muddled."

A t home, Obama was not enjoying much more success. With gun control and the rest of his agenda stalled on Capitol Hill, Obama essentially gave up on legislating. In early 2014, he traveled to Capitol Hill to declare independence from Congress in his State of the Union address and vowed to tackle economic disparity with a series of limited initiatives on jobs, wages and retirement that he could take without legislative approval.

He promised "a year of action" as he sought to rejuvenate a presidency mired in low approval ratings. "I am eager to work with all of you," he told lawmakers from the rostrum in the House chamber. "But America does not stand still – and neither will I. So wherever and whenever I can take steps without legislation to expand opportunity for more American families, that's what I'm going to do." Still, as he vowed to act "with or without Congress," his defiant approach was more assertive than any of the individual policies he advanced.

His staff called it the "pen and phone" strategy – he would use his pen to sign executive orders and his phone to lean on important figures like governors, business executives and labor leaders to accomplish what a Congress riven by partisanship would not or could not. It was an alliterative

SERGEY PONCMAREV/NEW YORK TIMES

Campaign poster for Bashar al-Assad on a destroyed building in Homs, Syria, June 15, 2014.

smokescreen to obscure Obama's retreat from the field. But weakened as he was, Obama was determined to make the most of what he could do in the magisterial space of the Oval Office. In the months to come, he signed a series of executive orders to raise the minimum wage from $7.25 to $10.10 an hour and set other employment standards for employees of federal contractors. Since he could not unilaterally order such changes for the private sector as a whole, he would use the federal government's leverage as a paying customer to force at least some private employers to adopt the changes he favored. Because of Washington's vast reach, that move alone could affect up to 29 million workers. And to an important degree, he succeeded in setting the terms of the national conversation, so that even though Congress refused to go along with a minimum wage hike, many states, localities and even companies like Walmart, Costco, Gap, Ikea and Disney raised pay floors on their own.

Many of Obama's executive actions, to be sure, were penny-ante stuff, more symbolic than significant. He grandly announced the issuance of small-bore grants for various goals even though they represented barely an asterisk in the overall federal budget. He politely asked business leaders to hire longtime unemployed workers since he could neither force them to nor entice them to with incentives. He set out to reorganize federal job training, a longtime bipartisan goal that nearly every recent president had tried to accomplish, only to have their successors find the programs just as unsatisfying.

But other unilateral moves had wider reach, especially labor regulations that made millions more workers eligible for overtime pay and sought to extend basic workplace protections to the so-called gig economy of independent contractors like those working for Uber. Rhetorically, at least, these efforts stemmed from Obama's 2011 speech in Osawatomie, Kansas, which Dan Pfeiffer called "perhaps the most substantively important speech of the Obama presidency." Obama's condemnation of income inequality, Pfeiffer said, created "a set of marching orders to the entire government." By his last year in office, Obama had put in place more than 500 regulations with significant impact, making him perhaps the most aggressive wielder of executive power in modern times, to the point that Republicans accused him of imperial overreach.

One of the areas where he had the broadest power to act on his own was in fighting climate change. Having given up on legislation after the Democratic Congress in his first two years in office failed to pass a bill creating a cap-and-trade system, Obama now turned to the Environmental Protection Agency to use its sweeping authority to achieve the same goal. In June, the administration announced a proposed rule that would set state-by-state limits on carbon emissions and let each state decide how to meet those targets. The overall goal was to slash pollution from existing power plants by 32 percent from 2005 levels by 2030. The far-reaching rule would effectively

O bama uses the power of his pen to improve the pay of millions of workers.

reshape the nation's energy industry without a vote of Congress, likely forcing hundreds of coal-fired plants to close their doors. The power plant rule came on top of new regulations requiring new cars and light trucks to be so fuel-efficient that they would get fifty-five miles per gallon by 2025, reducing the consumption of oil and emissions at the same time. Obama seemed to be on stronger legal ground with his climate push because the Supreme Court had already ruled that under the Clean Air Act, the E.P.A. had to regulate carbon emissions. But with tens of billions of dollars at stake, industry opponents still mounted a legal challenge.

The GOP hierarchy wants an immigration deal. The Tea Party does not.

The other major initiative Obama decided to pursue on his own was immigration reform. That had been the one area after his re-election where he harbored hopes of reaching a bipartisan compromise with Republicans, given that opposition party leaders wanted to stop alienating Hispanic voters who were becoming a larger force in the electorate. A group of senators from both parties formed what they called the Gang of Eight to broker an agreement that passed, 68 to 32, in 2013 only to die in the House. A year later, Speaker John Boehner and other Republican leaders resolved to fashion a plan that would finally settle the matter and take it off the table for the next election.

Obama was happy to work with Boehner. After all, the president was under enormous pressure from Hispanic leaders and advocates of liberalized immigration, who had grown impatient and restless, especially given Obama's record of deporting more than 2 million people by that point. In March, Janet Murguia, president of the National Council of La Raza, denounced Obama in a speech as the "deporter-in-chief," a line that deeply irked the president. During a subsequent meeting with activists, he scolded her, saying that if advocates for reform fought among themselves, they would only take the onus off Republicans.

But as much as the business-oriented, poll-reading Republican hierarchy wanted a deal, the ascendant Tea Party wing of the party did not. They saw any easing of the rules as an illegitimate amnesty. Immigrants who were in the country illegally had broken the law and were taking jobs at a time when there were still millions of American citizens out of work. The Republican rebels made clear they would punish any leaders who cut a deal with Obama.

They proved their power in June, when a little known conservative college professor came out of nowhere to upset Representative Eric Cantor in

DOUG MILLS/NEW YORK TIMES

reshape the nation's energy industry without a vote of Congress, likely forcing hundreds of coal-fired plants to close their doors. The power plant rule came on top of new regulations requiring new cars and light trucks to be so fuel-efficient that they would get fifty-five miles per gallon by 2025, reducing the consumption of oil and emissions at the same time. Obama seemed to be on stronger legal ground with his climate push because the Supreme Court had already ruled that under the Clean Air Act, the E.P.A. had to regulate carbon emissions. But with tens of billions of dollars at stake, industry opponents still mounted a legal challenge.

The GOP *hierarchy wants an immigration deal. The Tea Party does not.*

The other major initiative Obama decided to pursue on his own was immigration reform. That had been the one area after his re-election where he harbored hopes of reaching a bipartisan compromise with Republicans, given that opposition party leaders wanted to stop alienating Hispanic voters who were becoming a larger force in the electorate. A group of senators from both parties formed what they called the Gang of Eight to broker an agreement that passed, 68 to 32, in 2013 only to die in the House. A year later, Speaker John Boehner and other Republican leaders resolved to fashion a plan that would finally settle the matter and take it off the table for the next election.

Obama was happy to work with Boehner. After all, the president was under enormous pressure from Hispanic leaders and advocates of liberalized immigration, who had grown impatient and restless, especially given Obama's record of deporting more than 2 million people by that point. In March, Janet Murguia, president of the National Council of La Raza, denounced Obama in a speech as the "deporter-in-chief," a line that deeply irked the president. During a subsequent meeting with activists, he scolded her, saying that if advocates for reform fought among themselves, they would only take the onus off Republicans.

But as much as the business-oriented, poll-reading Republican hierarchy wanted a deal, the ascendant Tea Party wing of the party did not. They saw any easing of the rules as an illegitimate amnesty. Immigrants who were in the country illegally had broken the law and were taking jobs at a time when there were still millions of American citizens out of work. The Republican rebels made clear they would punish any leaders who cut a deal with Obama.

They proved their power in June, when a little known conservative college professor came out of nowhere to upset Representative Eric Cantor in a primary in his Virginia home district. Cantor had been the conservative champion in the Republican leadership, the voice of the base often curbing Boehner's deal-making instincts. When Cantor lost, there were no tears shed in the White House. His relationship with Obama had been prickly from the start, when Cantor joined Republicans plotting to undercut his presidency on the very day of his inauguration and Obama put down the upstart congressman during a later meeting by pointedly reminding him who won the election. Obama considered Cantor a partisan obstructionist and his main bête noire in the House. Cantor viewed Obama as an aloof liberal intent on shoving his agenda down the throat of Congress.

But over the past year or so, Cantor had moved to find ways to resolve the fiscal fights over taxes and the government shutdown. And even though he opposed Obama's immigration plan, he had signaled willingness to consider more limited measures like legalizing the children of adults who came to the country illegally. For that, he was judged insufficiently stalwart in standing up to Obama.

"It is incredible to me that Eric Cantor moved from the singular, highest-profile, most-important political figure on Capitol Hill stopping the president's agenda to the guy who was the chief compromiser with the president," said John Murray, a Cantor strategist. "The disconnect there is insane. It's so out of whack with reality."

Or perhaps reflective of the new reality. Obama began to think about how else he could use his pen.

United States Border Patrol agents detain a group caught hiding in a grove of trees just across the Rio Grande, McAllen, Texas, March 25, 2014.

TODD HEISLER/NEW YORK TIMES

President Obama on "Between Two Ferns" with comic Zach Galifianakis,
February 24, 2014.

'A Little Bit of a Rebel'

The first social media president finds new ways to get message out

Any president has to give up so many things – privacy, a personal life and anonymity, among others. But one thing President Obama was not willing to give up was his BlackBerry. Never mind the security concerns, he insisted that after taking office he still be allowed to carry a smart telephone that he could use for email. So the Secret Service and other government agencies developed a specially designed device that, they hoped, would at least keep the president's communications secure.

No other president had kept a phone much less used email regularly while in the White House, but then again Obama was a technological pioneer in all sorts of ways. He was the first president to set up a Facebook page, the first to write messages on Twitter, the first to answer questions on Reddit and Google+, the first to post an essay on Medium and the first to have accounts with Instagram, Snapchat, Vine, Tumblr and Flickr. With the help of the first White House videographer, his team aired essentially its own television program on the White House web site every Friday called *West Wing Week*.

Obama had a staff of twenty to manage those accounts, but by any measure, he was the first social media president. He was also a bit of a gearhead. He was the first commander in chief to receive his daily intelligence briefing on an iPad and he used it at night to scan the Internet for news stories of interest. During a trip to Alaska to highlight climate change, he was given a GoPro camera and a selfie stick to take his own photographs and video of disappearing glaciers, images that were shared online.

Obama eschewed traditional East Room news conferences in favor of unconventional outlets. Although he gave many one-on-one interviews to carefully selected mainstream journalists, often on predetermined topics, he all but ignored the White House reporters who covered him every day and were most attuned to the sometimes subtle policy changes and truth shading that a president tries to get away with. Obama took questions from the pool of journalists that followed him most closely barely a third as often as George W. Bush and less than a fifth as often as Bill Clinton. Even Ronald Reagan, famous for circumventing the media, took questions from White House pool reporters far more often than Obama.

But he gave interviews to all sorts of new-generation media figures. He traded deadpan insults with Zach Galifianakis on the quirky show *Between Two Ferns*. He sat down with a YouTube host named GloZell Green, who was famous for wearing bright green lipstick and once on camera soaked in a bathtub filled with milk and Fruit Loops. After his final State of the Union address, Obama chatted with a young man named Adande Thorne, a self-described "time traveler" and "professional cuddler" who used the screen name sWooZie and asked Obama for his favorite *Star Wars* character ("I've got to go with Han Solo," Obama answered. "He's a little bit of a rebel.")

If some of that came across as a little bit unpresidential, it also seemed necessary to Obama and his staff in an era when even 500 channels were no longer enough for many Americans and no single method allowed the White House to reach large segments of the voting public.

"Ultimately, what all of this is about," said Dan Pfeiffer, one of the architects of the strategy, "is finding ways to communicate with people in a time when media has become so disaggregated that simply communicating through the traditional means is woefully insufficient."

His would-be successors followed suit. Donald Trump was a ferocious Twitter user and Hillary Clinton found herself sitting between those ferns with Galifianakis. What was once a little bit rebellious now had become the default.

DOUG MILLS/NEW YORK TIMES

CHAPTER IX

'Haunted By Those Deaths'

A new, grisly and alarming black-hooded terrorist movement calling itself the Islamic State arises in Iraq and Syria, forcing Obama to get back into a war he wanted nothing to do with.

On New Year's Day, just hours after Americans welcomed the arrival of 2014 with fireworks and festivities, President Obama and his advisers tuned in their televisions to find a different, darker sort of celebration. Convoys of up to 100 trucks flying the black flag of Al Qaeda and armed with mounted heavy machine guns and antiaircraft guns stormed into the western Iraqi cities of Falluja and Ramadi. The Islamic extremists who had ruled there during the grim and bloody days of the previous decade cheered. They were back.

Two years after the last American troops pulled out of Iraq, the enemy once driven from the field had reconstituted itself and returned, this time vowing to create a caliphate, or an Islamic state, stretching across national borders. Operating from neighboring Syria, where they were taking advantage of the chaos of the three-year-old civil war, the Sunni Muslim militants were now calling themselves the Islamic State, or ISIS, ISIL or Daesh in some renditions. Unlike the original Al Qaeda, they aspired to hold territory. Indeed, they were intent on redrawing the map of the Middle East.

The sight of black flags flying once again in that part of Iraq sent a chill through the American military, which fought some of its fiercest battles there in the war that followed the invasion of 2003. Many veterans bristled at the thought of all that blood being spilled only to see the extremists take over again. But the fall of Falluja and Ramadi was the latest stage in a resurgence of radicalism in the region that had transformed the dreams of the Arab Spring into the nightmares of a jihadist winter. Egypt's democratically elected government had been ousted by the military. Libya was in chaos, riven by militias vying for power. Syria had degenerated into a cauldron of rebellion and terrorism. And now Iraq faced a renewed threat of being torn apart.

As disturbing as he found the latest developments, Obama was determined not to let the United States be dragged back into a war that he had opposed from the start and had promised to end. Obama was convinced that the United States was too quick to pull the military lever whenever it confronted a foreign crisis. He would not repeat what he considered George W. Bush's mistake. In Obama's mind, not every extremist with a gun posed an existential threat to the United States – and if they did not, then America should restrain itself rather than get sucked into another vortex of sectarian rivalry and ethnic violence.

Kashmiri demonstrators holding the ISIS flag in Srinagar, India, July 18, 2014.

"The analogy we use around here sometimes – and I think is accurate – is if a JV team puts on Lakers uniforms, that doesn't make them Kobe Bryant," he told *The New Yorker's* David Remnick, meaning junior varsity. Obama drew a distinction between Al Qaeda and "jihadists who are engaged in various local power struggles and disputes, often sectarian."

"But that JV team just took over Falluja," Remnick pointed out.

"I understand," Obama said. But terrorism is a global phenomenon and he argued that Americans should not "think that any horrible actions that take place around the world that are motivated in part by an extremist Islamic ideology is a direct threat to us or something that we have to wade into."

Crises in Iraq and Syria, and then trouble in Ukraine too.

In the two years since pulling out of Iraq, Washington had engaged in an awkward dance with Baghdad over how involved the Americans would be now that their military mission was over. As security worsened, American officials tried to reinsert themselves by proposing a joint intelligence center and offering other support, only to be brushed off by Prime Minister Nuri Kamal al-Maliki, who was eager to demonstrate his independence from the United States. But when violence began spilling over the border from Syria, it was Maliki who sought American help, only to find a reluctant partner.

In the months leading up to the takeover of Falluja, suicide bombings in Iraq spiked to fifty a month, up from just five a month when the Americans left. The Americans were so removed from the brewing crisis that they were flying just one surveillance flight a month at the time. Obama's administration sent a handful of Special Operations troops to advise Iraqis on targeting, but efforts to provide Apache helicopters and F-16 fighter jets stalled in Congress, where lawmakers were wary of empowering Maliki, a Shiite who had ruled with an increasingly sectarian hand since the American withdrawal, provoking Sunni resentment.

After Falluja fell, Obama resisted a military response and focused instead on pressing Maliki to hold genuinely free and fair elections in April in hopes of undercutting the popular resentment that was fueling the jihadist movement. But in the White House, the assumption was that Falluja and Ramadi were anomalies, longtime hotbeds of Sunni extremist sentiment that could essentially be walled off and contained, eventually even rolled back.

That was an assumption others warned against. Intelligence agencies had been raising alarms about the Islamic State for months, only to grow discouraged that the White House seemed not to take it seriously enough. Lieutenant General Michael T. Flynn, director of the Defense Intelligence Agency, even took his concerns public in his annual threat assessment to Congress. "ISIL," he told lawmakers six weeks after the jihadists muscled their way into western Iraq, "probably will attempt to take territory in Iraq and Syria in 2014, as demonstrated recently in Ramadi and Falluja."

Obama was not convinced. He wanted to end wars, not start them, and he gave a major speech at the United States Military Academy commencement ceremony at West Point intended to forswear future adventurism. "I am haunted by those deaths," he said of casualties resulting from operations he had ordered. From now on, when the United States was not directly threatened, he said, "the threshold for military action must be higher."

If Falluja were all that would confront Obama in 2014, that would still make it a challenging enough year. But 2014 would soon prove to be Obama's *annus horribilis*. By February, he not only had a growing crisis in Iraq and Syria but a new cold war developing in Eastern Europe.

For months, the former Soviet republic of Ukraine had been at the center of a geopolitical tug of war between its former masters in Moscow and a beckoning new Europe. President Viktor Yanukovych negotiated a trade agreement with the European Union only to reverse himself and renounce it after Russia offered him a $15 billion loan.

Pro-western demonstrators flooded the streets of Kiev, the capital, leading to a violent clash that killed about 100 protesters in the city's Maidan Square. A furious backlash over the deaths pushed Yanukovych to flee and the opposition took control. But Vladimir Putin was not about to accept the turn of fortunes. In a move that shocked the world, he sent masked Russian troops disguised in unmarked green uniforms – "little green men," as they became known – to the Ukrainian peninsula of Crimea, where many ethnic Russians lived and Moscow maintained a military base. Crimea had been a flashpoint between Russia and Ukraine ever since the end of the cold war. Historically a part of Russia, Crimea had been transferred by the Kremlin to control of the Ukrainian Soviet Republic in 1954 as a sop to the junior partner in the Soviet Union. When the union fell apart in 1991 and Ukraine became its own country, it kept Crimea, much to the consternation of nationalists in Moscow. With the ouster of Yanukovych, Putin decided the time had come to take it back. Within days, the Russians staged a referendum in which Crimean voters opted to break away from Ukraine. Putin then annexed the peninsula.

Suddenly, a relatively contained crisis in a second-tier Eastern European country turned into the most combustible confrontation between East and West since the end of the Cold War. Not satisfied with just Crimea, Russia escalated the clash by fomenting a separatist uprising in eastern

Ukraine, threatening to rip the country in half. A few weeks earlier, Obama had had only limited interest in whether Ukraine was anchored in Europe or remained under the influence of Moscow – he even referred to it as *the* Ukraine, unknowingly using an outdated formulation left over from the Soviet era that Ukrainians considered insulting. But once Russia used force to redraw the boundaries of Europe established nearly a quarter-century earlier, the president felt obliged to respond.

The turn of events represented the final collapse of Obama's efforts to restore relations with Moscow. When he took office, the two powers were at odds over Russia's 2008 war with the tiny former Soviet republic of Georgia. To bridge the divide, Obama resolved to "reset" the relationship, but the strategy got off to an embarrassing start when Hillary Clinton presented her Russian counterpart with a button marked with a Russian word she thought meant "reset," but actually translated to "overcharge."

The reset strategy was to bypass Putin and instead build up ties with his protégé, Dmitri Medvedev, whom he had installed as president when he formally stepped down in accordance with Russia's constitutional two-term limit. No one was fooled into thinking that Putin, who took the title of prime minister instead, had genuinely surrendered power, but Obama gambled that he could forge a personal connection with Medvedev, a more western-oriented lawyer of the same generation. On a hundred-degree day in June 2010, Obama took Medvedev to Ray's Hell Burger just outside Washington and talked about cooperation over cheeseburgers and fries. Over the course of a couple years, Obama cut a variety of agreements with him, including the New Start nuclear arms control treaty, a supply corridor to Afghanistan, United Nations sanctions on Iran and acquiescence for the war in Libya.

But Putin's decision to resume the presidency in 2012, fueled in part by his pique over Medvedev's failure to stand up to the west over Libya, effectively ended the reset. Putin publicly accused Clinton of inciting protests against his return to power. He presided over a harassment campaign against Obama's ambassador to Moscow, Michael McFaul, even before offering shelter to Edward Snowden, the American national security leaker. While they collaborated on destroying Syria's chemical weapons, Obama and Putin operated on radically different wavelengths. Putin, Obama said at one point, had a "kind of slouch" that made him look "like that bored schoolboy in the back of the classroom."

The bored schoolboy was now challenging the American president with a war of aggression in Europe. Obama crafted a response intended to quarantine Russia and turn it into an international pariah. In conjunction with Europe, he forced the ouster of Russia from the Group of Eight major powers, cut off a variety of civilian and military cooperation programs and imposed a series of escalating travel and financial sanctions. But Europe had far deeper economic ties to Russia and was far more skittish

Russian President Vladimir Putin at a ceremony in Sevastopol, Crimea, May 9, 2014.

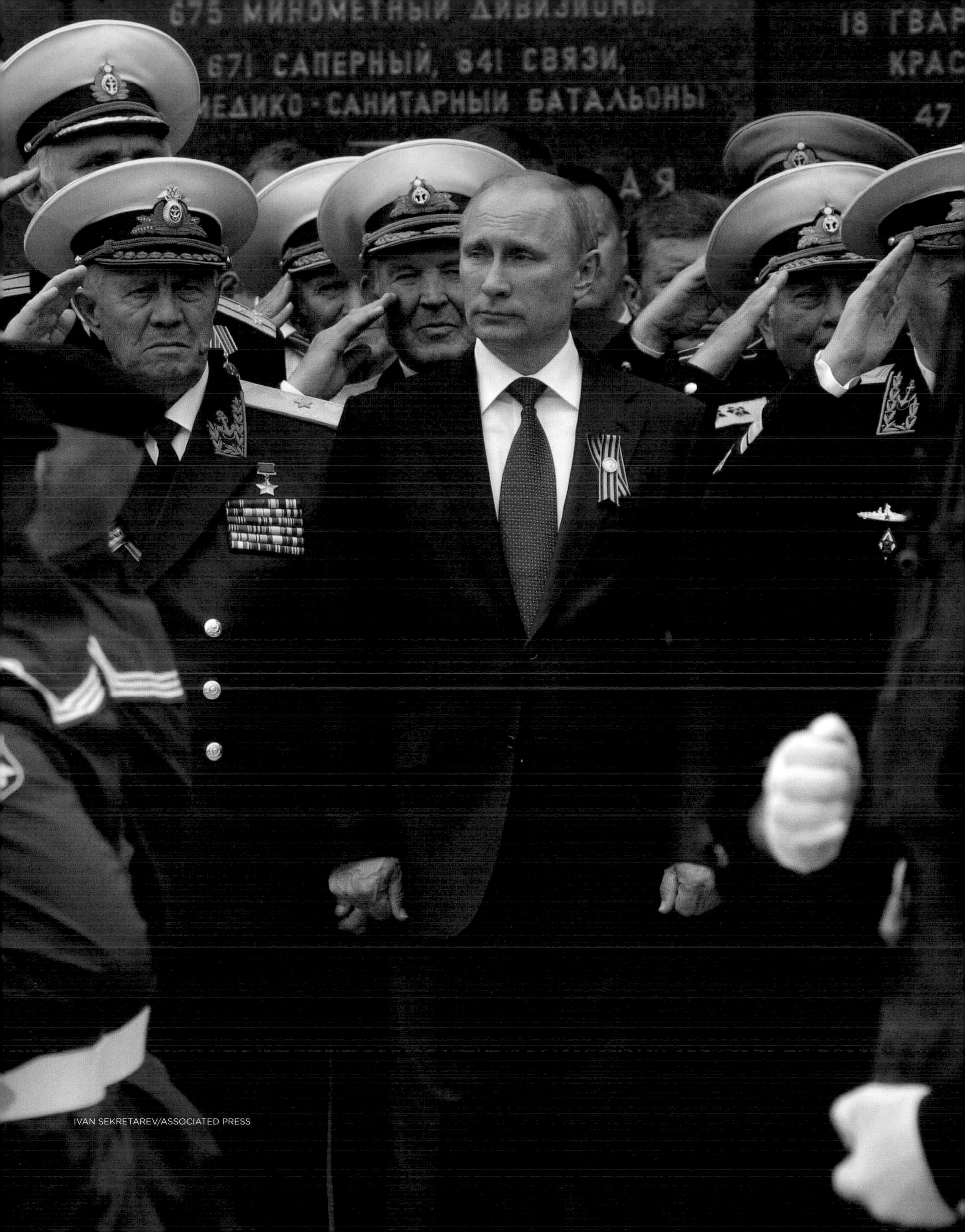

675 МИНОМЕТНЫЙ ДИВИЗИОНЫ
671 САПЕРНЫЙ, 841 СВЯЗИ,
МЕДИКО-САНИТАРНЫЙ БАТАЛЬОНЫ
18 ГВАР
КРАС
47
IVAN SEKRETAREV/ASSOCIATED PRESS

about confronting Moscow. To preserve solidarity, Obama limited the sanctions and other actions to no more than European leaders would agree to. And wary of being drawn into an armed clash with a nuclear superpower, Obama similarly resisted calls to ship arms to the Ukrainians, much less offer more overt military aid. Undeterred, Russia shipped weapons to its separatist allies in eastern Ukraine – and on July 17 an antiaircraft battery it provided the insurgents was used to shoot down Malaysia Airlines Flight 17, a civilian passenger jet passing overhead, killing all 298 on board, including eighty children.

"Russia is once again isolating itself from the international community, setting back decades of genuine progress," Obama said soon afterward as he ratcheted up sanctions again. "It didn't have to come to this. It does not have to be this way. This is a choice that Russia – and President Putin in particular – has made."

The challenges of 2014 kept coming, one after the other in a cascade that left Obama and his advisers wondering at times whether they could ever get out from under them. Obama's proactive initiatives were more or less lost in the inexorable wave of crises. For a time, a year earlier, Obama had seemed to be growing tired of the job. Now he faced questions about whether he was up to the job.

Spring brought fresh revelations about the deeply dysfunctional Department of Veterans Affairs, an agency long plagued by mismanagement and funding problems even as its mission grew more critical to so many American troops coming home from overseas battlegrounds with deep physical and psychological injuries. Americans were shocked by reports that Veterans Affairs officials manipulated data to hide long delays for patients seeing physicians.

The furor underscored a more fundamental danger for Obama as he once again found himself on the defensive over issues of basic management of the federal government. For a president who came to office hoping to restore public faith in government as a force for good in society, the mess at Veterans Affairs, coming after the botched rollout of the health care web site and the politicized decisions at the Internal Revenue Service, called into question Obama's mastery of the Washington bureaucracy over which he presided.

In the halls of the West Wing, there was more palpable concern over the veterans' situation than there ever was about other scandals that afflicted the administration, like the Benghazi talking points or the I.R.S. misconduct. If those controversies riled Republicans, poor treatment of veterans had the potential to offend a broader portion of the public across party lines, as evidenced by the outcry from Democratic members of Congress demanding the resignation of Eric Shinseki, the secretary of veterans affairs.

For once, Obama went along with those who wanted heads to roll.

The streets surrounding Kiev's Independence Square in Ukraine remain a nationalist opposition encampment, March 5, 2014.

TYLER HICKS/NEW YORK TIMES

Opponents of Ukraine's interim government and pro-secession demonstrators rally in front of Lenin's statue in Freedom Square, Kharkiv, Ukraine, March 15, 2014.

Like Bush before him, Obama had long rejected the idea of dismissing loyal advisers in the face of criticism just because that was how Washington worked. He had adamantly refused to push out Kathleen Sebelius, the secretary of health and human services, after the health care debacle and similarly resisted tossing other top officials overboard when things went wrong. Indeed, Obama had never before pushed out one of his own appointees with as high a profile as Shinseki in the thick of a crisis amid the braying of the media and the political class. But now he wasted little time showing Shinseki the door.

A swap for the release of a U.S. war prisoner is criticized.

A ritual sacking in Washington typically released the pressure of a controversy and pushed it off the front pages. In this case, however, what diverted attention from the veterans' mistreatment was yet another uproar that erupted the day after Shinseki was told to clean out his office. On orders from Obama, American troops met with Taliban fighters to conduct a swap, picking up Sergeant Bowe Bergdahl, the only American prisoner of war from the conflict in Afghanistan, on May 31 in exchange for the release of five detainees from Guantánamo Bay, Cuba. A video of the exchange later released by the Taliban showed a Black Hawk helicopter touching down in an arid field and American special forces troops emerging. They briefly shook hands with Taliban gunmen, then took Bergdahl to the helicopter, whose rotors never stopped spinning. Dressed all in white with a checkered scarf over his shoulders, the twenty-eight-year-old Bergdahl looked dazed, his eyes blinking. The American troops patted him down to make sure he was not laced with hidden weapons, then put him on the helicopter and lifted off. The encounter lasted just seconds.

The relief over his release, however, barely lasted longer. Obama appeared in the Rose Garden alongside Bergdahl's ecstatic parents to hail his freedom. But as the details emerged, Obama was quickly accused of negotiating with terrorists despite longstanding policy and castigated for letting five dangerous men back onto the battlefield. In making the trade, Obama ignored a law passed by Congress requiring thirty days' notice before any Guantánamo detainee was freed. And much of the sympathy for Bergdahl after five years of captivity dissipated with reports that he been captured after walking away from his unit, raising questions about whether the United States should trade enemy fighters for a deserter.

Obama defended the decision, saying that the urgency of the situation made it impractical to give notice to Congress and that the five

Guantánamo detainees were turned over to the Persian Gulf state of Qatar, which promised to keep them under control and bar them from traveling for a year. "The United States has always had a pretty sacred rule," Obama told reporters during a visit to Warsaw, "and that is: we don't leave our men or women in uniform behind." Whether Bergdahl deserted or not, the president added, did not change that. "Regardless of circumstances, whatever those circumstances may turn out to be, we still get an American prisoner back. Period. Full stop. We don't condition that."

Afghanistan was not the main focus of attention in the Situation Room that summer, however. Within weeks of the Bergdahl trade, all eyes in the White House were trained squarely on Iraq as thousands of fighters from the Islamic State swept through the northern part of the country, seized the major city of Mosul and drove into Tikrit, the ancestral home of Saddam Hussein. Suddenly, the Sunni extremists were not contained in the Sunni extremist part of the country – they were on the march through regions where they had less natural popular support and were even bearing down on the capital of Baghdad.

Just as Bush had before him, Obama found that any faith he had in the Iraqi security services was badly misplaced. For all of their American training and American-style uniforms, Iraqi troops simply melted away in the face of an aggressive, even fanatical, enemy. Without help, it was unclear how Iraq would resist. And so Obama reluctantly agreed to send 300 Special Operations troops back to Baghdad, not to engage in combat but to try to help the Iraqis organize their own forces more effectively. It was a small deployment, but a turning point for Obama.

With jihadists carving up Iraq, the Islamic State now controlled a wide swath of the Middle East, imposing a harsh form of Islam on its newly captured territory and threatening those who did not meet their religious standards. Obama was open to taking more direct action and even authorized a secret commando operation into Syria in July to try to rescue Americans being held hostage, only to be deflated when the troops failed to find them where they thought they would be. "Dry hole," came the dispiriting news over the radio.

The militants won more stunning victories against the Kurds, America's most loyal and reliable allies in the country, and they drove thousands of Yazidis, another religious minority, to Mount Sinjar, where the radicals were threatening to wipe them out. There was also continuing fear that the Islamic State would capture the strategic Haditha Dam on the Euphrates River and open its floodgates, releasing a wall of water that would overwhelm nearby towns and villages.

In early August, Obama took a fateful step. He ordered the Pentagon to launch a series of airstrikes to aid the Kurds and save the Yazidis. In sending warplanes back into the skies of Iraq, Obama found himself exactly

ANDREW CRAFT/FAYETTEVILLE OBSERVER

Sergeant Bergdahl leaves the courthouse after his arraignment in Fort Bragg, North Carolina, December 14, 2015.

where he did not want to be. The president who had vowed to end the war in Iraq was starting another one – or arguably jumping back into the old one, which was never genuinely finished. He comforted himself by focusing on the fact that he was not deploying a large ground force the way Bush did. He would not get America enmeshed in nation building the way Bush did. He would keep the mission limited and manageable. Yet his presence in the State Dining Room the night he announced the new mission testified to the bleak reality that the tide of events in that ancient land had defied his predictions and aspirations. Just three months earlier, he had told cadets at West Point that he was raising the bar for military action. Now he was crossing over the bar all over again.

"I know that many of you are rightly concerned about any American military action in Iraq, even limited strikes like these," Obama told the nation, almost as if trying to reassure himself. "I understand that. I ran for this office in part to end our war in Iraq and welcome our troops home, and that's what we've done. As commander in chief, I will not allow the United States to be dragged into fighting another war in Iraq."

TYLER HICKS/NEW YORK TIMES

F/A-18 fighter-bombers aboard the U.S.S. Carl Vinson in the Persian Gulf carry out daily attacks against Islamic State targets in Iraq and Syria, and support Iraqi ground troops, December 8, 2014.

A rescue in Kurdistan, and a divisive Iraqi leader departs.

Among the reasons Obama was reluctant to agree to the airstrikes was fear of bolstering Maliki as prime minister. Obama, aides said, did not want the United States to be "Maliki's air force." To the Americans, Maliki was the source of much of the problem. The Shiite prime minister had turned increasingly authoritarian since the departure of American troops at the end of 2011– indeed, within days of the withdrawal, he arrested a Sunni vice president, foreshadowing a more sectarian approach. In cracking down on Sunnis, Maliki fed resentment of his Shiite-led government and seeded the ground for the arrival of the Islamic State. Now Obama was ready to cut the cord. At the urging of the Americans, Iraq's president in August tapped another member of Maliki's party to take over as prime minister, Haider al-Abadi. Maliki hesitated for a few days, stirring fears that he would use force to retain power, then finally stepped aside. Obama and Joseph Biden each called to congratulate Abadi and came away hopeful that the new Iraqi leader would take a more inclusive approach, undercutting Sunni support for the Islamic State.

Iraq, though, was only part of the problem. It would mean little if the United States took on the Islamic State on one side of the border and did nothing about it on the other side in Syria. The jihadists did not respect lines on the map. And they showed in grim fashion that they would use

A fighter-bomber taking off in the Persian Gulf, December 8, 2014.

their territory to produce terror in far-off America. In quick succession, they released videos showing terrorists beheading two American journalists, James Foley and Steven Sotloff, as they were forced to wear Guantánamo-style orange jumpsuits and kneel on the ground to await their grisly fate. The videos shocked Americans and produced calls for revenge. Obama seemed genuinely troubled by the murders, but unintentionally sent the opposite message by heading to the golf course immediately after denouncing the Islamic State's actions. Obama was determined not to let terrorists dictate the president's schedule, but even some Democrats thought the quick juxtaposition of grief and golf was unseemly.

As Obama considered how to respond, he grappled with the lines that the Islamic State ignored. In Iraq, he had the invitation of the government to operate inside its territory and the cooperation of the Iraqi army to fight the enemy. But he had no such alignment with the government of Syria and no such allies on the ground in that war-torn country. Obama finally agreed to try to create from scratch a ground force in Syria by training and equipping a rebel army, much as Hillary Clinton and David Petraeus had recommended before. And in a dramatic intervention, Obama ordered American airstrikes on Islamic State forces inside Syria, reasoning that he had the right to act in the nation's self-defense.

In announcing his decision to extend the bombing campaign into Syria, Obama tried to strike a balance, again presenting himself as the anti-Bush even as he ordered a military action that Bush himself had not. Obama talked almost as much about what he would not do – "We will not get dragged into another ground war in Iraq" – as what he would do to counter the Islamic State.

But he also advanced an argument that in some ways mirrored Bush's much-debated strategy of pre-emption – that is, acting to forestall a potential threat rather than waiting for it to gather. Obama acknowledged that the Islamic State did not pose a direct threat to the United States at that time, but he contended that "if left unchecked" it could.

Obama's measured approach reflected a country weary of war in the Middle East and wary of another one. While commanders in chief typically enjoy a surge in public support when they take the nation into conflict overseas, Americans did not exactly rally behind Obama this time around. A fresh battery of polls indicated that most Americans did want him to go after the Islamic State, yet disapproved of his leadership.

In other words, they supported the policy but not the president.

Just how much they did not support him became clear in November, when voters repudiated Obama by handing Republicans control of the Senate and bolstering their majority in the House. Just two years after Obama's re-election, the midterm results underscored how far he had fallen in the public estimation. Nearly six out of ten voters interviewed by pollsters as they exited balloting stations expressed negative feelings about his administration. For every two voters who said they cast ballots to back Obama, three said they were voting to express their opposition to him.

While winning two historic elections himself, Obama in the course of his presidency had presided over the disintegration of his party on Capitol Hill. In six years, Democrats had lost a net thirteen seats in the Senate and sixty-eight in the House, the most dramatic reversal for an incumbent president's party in more than a half-century. The 2014 midterm election climaxed a year in which almost everything seemed to go wrong for Obama, and the Republican victory appeared to foreshadow a challenging final two years in office for the president with minimal chance for significant legislation.

But the one person in the White House who did not seem all that upset was Obama. "We got beat," he admitted publicly afterward. But he consciously made a point of avoiding any kind of memorable, headline-friendly word like "shellacking," the term he used after the 2010 midterm elections. Moreover, he sounded anything but defeated. He dismissed the notion that the election was a referendum on his leadership. The electoral map was stacked against him, he argued, making Democrats underdogs from the start. His staff told him that no president since the 1950s had as many vacant Senate seats up for grabs in states lost by the president. "This is probably the worst possible group of states for Democrats since Dwight Eisenhower," Obama told an interviewer on Election Day. And privately he groused that his own party had kept him off the campaign trail, with many of its most embattled candidates refusing to let him come to their states or districts, meaning he never really got the chance to make his case. In the last days of the campaign, he was brought into just five states to campaign, compared with the ten visited by Bush in similar circumstances in 2006.

In a way, although he would not say this out loud with the cameras on, Obama felt liberated by the defeat of the Democrats. Now, at least, he no longer had to defer to Senator Harry Reid of Nevada, the cantankerous Democratic leader in the upper chamber who often made the president's life difficult. Now Obama no longer had to subordinate his own priorities to those of a vulnerable congressional caucus obsessed about the next election. Now he could essentially bypass his own petulant party allies to deal directly with Republican leaders in areas where they might come to agreement and publicly take them on in areas where they could not.

In the days following the election, Obama seemed almost revitalized and determined to advance his agenda using the power he already had – and the power that he was about to claim. He wasted little time exercising it. He started by weighing in on a long-running debate over "net neutrality," urging his appointees on the Federal Communications Commission to regulate the Internet as a public utility like electricity and telephone service. He told the F.C.C., with three Democratic appointees to two Republicans, that

A car bomb explodes at a rally for a Shiite militant group, where three such explosions killed more than 30 people on April 25, 2014 in Baghdad.

'Feeling Pretty Good'

Fiercely competitive, a hoopster turns to greener pastures

If President Obama was in town for the weekend and the weather was even passable, it was a fair bet he could be found on a golf course. Like most of his modern predecessors, Obama found release on the links, a chance to escape the confines of his admittedly grand white home, spend a few hours outdoors and even put out of mind, however briefly, the troubles of the nation and the world.

At forty-seven, Obama arrived at the White House one of the youngest presidents, still energetic, trim and fit. He loved basketball and played frequently, the first occupant of the West Wing to shoot hoops on a regular basis. Indeed, he had the White House tennis court retrofitted so it could be used as a regulation-sized basketball court. For his second birthday in the White House, he played with some of the all-time greats, including Alonzo Mourning, Bill Russell, Grant Hill, Magic Johnson and LeBron James.

On the court, Obama was famous for his intense game, trash-talking aides he did not think were carrying their weight. At one early game, he was playing physical defense when a young official from the Congressional Hispanic Caucus who had been invited to play accidentally slammed his right elbow into Obama's mouth, causing a wound that required twelve stitches. In a show of forgiveness, Obama sent him a three-photograph sequence of the episode framed and signed to "the only guy who ever hit the president and never got arrested." Still, there was a limit to amnesty; the man with the sharp elbow was never invited back.

As his presidency wore on and his hair turned gray, though, Obama increasingly turned to golf instead of basketball. He still loved basketball – he stayed up late to catch ESPN's *SportsCenter* and made a point of releasing his own NCAA March Madness tournament brackets every spring (although he only picked one champion correctly in his eight years in office). When his hometown Chicago Bulls fired the coach, Tom Thibodeau, Obama took to Twitter to lament the move.

But by his own admission, he was slowing down. "I used to play basketball more," he told the comedian Marc Maron in 2015. "But these days, I've gotten to the point where it's not as much fun because I'm not as good as I used to be and I get frustrated." He added: "Now I'm one of these old guys who's running around. The guys I play with – who are all a lot younger – they sort of pity me and sympathize with me. They tolerate me, but we all know I'm the weak link on the court and I don't like being the weak link."

So golf became his leisure time preoccupation. He usually played with a set of younger aides or old friends, staying away from other politicians who would pepper him with unwanted requests or advice. His one game with House Speaker John Boehner only caused problems for Boehner with his Republican base and was never repeated. For Obama, golf was a boys' outing; women were almost never invited. But he was relentlessly honest, unlike Bill Clinton who regularly took mulligans.

By his last summer in office, Obama had played his 300th round, making him the most avid presidential golfer since Dwight Eisenhower. Where George W. Bush gave up golf in office to avoid looking insensitive to troops fighting overseas, Obama ignored critics who mocked what they deemed his golfing-while-Rome-burns pastime.

Others teased him about his performance. Michael Jordan publicly called the president "a hack" golfer. But Obama reportedly brought his score down into the 80s. As he talked one day with Thomas Friedman of *The New York Times,* he prefaced his perorations on the Middle East to crow that he had just played his best game ever.

"Had an 80 last week," Obama said. He had "a fifteen-foot putt for 79. I was feeling pretty good. I missed it by about that much."

President Obama and House Speaker John Boehner at the Andrews Air Force Base course in Maryland, June 18, 2011.

The president plays a little basketball during the annual Easter Egg Roll at the White House, April 25, 2011.

Going for a rebound in a game with congressmen at the White House, October 8, 2009.

Singing "Amazing Grace," Charleston, South Carolina.

METHODIST
AFRICAN EPISCOPAL

CHAPTER X

'Could Have Been Me'

Eager to be judged not as a black president but as a unifier, Obama is confronted with a series of killings that bring the country's race relations to a boil.

President Obama joins hands with civil rights activists Amelia Boynton Robinson and Representative John Lewis as they cross the Edmund Pettus Bridge, Selma, Alabama, March 7, 2015, marking the 50th anniversary of the 'Bloody Sunday' March.

DOUG MILLS/NEW YORK TIMES

President Obama was sitting on Marine One as the iconic white-topped helicopter lifted off from the South Lawn of the White House. He was thinking about race in America. Here he was, the first black man to live in the executive mansion built in part by slaves and command the tools of the presidency like the aircraft ferrying him to his next destination, a living symbol of progress in a country long divided along lines of color. But he was heading off to South Carolina to deliver the eulogy for a black pastor and eight of his parishioners gunned down in church on June 17, 2015, by a twenty-one-year-old white supremacist, the kind of mindless act of hate that seemed to belie the hope his election had inspired.

"When I get to the second part of referring to 'Amazing Grace,'" he ventured out loud as he thought about his speech, "I think I might sing."

Sing? That was not something presidents typically did, not in public, especially not in the age of YouTube when every moment lives on forever. Michelle Obama and the president's senior adviser, Valerie Jarrett, seemed skeptical. "Why on earth would that fit in?" the first lady asked.

The president demurred. Maybe he would not do it. He was not sure. "We'll see how it feels at the time," he said.

It must have felt okay, because from the pulpit of the stately Emanuel African Methodist Episcopal Church in Charleston later that day, Obama came to the end of a forty-minute eulogy delivered in revivalist cadences, paused and then began singing, alone, the opening refrain of "Amazing Grace."

Amazing Grace, how sweet the sound
That saved a wretch like me.

Something about that moment captured the roiling emotions of a nation struggling to make sense of racial violence in what was supposed to be an era that had moved past that. For all the heady assumptions about the larger meaning of his election, Obama's presidency revealed just how far the nation had yet to go when it came to bridging the enduring divisions that once led it into civil war. A series of deadly encounters between police officers and young black men, riots in the streets of cities big and small and the massacre of African-American churchgoers praying to God put race back on the table in Obama's later years in office.

Many presidents have governed during times of racial tension, but Obama was the first to glance in a mirror and find a face that looked like those on the other side of history's ledger. While his first term was consumed with the economy, war and health care, his second kept coming back to the societal scars that were not healed by his ascension. A president who initially eschewed focusing on race, eager to be judged as a president who happened to be black, not as a black president, now seemed to find his voice again as he lamented the fate of young men like Trayvon Martin, Michael Brown and Freddie Gray.

Despite an election breakthrough, old hatreds find new life.

Obama was not able to resolve those tensions during his eight years, nor could he be expected to, but many debated whether his presidency had helped or hurt. To many of his supporters, it was self-evident that the ferocity of opposition to him was fueled by racism, that his detractors simply could not stomach the sight of an African-American in power. The unrelenting antagonism by Republicans in Congress had to be a function of race, they concluded, to the point that it became an article of faith in some circles: *They would never do that to a white president.* That was a conviction shared by some of those close to Obama and, some said, at some moments by the president himself. At times, it felt like Obama's presidency had given new life to old hatreds rather than bury them. "For many people, it feels worse because we have seen such a reaction to this presidency that has been really alarming and without question from many quarters has been based in part on his race," said Sherrilyn Ifill, president of the NAACP Legal Defense and Educational Fund.

Others argued that such a conclusion said more about the racial lens of Obama and his supporters than that of the other side, that America's corrosive politics had resulted in virulent and ugly opposition to white presidents like George W. Bush and Bill Clinton too. To be sure, Obama had faced stubborn assertions that he was not born in the United States, but Clinton was accused by some of involvement in the supposed murder of his aide Vincent Foster, who committed suicide, and Bush was accused by others of complicity in the terrorist attacks of September 11, 2001. At one point, moviemakers released a film imagining Bush's assassination. To the extent that racial tensions had been exacerbated during Obama's presidency, some of his critics maintained that Obama himself was at least partly to blame for embracing the politics of grievance and undercutting police officers with snap judgments in disputed cases. "President Obama, when he was elected, could have been a unifying leader," said Senator Ted Cruz of Texas, who was preparing a campaign for the Republican presidential nomination in hopes of succeeding Obama. "He has made decisions that I think have inflamed racial tensions."

One thing that was not debatable was that the vision of a post-racial society remained far away by the end of Obama's presidency. He presided over a country where blacks were still twice as likely to be unemployed as whites, where gaps in income and wealth between races were widening rather than closing, where blacks were five times likelier to be in prison and young black men nine times as likely to be killed in a homicide as their white counterparts and where blacks got sick more, died younger and owned less. Frustrated activists felt compelled to organize behind a slogan that might have seemed unnecessary with an African-American in the White House: Black Lives Matter. "His candidacy suggested we had reached a new moment in America," Ifill said, "and I think some people overestimated the meaning of that moment."

Obama maintained that his economic and health care policies, if not overtly targeted to benefit minorities, had a disproportionate impact on African-Americans and other disadvantaged groups. Indeed, 1.7 million more blacks had health insurance coverage by 2015 than before Obama's program, a proportionately greater change than among whites. And Valerie Jarrett maintained that his mere presence in the office made a huge difference in setting expectations for a whole new generation of young Americans who came of age not knowing any other presidents. "By breaking through that barrier, there are children growing up today who think it's perfectly normal to have an African American president because that's all they have ever known," she said.

Obama arrived at the White House understanding how he had gotten there. He placed a bust of the Rev. Dr. Martin Luther King Jr. in the Oval Office and hung a framed copy of the program from the March on Washington of 1963. On his custom-designed office rug, he included one of King's favorite quotations (often credited to the civil rights leader but actually just adopted and popularized by him): "The arc of the moral universe is long, but it bends towards justice."

Obama had spent years reflecting on race in America and his own identity as the son of a black father from Kenya he met just once and a white mother from Kansas who took him to live overseas but eventually sent him to live with his white grandparents. His early memoir, *Dreams From My Father*, written as the first African American to serve as president of the *Harvard Law Review*, explored his own struggles to straddle lines between white and black and to define what it meant to be an American. With the bracing candor and self-absorption of youth, Obama wrote about race in an unvarnished way that no one planning a political career would ever have

Michael Brown, Sr., cries out as his son Michael's casket is lowered, St. Louis, August 25, 2014.

done. But now he was a politician, not an author. And consumed as he was by the greatest economic crisis in decades and two overseas wars to end, he entered office reluctant to talk about race.

When Attorney General Eric Holder said in 2009 that the United States was "a nation of cowards" on the subject, Obama quietly reined him in, making clear he did not want such a conversation. On the few occasions that he did step into racial controversy, he found himself burned. After a friend of his, Professor Henry Louis "Skip" Gates Jr., the eminent Harvard University historian, was arrested in his own home by a white police officer even after confirming that he was not an intruder, Obama said the police had "acted stupidly." He was surprised by the resulting uproar among those who complained about him inserting himself into a local dispute and second-guessing a law enforcement officer. To try to smooth over the flap, Obama invited both Gates and the officer to the White House to join him and Joseph Biden for a beer on the South Lawn, in what was quickly dubbed "the beer summit" by the media.

After winning a second term, Obama begins talking about race more often.

After Trayvon Martin, a seventeen-year-old African-American, was shot to death by a white man in Florida, Obama noted that "if I had a son, he'd look like Trayvon." But otherwise, he steered away from extended discussion of race relations in America during his first term, much to the consternation of some African-American figures who accused him of betraying his special historical responsibility. Cornel West, the outspoken Princeton University professor, called Obama, "a black mascot of Wall Street oligarchs" and a "Rockefeller Republican in blackface." Tavis Smiley, the radio host, accused Obama of being "timid" on issues that had really mattered to Martin Luther King. "If you're not going to address racism, if you're not going to address poverty, if you're not going to address militarism, if you're going to dance around all three of them, then you're not doing justice to Dr. King," Smiley said.

After his re-election, liberated of worries of political consequences, Obama began talking about race more often. In the days after securing a second term, he told aides that he wanted to overhaul criminal justice policies that disproportionately affected young African-American men. He also said he wanted to focus more on income inequality and he used his inaugural address to pledge to fight what he saw as restrictions on voting rights.

In part, his increased public focus on race was a function of the calendar – a series of fifty-year anniversaries from the civil rights era prompted him to reflect on the progress, or lack thereof, over his lifetime. He addressed commemorations of the March on Washington, the passage of the Civil Rights Act and the police beatings in Selma, Alabama. But his changing focus also owed to disturbing events across the country.

Michael Brown's killing touches off angry protests and challenges a president.

The acquittal of Trayvon Martin's killer in July 2013 prompted Obama to reflect publicly on the case in a more fulsome and personal way than he had before. "Trayvon Martin could have been me thirty-five years ago," he said. He talked about his own experiences of being followed while shopping in a department store or hearing car door locks when he crossed the street. "It's inescapable for people to bring those experiences to bear," he said.

Then came Ferguson, Missouri, where a white police officer shot to death Michael Brown, an unarmed eighteen-year-old African-American who was reported to have his hands up when the bullets slammed into him. The episode touched off angry protests and riots in the summer of 2014, and eventually a federal investigation showing that authorities there targeted black residents. Obama was on vacation at Martha's Vineyard, where he huddled with Eric Holder. A photograph of the two released by the White House unintentionally captured the contrasting approaches of the two men, the most powerful African-American officials in the country. Holder was the one leaning forward, both in the photograph and on the issues underlying the crisis in Ferguson. Obama, sitting back in his chair with two fingers pressed to his temple as he listened intently, was the one seemingly holding back, contemplative, even brooding, as if seeking to understand how events could get so out of hand.

After all, Holder grew up in the civil rights era and felt its legacy acutely. His sister-in-law integrated the University of Alabama. Obama, a decade younger, was removed from that experience by time, geography and family background, growing up largely in white households an ocean away in Hawaii and Indonesia. As a result, Obama was always somewhat suspect to more outspoken black activists who concluded that he could not feel intuitively what they did. "There is no blood flowing through the veins with empathy," said Michael Eric Dyson, a prominent author and Georgetown University professor.

A grand jury eventually declined to indict the Ferguson police officer, who argued that he had felt threatened during an altercation amid evidence that contradicted the report that Michael Brown's hands were actually up. Convinced of another cover-up by the white establishment, protesters

The White House is illuminated in rainbow colors after a Supreme Court ruling legalized gay marriage, June 26, 2015.

"All the News That's Fit to Print"

The New York Times

Late Edition

Today, mostly cloudy, afternoon rain, windy, cooler, high 71. Tonight, heavy rain, thunder, flooding, low 64. Tomorrow, a thunderstorm, high 78. Weather map, Page C8.

VOL. CLXIV ... No. 56,910   © 2015 The New York Times   NEW YORK, SATURDAY, JUNE 27, 2015 $2.50

'EQUAL DIGNITY'

5-4 Ruling Makes Same-Sex Marriage a Right Nationwide

Michael Crow and Robert Woodcock

Breanne Brodak and Cortney Tucker

Traci Bliss Panzner and Julie Ann Lake

George Harris and Jack Evans

Natalie, Christina and Alice Leslie

Christopher Brown and Tom Fennell

Kenneth Denson and Gabriel Mendez

Crystal Zimmer and Lena Williams

Marge Eide and Ann Sorrell

Barbara Schwartz and Julia Troxler

Lori Hazelton and Stephanie Ward

Terrence McNally and Thomas Kirdahy

Forceful Dissents From the Court And Nation

By ADAM LIPTAK

WASHINGTON — In a long-sought victory for the gay rights movement, the Supreme Court ruled by a 5-to-4 vote on Friday that the Constitution guarantees a right to same-sex marriage.

"No longer may this liberty be denied," Justice Anthony M. Kennedy wrote for the majority in the historic decision. "No union is more profound than marriage, for it embodies the highest ideals of love, fidelity, devotion, sacrifice and family. In forming a marital union, two people become something greater than once they were."

Marriage is a "keystone of our social order," Justice Kennedy said, adding that the plaintiffs in the case were seeking "equal dignity in the eyes of the law."

The decision, which was the culmination of decades of litigation and activism, set off jubilation and tearful embraces across the country, the first same-sex marriages in several states, and resistance — or at least stalling — in others. It came against the backdrop of fast-moving changes in public opinion, with polls indicating that most Americans now approve of the unions.

The court's four more liberal justices joined Justice Kennedy's majority opinion. Each member of the court's conservative wing filed a separate dissent, in tones ranging from resigned dismay to bitter scorn.

In dissent, Chief Justice John G. Roberts Jr. said the Constitution had nothing to say on the subject of same-sex marriage.

"If you are among the many Americans — of whatever sexual orientation — who favor expanding same-sex marriage, by all means celebrate today's decision," Chief Justice Roberts wrote. "Celebrate the achievement of a desired goal. Celebrate the opportunity for a new expression of commitment to a partner. Celebrate the availability of new benefits. But do not celebrate the Constitution. It had nothing to do with it."

In a second dissent, Justice An-

Continued on Page A11

"It would misunderstand these men and women to say they disrespect the idea of marriage. Their plea is that they do respect it, respect it so deeply that they seek to find its fulfillment for themselves."

JUSTICE ANTHONY M. KENNEDY, from the majority opinion

Historic Day for Gay Rights, but a Twinge of Loss for Gay Culture

By JODI KANTOR

From Capitol Hill in Seattle to Dupont Circle in Washington, gay bars and nightclubs have turned into vitamin stores, frozen yogurt shops and memories. Some of those that remain are filled increasingly with straight patrons, while many former customers say their social lives now revolve around preschools and playgrounds.

Rainbow-hued "Just Be You" messages have been flashing across Chase A.T.M. screens in honor of Pride month, conveying acceptance but also corporate blandness. Directors, filmmakers and artists are talking about moving past themes of sexual orientation, which they say no longer generate as much dramatic energy.

The Supreme Court on Friday expanded same-sex marriage rights across the country, a crowning achievement but also a confounding challenge to a group that has often prided itself on being different. The more victories that accumulate for gay rights, the faster some gay institutions, rituals and markers are fading out. And so just as the gay marriage movement peaks, so does a debate about whether gay identity is dimming, overtaken by its own success.

"What do gay men have in common when they don't have oppression?" asked Andrew Sullivan, one of the intellectual architects of the marriage movement. "I don't know the answer to that yet."

John Waters, the film director and patron saint of the American marginal, warned graduates to heed the shift in a recent commencement speech at the Rhode Island School of Design. "Refuse to isolate yourself. Separatism is for losers," he said, adding, "Gay is not enough anymore."

No one is arguing that prejudice has come close to disappearing, especially outside major

Continued on Page A12

THE OPPOSITION Many conservatives hope that stronger legal protections for religious beliefs and other exemptions will allow them to avoid any involvement in same-sex marriages. PAGE A14

THE REACTION It was a day of celebration for some, denunciation for others and delays and confusion in some of the country's most conservative pockets. PAGE A13

THE CHIEF JUSTICE Even though he wound up in the minority, the views of Chief Justice John G. Roberts Jr. came across as consistent and principled. PAGE A13

returned to the streets not just in Ferguson but around the country. Then came Staten Island, where another grand jury declined to indict a police officer in the death of Eric Garner, an African-American who called out, "I can't breathe," as he was restrained by a choke hold. Then came Baltimore, where Freddie Gray, a twenty-five-year-old African-American, died while in police custody. Some of the Baltimore protesters turned violent, looting stores, setting fires and throwing rocks and cinder blocks at police officers. Obama, trying to settle the streets, appealed for calm and lamented the cycle of poverty and hopelessness. At the same time, he condemned the "criminals and thugs" who were taking advantage of the situation, a line that aggravated some of the activists.

I n June 2015, a young white racist named Dylann Storm Roof joined a group of African-Americans to pray at Emanuel African Methodist Episcopal Church in Charleston before pulling out a gun and opening fire. Bug-eyed with a bowl haircut, a broken family and a history of drug use, the twenty-one-year-old Roof had descended into hate and extremism in the months leading up to the slaughter, spewing racist views and posting a photograph of himself on Facebook wearing a black jacket with flags of apartheid-era South Africa and white-ruled Rhodesia. Among those he killed was the Reverend Clementa Pinckney, who was both the church pastor and a state senator – and whom both Obama and Biden had met during past campaigning in South Carolina.

Before 6,000 fellow mourners at T.D. Arena in Charleston, not far from the church, Obama eulogized Pinckney with the rhythm and tone of a pastor himself. "Maybe we now realize the way racial bias can infect us even when we don't realize it," Obama said behind Pinckney's coffin, draped in a blanket of red roses. "So that we're guarding against not just racial slurs, but we're also guarding against the subtle impulse to call Johnny back for a job interview, but not Jamal. So that we search our hearts when we consider laws to make it harder for some of our fellow citizens to vote." By treating every child as important regardless of skin color and by opening up opportunities for all Americans, Obama said, "we express God's grace."

Obama's sermon – one of the preachers referred to him as the "Reverend President" – harkened back to his speech on race during his 2008 campaign, when he was forced to repudiate his own pastor, Rev. Jeremiah Wright, whose inflammatory, hate-filled rhetoric belied Obama's message of racial harmony and threatened his nascent candidacy. But as his second term progressed, Obama increasingly resolved to lean forward as Eric Holder had and tried in various ways to take the initiative on issues related to race.

Most prominent was his drive to overhaul a criminal justice system that he saw as tilted against African-Americans. A month after his eulogy in South Carolina, Obama addressed the annual convention of the N.A.A.C.P.

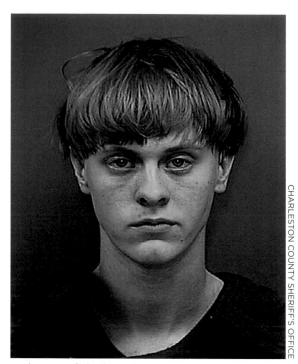

Dylann Roof's booking photo.

President Obama at the memorial service for the Reverend Clementa Pinckney, who was among the victims of a mass shooting at Emanuel African Methodist Episcopal Church, Charleston, South Carolina. Pinckney's wife, Jennifer Benjamin Pinckney, holds daughter Malana, June 26, 2015.

Visiting the facility in El Reno, Oklahoma, July 16, 2015, President Obama becomes the first sitting president to set foot in a federal prison.

'Hanging Out with Hollywood'

Entertaining at the White House is back in a big way

The giveaway was a tweet from the Reverend Al Sharpton. "Leaving the White House party w/POTUS and FLOTUS," he wrote on Twitter in the early morning hours in spring 2015, using acronyms for the president and first lady of the United States. "Awesome to see Prince and Stevie Wonder on keyboards together. Unbelievable experience."

Unbelievable and, until that point, almost unknown. Secretly, the Obamas had gathered 500 people for a star-studded party at the White House where Prince and Stevie Wonder, two of the world's most famous singers, performed. On hand were professional athletes, Wall Street executives, Washington lobbyists, movie stars, members of the Cabinet and plenty of others. The White House called it a private affair paid for by the Obamas and declined to give details.

White House veterans dating to the Lyndon B. Johnson administration could not remember such a large party being held at 1600 Pennsylvania Avenue in secret. But after the early-to-bed presidency of George W. Bush, the Obamas brought entertaining back to the White House in a big way, both openly and behind closed doors. Over their eight years, they gave the White House stage to Irish fiddlers, mariachi bands, pop stars and jazz singers. They sponsored the first White House poetry jam featuring James Earl Jones as Othello. They started an annual tradition of hosting a Passover seder. They held dinners for thinkers and filmmakers like Ken Burns. They even brought the cast of the Broadway hit *Hamilton* to perform at the White House.

Most of this was for fun, or to highlight the arts, not so much for political schmoozing or high diplomacy. Obama did not particularly care for formal, black-tie state dinners for visiting foreign leaders any more than Bush did – and not just because wannabe reality television stars gate-crashed his first one. Obama held only a few more state dinners than his predecessor did and far fewer than Ronald Reagan, Bill Clinton or the first George Bush did.

Instead, Obama preferred to hang out with celebrities and enjoyed an eclectic blend of music and art. The list of those who performed at the White House during the Obama era amounted to a who's who of American entertainment. Among them: Burt Bacharach, Joan Baez, Joshua Bell, Tony Bennett, Leon Bridges, Natalie Cole, Sheryl Crow, Gloria Estefan, Jennifer Hudson, Mick Jagger, Booker T. Jones, B.B. King, Nathan Lane, Queen Latifah, Cyndi Lauper, John Legend, Lyle Lovett, John Mellencamp, Smokey Robinson, Paul Simon, Jordin Sparks, Mavis Staples, James Taylor and Justin Timberlake. And of course, Stevie Wonder, an Obama family favorite.

The Obamas seemed to be especially fond of Beyoncé and her husband, Jay Z, and the president often enlisted celebrities for political causes, discussing Sudan with George Clooney and climate change with Leonardo di Caprio. But he was sensitive about how their presence would be perceived, saying he knew that "somehow it'll be tagged as Obama hanging out with Hollywood stars."

There were also moments of tension with some of those Hollywood stars who grew disenchanted with the president. After the actor Matt Damon criticized him over drone strikes and secret surveillance, Obama fired back with a joke at a black-tie dinner. "Matt Damon said he was disappointed in my performance," Obama said. "Well, Matt, I just saw *The Adjustment Bureau*, so right back at you, buddy."

But Obama was an eager consumer and promoter of popular culture. He released his playlists on Spotify, including songs like "Ain't Too Proud to Beg" by the Temptations, "Paradise" by Coldplay, "Boozophilia" by Low Cut Connie and, of course, "Another Star" by Stevie Wonder. The lists had impact. Streams of Low Cut Connie jumped nearly 3,000 percent overnight.

The professionals were impressed. Rarely had there been a president as attuned to popular culture as Obama. As the spokesman for Spotify said, "If he wants a job curating music when this presidential gig is over, we'd take him in a second."

President Obama and Secretary of State John Kerry at the United Nations, September 28, 2015.

DOUG MILLS/NEW YORK TIMES

CHAPTER XI

'Never Fear to Negotiate'

Fulfilling a pledge to engage with long-term antagonists, the president moves to end the half-century American isolation of Cuba and forges a nuclear arms agreement with Iran.

President Obama meets with Cuban President Raul Castro, Havana, March 21, 2016.

A week before Christmas 2014, President Obama marched into the Cabinet Room of the White House to make a stunning announcement televised around the world. Nearly fifty-four years after the United States broke off relations with Fidel Castro's Cuba, Obama declared that he was ordering the restoration of ties and the reopening of an embassy in Havana in a dramatic act intended to sweep aside one of the last vestiges of the Cold War. "These fifty years have shown that isolation has not worked," he said. "It's time for a new approach."

Obama rarely displayed much emotion in public, but anyone who had followed him over the years could detect a sense of satisfaction that day in the hint of a grin on his face and the tone of vindication in his voice. The surprise decision capped eighteen months of secret talks prodded in part by Pope Francis and concluded by a telephone call between Obama and President Raul Castro. The historic deal broke an enduring stalemate between two countries divided by just ninety miles of water but oceans of mistrust and hostility dating from the days of Theodore Roosevelt's charge up San Juan Hill and the nuclear brinkmanship of the Cuban missile crisis.

The opening to Cuba was part of a broader effort by the president to transform America's relations with the world and reach out to its enemies. When he first ran for president, Obama promised to talk with leaders of renegade states like Cuba, Iran, Syria, North Korea and Venezuela without precondition in his first year in office. While his promise was ridiculed during the campaign by Hillary Clinton as "irresponsible and frankly naïve," and John McCain said it betrayed his "inexperience and reckless judgment," Obama pointed repeatedly to John F. Kennedy's inaugural maxim, "Let us never negotiate out of fear but let us never fear to negotiate." At his own inauguration, Obama addressed the nation's most intransigent adversaries by promising to "extend a hand if you are willing to unclench your fist."

It didn't happen in his first year or without preconditions, nor did it happen across the board. But deep into his second term, Obama was ready to follow through on the thrust of his promise with two of the five rogue states mentioned in his original campaign, Cuba and Iran. As with his

Workers hanging the seal of the United States at the reopened American Embassy, Havana, August 14, 2015.

diplomatic overture to Havana, Obama decided it was time to talk with Tehran, now more than three decades after the Islamic revolution and the subsequent 444-day hostage crisis that gripped the world, doomed Jimmy Carter's presidency and touched off a relentless ideological struggle for influence in the region. As with Cuba, Obama authorized secret talks that, in this case, eventually led to an agreement curbing Iran's nuclear program in exchange for the lifting of international sanctions.

Obama explained his thinking about such diplomatic initiatives to Thomas Friedman of *The New York Times*, arguing that it was better to see if talking would work. "We are powerful enough to be able to test these propositions without putting ourselves at risk," he said when the two sat down for a one-on-one conversation in the Oval Office. Cuba was not a country "that threatens our core security interests" and even if Iran was more dangerous, the mullahs understood that they could not hope to match the power of the United States.

The Iran deal widens the rift between Obama and Israel's leadership.

"You asked about an Obama Doctrine," he told Friedman. "The doctrine is: We will engage, but we preserve all our capabilities."

Not everyone was impressed. For all the self-congratulations, Republicans and even some Democrats viewed Obama's outreach to Cuba and Iran as dangerously misguided. Cuba had done nothing to ease its iron grip over its own people and reopening relations would simply reward the hemisphere's most brutal dictatorship. Iran had a record of cheating when it came to building a nuclear capability and would simply use the estimated $100 billion it would recoup after sanctions were lifted to finance further terrorism and instability in the Middle East.

Moreover, the Iran deal widened a rift between Obama and the leadership of Israel, never close to begin with. While five other international powers – Britain, France, Germany, Russia and China – signed off on the Iran deal, America's closest friend in the region definitively did not. Indeed, Prime Minister Benjamin Netanyahu became the world's leading opponent of the agreement, dismissing Tehran's promises to abide by new restrictions and calling the deal an existential threat to his small state that would only trigger an arms race with Arab states wary of Iranian aspirations to regional hegemony. He went so far as to accept an invitation from John Boehner to address a joint meeting of Congress to attack the president's diplomacy with Iran, a spectacle with few if any modern precedents and one that outraged Obama.

President Obama and Prime Minister Shinzo Abe at the Ise Shrine, Japan, May 26, 2016.

"This deal won't be a farewell to arms – it would be a farewell to arms control," Netanyahu declared on March 3, 2015, from the rostrum of the majestic chamber of the House of Representatives, where Republicans greeted him with standing ovations even as dozens of Democrats, including Joseph Biden and Nancy Pelosi, the House minority leader, stayed away. "And the Middle East would soon be crisscrossed by nuclear tripwires. A region where small skirmishes can trigger big wars would turn into a nuclear tinderbox."

For Obama, the gambits with Cuba and Iran represented a conflict of visions between his faith in diplomacy as the most rational way to resolve differences between international actors and his critics' deep skepticism over the wisdom of negotiating with what they saw as adversaries that should not be trusted. It was something of a season for diplomacy – in addition to the Cuba opening and the Iran nuclear deal, Obama was putting the finishing touches on a sweeping Asian-Pacific trade pact that would encompass 40 percent of the world's economy and pushing for a global climate change accord that would commit even outliers like China and India to fighting toxic emissions.

"Part of our goal here has been to show that diplomacy can work," Obama told Friedman in a second interview after the Iran agreement was sealed in July 2015. "It doesn't work perfectly. It doesn't give us everything that we want." But, he added, "what we can do is shape events in ways where it's more likely that problems get solved, rather than less likely, and that's the opportunity we have now."

Obama's symbolically rich trip to Africa came during this period of outreach. During his entire first term, Obama spent just about twenty-four hours in sub-Saharan Africa, and even then on the other side of the continent from his father's home. Some critics said that the first president with African roots was doing less for Africa than the white president he had succeeded. With re-election behind him, Obama now showed fresh interest in Africa, launching a Power Africa initiative intended to spread electricity through the continent, hosting a summit meeting in Washington for African leaders and pushing a renewal of an African trade preference program through Congress.

Obama seemed moved to be back in his father's homeland, but the trip that July was surreal and strangely impersonal at the same time. The first time he had visited Kenya, as a young man, he was by his own account seeking to fill "a great emptiness" he felt inside and figure out how he fit in. On that trip, he rode in from the airport in his half-sister's beat-up car with a muffler that fell off during the drive. Now he returned with an entourage of hundreds, an armored car with a working muffler and no question about his place in the world.

"Obviously, this is personal for me," he said after arriving. "My father

President Obama and Pope Francis at the White House, September, 2015.

came from these parts and I have family and relatives here." His half-sister, Auma Obama, told an excited crowd at a stadium that he was one of them. "He's not just our familia," she said. "He gets us. He gets us."

Still, Obama made clear that he resented the security bubble that prevented him from visiting his father's village or even just strolling around the capital, Nairobi, as he did when he visited as a young man. For security reasons, the streets had been swept of people, and the city had an eerie, empty feeling. With Obama unable to come to them, dozens of cousins and step-aunts and other members of his extended family, some of whom he had never met, were brought for dinner with him at his well-appointed and heavily guarded hotel in Nairobi. As journalists were brought in to snap a few quick pictures, they could see the president looking to his right and looking to his left, clearly not really recognizing all of the people around him who claimed kinship.

"Part of the challenge that I've had during the course of my presidency is that, given the demands of the job and the bubble, I can't come here and just go upcountry and visit for a week and meet everybody," Obama lamented. "I'm more restricted, ironically, as president of the United States than I will be as a private citizen."

But with his unique status as the first American president descended from Africa, Obama used the visit to Kenya and nearby Ethiopia to send a message to a continent ruled by potentates clinging to power. It was time to stop rewriting constitutions and rigging elections.

"Nobody should be president for life," he said in a speech at the African Union in Addis Ababa.

Obama was back on the world stage a couple months later as he hosted Pope Francis for his first visit to the United States. Standing together on a sunny day in September 2015 on the South Lawn of the White House, Obama welcomed Francis with an elaborate arrival ceremony complete with fife and drum corps – but skipping the traditional twenty-one-gun salute, which might seem discordant for a man of peace. The president and the pontiff could hardly have come from more starkly disparate backgrounds, and yet commonalities now united the fifty-four-year-old community organizer from Chicago and the seventy-eight-year-old priest from Argentina, both presenting themselves as champions of the powerless.

Unlike his two immediate predecessors, Francis had embraced the social justice side of the Catholic message, putting him in sync with the liberal American president on many issues – so much so that critics derided him as "Obama's Pope." Obama had to be satisfied when the pope used the visit to effectively bolster the president's side of America's fractious debates over climate change, immigration and economic inequality. "You shake our conscience from slumber," Obama told him.

The pope had also been a key player in the clandestine negotiations that led to the Cuba opening, a critical intermediary who helped bring the two long-estranged neighbors together and forced them to take a chance on each other. The United States had broken off diplomatic relations with Cuba in January 1961, seven months before Obama was born – and made fitful efforts to topple Fidel Castro's regime, most disastrously in the Bay of Pigs operation. Ten presidents either failed or refused to bridge the gap, and the relationship remained frozen in time long after the fall of the Berlin Wall and collapse of the Soviet Union.

Obama was determined to succeed where his predecessors had not, convinced that the half-century trade and commercial embargo had failed to undermine the Castro government while worsening Washington's standing in Latin America. Once in office, he eased limits on people visiting relatives in Cuba and sending money to them, expanded cultural and academic exchanges and resumed talks on migration, drug trafficking and postal services. But the early thaw ended in late 2009 when the Havana government arrested Alan Gross, an American contractor distributing mobile telephones, laptops and other communications equipment in Cuba on behalf of the United States government.

The pope is key in bringing Obama and Raul Castro together.

After his re-election, Obama told aides he wanted to do "something big on Cuba" in his second term, and two White House officials, Benjamin Rhodes and Ricardo Zuniga, were assigned to establish a confidential channel. For eighteen months, they snuck out of Washington periodically to fly to Canada to meet Cuban counterparts, inventing cover stories to shroud their travels even from relatives.

To clear the way for broader changes, Obama knew he had to win Gross's freedom. Raul Castro's government insisted on a swap for the Cuban Five, spies who had long been locked up in American prisons and become folk heroes at home. But Obama was reluctant to agree to an explicit trade because it would imply that Gross really was a spy, as Cuba claimed.

Eventually, Obama's advisers came up with an alternative that would allow them to deny making a direct swap – Havana would release a Cuban imprisoned for spying for the United States in exchange for the three members of the Cuban Five who had not yet finished their federal prison terms. Gross would be released at the same time in a theoretically separate humanitarian gesture. Cuba would also release more than fifty political prisoners, while the United States would allow more travel, banking and commercial ties, although Obama could not lift the trade embargo entirely without Congress.

After battling rough seas and high winds, migrants arrive on the Greek island of Lesbos, October 1, 2015.

TYLER HICKS/NEW YORK TIMES

Pope Francis sent letters to both Obama and Castro urging them to follow through on a deal, and once the two sides negotiated the details, delegations visited the Vatican to present the package to the pope's advisers, all but cementing the agreement. "At that point, you're on the hook to the pope," Rhodes later said. Obama called Castro and talked for forty-five minutes, the first direct substantive contact between leaders of the two countries in more than fifty years. The next day, December 17, 2014, Gross walked out of a Cuban prison, boarded an American military plane and flew to Washington, happily devouring a corned beef sandwich on rye bread with mustard during the flight.

While his release was widely welcomed, not everyone was happy with the broader warming in relations. "This entire policy shift announced today is based on an illusion, on a lie, the lie and the illusion that more commerce and access to money and goods will translate to political freedom for the Cuban people," said Senator Marco Rubio, a Florida Republican and son of Cuban immigrants readying a race for the presidency.

Undeterred, Obama would go on to meet with Raul Castro on the sidelines of a regional summit several months later, and the American flag was raised over a new embassy in Havana not long after that. An enthusiastic Obama now set his sights on traveling to Cuba himself in his final year for what he hoped be a trip that would go into the history books.

Obama's accord with Iran also had its roots in a telephone call. Picking up where George W. Bush had left off, Obama came to office intent on tightening sanctions against the Islamic government to force it to give up its nuclear program. After choking off international financing and drying up its oil exports, Obama hoped to get Iran to the negotiating table and a newly elected, seemingly less extreme Iranian government appeared open to talking. When President Hassan Rouhani came to New York for the opening of the annual United Nations General Assembly session in September 2013, the White House explored the chances for a breakthrough.

What about a meeting between Obama and Rouhani? The White House wanted to know.

No, the Iranians said. A picture of the two shaking hands was a step too far for an Iranian president, even one styling himself as a reformer.

Okay, then, the White House asked, what about a telephone call?

Fine, the Iranians said, and gave the White House the number to call.

So as Rouhani rode in his car on the way to the airport to leave New York and return to Tehran, the phone rang and the White House connected him to Obama. The fifteen-minute conversation was the first between American and Iranian leaders since the hostage crisis of 1979-81.

Much like the Cuba outreach, Obama authorized a pair of top State Department officials, William Burns and Jake Sullivan, to kick off secret negotiations hosted by the Middle East country of Oman. Eventually the cloaked channel went public, other world powers were brought into the talks, and Secretary of State John Kerry took the lead. A longtime former senator, presidential candidate and early promoter of Obama, Kerry could hardly be more different from the president he now served. Where Obama was cautious and dubious, Kerry was energetic and optimistic. Where Obama described his approach to foreign policy as "don't do stupid stuff" (actually using a more risqué word), Kerry regularly declared that he would rather get "caught trying" than hold back. At one point, White House aides joked that Kerry was like the astronaut in the movie *Gravity*, somersaulting through space, untethered from the White House. At another point, even Obama felt compelled to rein him in. "John, don't go overselling it to me, brother," Obama told him in a meeting.

After painstaking negotiations, Kerry reaches a deal.

The Iran negotiation underscored how much Obama relied on a tight circle of advisers – and even more so his own judgment. During a secure video conference call with negotiators to settle on the final terms that would be acceptable for a deal with Iran, Obama methodically outlined his bottom lines on various issues one after the other. Advisers nodded in agreement. Obama encountered no real resistance, no dissent that would give him pause, no objection from anyone telling him he was giving away too much.

In part, the consensus owed to how long the talks had lasted, narrowing the remaining issues by that point. But it also underscored how policy was made in the final stretch of Obama's administration. An untested president who entertained fierce disputes when he arrived in office now had enough experience to know his own mind and needed, or invited, less debate. The so-called team of rivals he assembled at first had been replaced by a team of facilitators who channeled his ideas and executed his policies. "It's not our job to question him," said one former adviser. "It's our job to figure out what he wants and get it done." Not everyone thought that was healthy. "The president suffers when he doesn't have that kind of robust debate," Robert Gates said as he watched from the outside.

By the summer of 2015, after painstaking negotiations, Kerry reached a deal: Iran would shutter its heavy-water reactor, ship nearly all of its nuclear fuel out of the country and dismantle two-thirds of its centrifuges. With intrusive international inspections, the Americans argued that the rollback should make it impossible for Iran, if it decided to cheat, to actually develop

Iranian President Hassan Rouhani, United Nations,
September 25, 2014.

a bomb in less than a year, a long enough "breakout" time for the world to react. In exchange, American and international sanctions were to be lifted, freeing up long-frozen funds for a cash-starved government.

For good measure, Obama's aides also secretly negotiated the resolution of a longstanding dispute over military equipment that the United States sold Iran before the Islamic revolution of 1979 and then never delivered. The administration agreed to return $400 million in Iranian payments along with $1.3 billion in accrued interest, sending the first installment in giant pallets of cash.

The Iran accord done, Obama finalizes an Asian economic pact.

At the same time, Obama's team won the release of four Iranian Americans held by Tehran on spurious charges in exchange for seven Iranian or Iranian-Americans imprisoned in the United States for violating the sanctions. The White House insisted that the release of the prisoners was unrelated to the money being sent to Tehran, but to many critics it smacked of ransom. And even that deal almost collapsed at the last minute as Iranian authorities at the Tehran airport tried to stop the wife and mother of one of the Americans, Jason Rezaian, *The Washington Post's* bureau chief who had spent 545 days in captivity, from leaving with him. An American official said it "was like a scene out of *Argo*," the Ben Affleck movie about the Carter-era hostage crisis.

For many Iranians, the deal offered a bright moment of hope that their country would finally rejoin the community of nations and escape the shackles of sanctions that had helped cripple their economy. "I am desperate to feed my three sons," Ali, a fifty-three-year-old cleaner, told a *New York Times* reporter in Tehran. "This deal should bring investment for jobs so they can start working for a living."

But for many Israelis, it seemed a betrayal. Benjamin Netanyahu called it "a historic mistake." The deal, he and other critics said, would only postpone Iran's quest for a nuclear bomb, not end it permanently, even if inspectors could detect any cheating. Obama was allowing a country that regularly threatened Israel's very existence out of the diplomatic and economic isolation that the world had effectively imposed.

Pugnacious and determined, Netanyahu made common cause with Republicans in Washington in hopes of blocking the agreement. He and Obama had never gotten along. Obama saw Netanyahu as enthralled with

a hard-line philosophy that blocked progress, and unwilling to make the necessary concessions to finally end the decades-long struggle with the Palestinians. Netanyahu considered Obama hopelessly naïve about one of the world's most volatile neighborhoods and insufficiently aware of just how threatened Israel really was.

Even before it ruptured over the Iran agreement, their tortured relationship had been a story of crossed signals, misunderstandings and slights, perceived and real. During one early meeting, Obama sat with his jaw clenched and his eyes narrowed as Netanyahu lectured him in front of television cameras on the realities of the Middle East. When Obama later talked with Thomas Friedman about the Iran deal, Friedman thought the president, in discussing his distress over being portrayed as anti-Israel, sounded more emotional than he ever had. Netanyahu had gotten under his skin. "You're fed up with him," Obama was overheard on another occasion telling his French counterpart with manifest frustration, "but I have to deal with him even more often than you."

For Obama and Netanyahu, a tortured relationship.

The Israelis were not the only ones unhappy about the deal. America's Arab allies, most notably the Sunni-led Saudi Arabia, had been waging a virtual proxy war against the Shiite-led Iran for years, and they now worried that the nuclear agreement would free up once-sanctioned resources for Tehran to flex its muscles even more around the region. Obama tried to reassure them with arms sales and a summit meeting at Camp David. But he dismissed their request for a mutual defense treaty along the lines of the one with Japan, and so King Salman of Saudi Arabia and most of the other Persian Gulf heads of state skipped the Camp David meeting, sending lower-level officials instead. The bid to repair relations with the Arab states led Obama to finally abandon his Arab Spring aspirations altogether when he restored the fraction of military aid to Egypt suspended after the military coup, even though the new leadership had not restored democracy as he had demanded. In the end, Congress was unable to stop the Iran nuclear deal, although Republican presidential candidates vowed to scrap it if they were to capture the White House.

President Obama and Israeli Prime Minister Benjamin Netanyahu, Oval Office, November 9, 2015.

The G7 leaders meet in Bavaria where they vowed to keep sanctions against Russia in place, June 8, 2015.

MICHAEL KAPPELER/REUTERS

Just three months after sealing the Iran deal, Obama finalized the Asian economic pact known as the Trans-Pacific Partnership, bringing together twelve nations, including Japan, Canada, Mexico, Malaysia and Australia, to create the largest regional trade accord in history. The agreement would phase out thousands of tariffs and other barriers to international trade, like Japanese regulations to keep out some American-made autos and trucks; it would establish uniform rules on corporations' intellectual property; and it would open the Internet even in communist Vietnam.

Rather than a revolt from Republicans, Obama this time faced one from his fellow Democrats, who argued that the deal would ship even more American jobs overseas and enrich companies at the expense of workers. Just to get this far, Obama had to overcome ardent resistance on the left, led by Senator Elizabeth Warren of Massachusetts, which he did by teaming up with John Boehner, Paul Ryan and other Republicans to get Congress to sign off on negotiating authority.

Now he looked ahead to another fight in his final year in office to get the actual agreement approved by Congress. But once again, he argued, diplomacy had paid off.

Obama had little time to savor his victories. In November 2015, terrorists from the Islamic State fanned out across Paris and killed 130 people in a series of bombings and shootings that panicked the French capital and horrified the world. A little more than two weeks later, a husband and wife inspired by the Islamic State shot up a holiday party in San Bernardino, California, killing fourteen people.

The carnage made clear that the Islamic State was no longer just a threat in the Middle East but in fact a fresh menace to America and Europe. Obama had been waging war against the group for more than a year with mixed results at best. A military program he authorized to train Syrian rebels to fight the Islamic State on the ground while American planes pounded the group from the air collapsed after it yielded only four or five trained fighters on the battlefield. The situation then grew exponentially more complicated when Russia suddenly intervened to save Bashar al-Assad's faltering government with its own airstrikes, many of them targeting allies of the United States.

Obama did not help himself by telling ABC News just a week before that Paris attack that the United States had effectively halted the spread of the Islamic State. "We have contained them," he said. He meant that American military action had stanched the group's territorial gains in Iraq and Syria, but in light of the mayhem in France and California, the terrorists seemed anything but contained, and the president seemed out of touch. His response after the attacks also tended toward the intellectual rather than

"All the News That's Fit to Print"

The New York Times

Late Edition

Today, windy, chillier, partly sunny, high 50. **Tonight,** mainly clear, cold, low 40. **Tomorrow,** mostly sunny, becoming milder in the afternoon, high 58. Weather map, Page C8.

VOL. CLXV . . . No. 57,050 — © 2015 The New York Times — NEW YORK, SATURDAY, NOVEMBER 14, 2015 — $2.50

PARIS TERRORIST ATTACKS KILL OVER 100; FRANCE DECLARES STATE OF EMERGENCY

Chaos and Horror Echo in the City Once Again

By LIZ ALDERMAN and JIM YARDLEY

PARIS — The night was chilly but thick with excitement as the big match between France's national soccer team and archrival Germany was underway at the national stadium in a northern suburb of Paris. President François Hollande watched with the crowd as the French players pushed the ball across midfield.

Then came the sharp, unmistakable crack of an explosion, overwhelming the roar of the crowd. A stunned moment passed. Players and spectators seemed confused, and eventually the awful realization swept through the stadium: Terror, for the second time this year, had struck Paris.

The symmetry could not be more jarring. A Parisian year that began with the bloodshed and chaos of the terrorist attacks at the satirical newspaper Charlie Hebdo and later at a Jewish grocery now had an even deadlier coda: With events still fluid and exact details unclear, the authorities said more than 100 people had been killed in a series of attacks across Paris. And dozens of people were taken hostage at a Parisian theater.

The urgent, bleating screech of sirens filled the evening air as police cruisers raced through the streets, uncertain if more mayhem was to come. Taxis ferried people home without charge as the police advised residents to stay inside. Ambulances screamed down the boulevards, as a stunned and confused French capital was again left to wonder: Why us? Once again?

"Paris has been hit again by terror tonight," Deputy Mayor Patrick Klugman said on Twitter.

For three days in January, Paris was gripped with fear as the police searched for Chérif and Saïd Kouachi after the two brothers attacked the Charlie Hebdo offices, a manhunt that ended with the Kouachis dying in a shootout. The terror only deepened when a third terrorist, Amedy Coulibaly, attacked a Jewish grocery, killing customers, before the police stormed the building and killed him.

Those attacks left France reeling for months, dredging up sadness and fury and horror. They also stirred a national debate over freedom of expression and the state of French Islam, a topic that has divided France like few others and seems certain to intensify now.

The attackers' names, or whether they are linked to radical Islamist groups, are not yet known. But some witnesses described militants shouting "God is great" in Arabic before open-

Continued on Page A8

THIBAULT CAMUS/ASSOCIATED PRESS

THEATER Terrorists shot numerous people and took others hostage at the Bataclan concert hall.

HOTEL
MEDECIN

PHILIPPE WOJAZER/REUTERS

RESTAURANT Emergency workers covered and removed bodies of victims after gunmen attacked.

IAN LANGSDON/EUROPEAN PRESSPHOTO AGENCY

STADIUM A man wounded outside the Stade de France, where a soccer match was in progress.

Series of Shootings and Blasts, Apparently Coordinated

By ADAM NOSSITER and RICK GLADSTONE

PARIS — The Paris area reeled Friday night from a shooting rampage, explosions and mass hostage-taking that President François Hollande called an unprecedented terrorist attack on France. His government announced sharply increased border controls and heightened police powers as it mobilized the military in a national emergency.

French television and news services quoted the police as saying that around 100 people had been killed at a concert site where hostages had been held during a two-hour standoff with the police, and that perhaps dozens of others had been killed in apparently coordinated attacks outside the country's main sports stadium and four other popular locations in the city. But estimates on the total number of dead varied.

Witnesses on French television said the scene at the concert hall, which can seat as many as 1,500 people, was a massacre, describing how gunmen with automatic weapons shot bursts of bullets into the crowd.

Ambulances were seen racing back and forth in the area into the early hours of Saturday, and hundreds of survivors were evacuated in police buses. French television said Paris hospitals were overwhelmed with wounded.

News agencies quoted Michel Cadot, head of the Paris police, as saying early Saturday that all the assailants involved in shootings or bombings were believed to be dead, and the Paris prosecutor's office said that eight attackers were dead, according to The Associated Press.

But the total number involved in the attacks, including accomplices still at large, remained unclear.

"We are going to try and determine what happened, determine what the profiles of these terrorists are, find out what their course of action was, find out if there are still accomplices or co-attackers," said François Molins, the public prosecutor for Paris.

The casualties eclipsed by far the deaths in Paris during the massacre at the satirical newspaper Charlie Hebdo and related assaults around the French capital by Islamic militant extremists less than a year ago.

Those attacks traumatized France and other countries in Europe, elevating fears of religious extremism and violent jihadists who have been radicalized by the conflicts in Syria and elsewhere in the Middle East and North Africa.

An explosion near the sports

Continued on Page A8

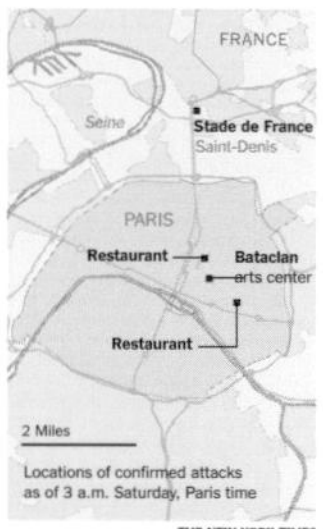

FRANCE
Seine
Stade de France
Saint-Denis
PARIS
Restaurant
Bataclan arts center
Restaurant
2 Miles
Locations of confirmed attacks as of 3 a.m. Saturday, Paris time

THE NEW YORK TIMES

Inside Sold-Out Concert Hall, A Siege and 'a Scene of Carnage'

By ADAM NOSSITER and ANDREW HIGGINS

PARIS — The band had been playing to the crowd at one of this city's most popular music venues, the Bataclan, for about an hour. The 150-year-old music hall was sold out for the show by the American group Eagles of Death Metal.

Suddenly, four men brandishing AK-47 assault rifles entered the hall. There were shouts of "Allahu akbar" just before the gunmen opened fire, and for about 20 minutes there was carnage.

Witnesses said the attackers also threw grenades into the crowd.

"When they started shooting, we just saw flashes," a witness named Gwen told French BFM-TV. "People got down on the ground right away. It was all dark."

In the scramble to survive, people climbed into the upper boxes of the hall, or cowered under seats. The musicians quickly fled the stage.

"It was a scene of carnage," Julien Pearce, a radio reporter who was inside the Bataclan, told Europe 1 radio.

The music hall can seat up to 1,500 people, but it was unclear how many were inside when the attack began. Some of the spectators managed to escape out back exits, but for minutes the gunmen shot unimpeded.

Continued on Page A8

Ban or No Ban, Fantasy Site's Back Door Is Open

By JAMES GLANZ and JACQUELINE WILLIAMS

Starting next week, the two leading daily fantasy sports sites will be barred from taking bets from a lucrative market: New York State. But one of them, DraftKings, leaves open a simple digital loophole that may let New Yorkers play anyway.

On Tuesday, the New York State attorney general ordered DraftKings and the other top site, FanDuel, to stop taking bets in the state, saying that daily fantasy sports is no different from online sports gambling, which is illegal in New York. With the hugely popular games coming under intense scrutiny, both companies say they will fight the action, and on Friday, both companies filed formal complaints.

But for DraftKings, the ruling and any courtroom battle may be easily circumvented. The New York Times, working with users in all six states where daily fantasy sports is already considered illegal, was able to make bets on the DraftKings site using the most basic, easily accessible service for disguising a computer's true location.

Called a proxy server, the service is available for a few dollars a month from numerous companies. It allows users in, say, Iowa — one of the states where daily fantasy is illegal — to appear to be logging on to a website from somewhere else. Although companies can use standard technol-

Continued on Page D6

Supreme Court Takes Abortion Case From Texas

By ADAM LIPTAK

WASHINGTON — The Supreme Court on Friday agreed to hear its first major abortion case since 2007, one that has the potential to affect millions of women and to revise the constitutional principles governing abortion rights.

The court's decision will probably arrive in late June, as the presidential campaign enters its final stretch, thrusting the divisive issue of abortion to the forefront of public debate. Other major rulings — on affirmative action, public unions, contraception coverage and possibly immigration — are also expected to land around then.

But it is the new abortion case, however it is decided, that is likely to produce the term's most consequential and legally significant decision. Many states have been enacting restrictions that test the limits of the constitutional right to abortion established in 1973 in Roe v. Wade, and a ruling in the new case, from Texas, will enunciate principles that will apply in all of them.

The case may turn out to be the third installment in a legal trilogy on the scope of the constitutional right to abortion, one that started with Roe and continued in 1992 with Planned Parenthood v. Casey.

The Casey decision said states may not place undue burdens on the constitutional right to abor-

Continued on Page A14

INTERNATIONAL A3-12

China's Loneliest Generation
China ended its one-child policy, but many, like Liu Jia, above, have mixed feelings about larger families. PAGE A4

U.S. Believes It Killed Jihadist
The Pentagon said it was "reasonably certain" a strike had hit "Jihadi John," the Islamic State executioner. PAGE A6

NATIONAL A13-17

Insults Pose Risks for Trump
As Donald J. Trump intensifies blistering attacks on his Republican rival Ben Carson, some political strategists say the effrontery could backfire. PAGE A15

Moms Can Keep Baby, for Now
A Utah judge reversed, at least temporarily, his order to take a foster child away from a lesbian couple. PAGE A13

BUSINESS DAY B1-7

Oil Price Continues to Slide
A global stockpile of three billion barrels, about a month of global production, is pushing down oil prices. PAGE B1

ARTS C1-7

Applauding the Newcomers
Immigration is divisive in politics, but on Broadway it's a reason to sing, with "Hamilton," "On Your Feet!" and "Allegiance," above, celebrating it. PAGE C1

EDITORIAL, OP-ED A22-23

Gail Collins PAGE A23

SPORTSSATURDAY D1-6

Russia Suspended From Track
A ban, which comes after sweeping doping allegations, could affect the ability of Russian track-and-field athletes to compete in next year's Olympics. PAGE D1

Missouri Football Coach to Quit
Gary Pinkel, who backed his players during the university's racial protests, cited illness in his decision. PAGE D3

OBITUARIES B8

A Jew Whose Twin Was a Nazi
Jack Yufe, who became a celebrity after he and his brother were part of a nature vs. nurture study, died on Monday at 82.

THIS WEEKEND

0 354613 9

channeling the visceral fear and outrage felt by many Americans; indeed, he saved his real passion for arguing with Republicans about whether the United States should admit Syrian refugees for fear that some might be Islamic State operatives or sympathizers.

Obama was personally irritated by what he saw as the jingoistic response to the attacks, particularly by Republican candidates in the emerging campaign to succeed him, and he resolved not to be railroaded into taking unwise military action. While even Hillary Clinton and other Democrats were calling for a no-fly zone, Obama rejected what he called "half-baked ideas" that amounted to "a bunch of mumbo-jumbo." Asked if those ideas included Clinton's, he demurred, saying she was not half-baked but then essentially dismissed her statements as mere campaign rhetoric that should not be taken seriously. "There's a difference between running for president and being president," he said.

Attacks in Paris and San Bernardino prove ISIS can reach beyond the Middle East.

In a private, off-the-record meeting later with opinion writers and columnists, Obama acknowledged he had been slow to respond to the understandable public anxiety and fear generated by the attacks. Perhaps one reason, he told the columnists, was that he did not watch much cable television – as much a jab at the media for sensationalizing terrorist attacks as an admission that he was not attuned to public sentiment. But he made clear he would not send large numbers of ground troops unless there was a terrorist attack that was so spectacular it disrupted the normal functioning of the United States.

The focus on the Islamic State detracted from one of Obama's most cherished policy goals even as it came to fruition. While advancing new regulations by the Environmental Protection Agency to limit emissions by power plants, he was putting the final touches on a global accord that would commit virtually all of the world's nations to take similar action to fight climate change, including longtime outliers like China and India.

To build support for the agreement, Obama flew north to become the first sitting president to visit Arctic Alaska, where he highlighted the impact of changing climate patterns on glaciers and wildlife. He journeyed to what seemed like the ends of the earth as he traveled across gravel and dirt roads to a town of 900 where caribou and moose antlers adorned wooden houses on pilings, and pickup trucks and all-terrain vehicles were the transportation of choice. Obama also joined Bear Grylls for an episode of his popular survivalist reality show, with the president helping make tea from catkins, eating a salmon prechewed by a bear and discussing why people would drink their own urine.

If that were not enough to set the stage for the global agreement, Obama waited until just before the final conference to announce that he was blocking construction of the Keystone pipeline that had become a cause célèbre for environmental activists.

Putting the final touches on a global climate change agreement.

With Kerry sealing the climate change deal after a last-minute scramble that nearly killed it, Obama signed the pact in Paris just weeks after the Islamic State attacks rattled the French capital, neatly encapsulating the twin sides of his foreign policy.

On the one hand, he was putting together international agreements with lofty goals like curbing nuclear proliferation, spreading free trade and stemming climate change, agreements that, flaws and all, were destined to have lasting impact long after Obama left office.

But for all his success at the bargaining table, he found himself still fighting the same war on terror he inherited from his predecessor and still trying to figure out how to defeat the same forces of darkness that were consuming one region and threatening the rest of the world.

The Obama Doctrine was still a work in progress.

Kim Williams, Alannah Hurley and President Obama inspect a silver salmon, Dillingham, Alaska, September 2, 2015.

CHAPTER XII

'A Personal Insult'

Facing the end of his presidency, Obama goes all out to defeat a candidate he cannot imagine succeeding him.

Candidate Trump at his campaign headquarters in the Trump Tower, May 4, 2016.

On a soggy winter afternoon in February 2016, President Obama traveled up the highway to a mosque in Baltimore. While President George W. Bush had made a point of visiting a mosque after the attacks of Sept. 11, 2001, to demonstrate that the newly declared war on terrorism was not a war on Muslims, Obama waited until his eighth and final year in office to finally cross the threshold of an Islamic center of religion in the United States.

The reasons were obvious. Even as his motorcade arrived at the Islamic Society of Baltimore, three out of ten Americans believed Obama himself was actually Muslim, even though he was not. Appearing in a mosque was not likely to correct those misperceptions. But Obama finally discarded any concerns because he was angry. The leading Republican running for president was none other than Donald J. Trump, the same man who had made such a spectacle of supposedly investigating whether Obama was actually born in the United States and had even hinted that the president was secretly Muslim. Now on the campaign stump, Trump was targeting Muslims as a group, vowing to temporarily ban them from entering the country to prevent terrorism.

"We have to understand an attack on one faith is an attack on all our faiths," Obama told the audience that day, barely containing his scorn. "And when any religious group is targeted, we all have a responsibility to speak up. And we have to reject a politics that seeks to manipulate prejudice or bias and targets people because of religion." Trump's name never passed Obama's lips, but it did not have to. Everyone understood exactly whom he was talking about. And in case they did not, he threw in an extra jab. "Thomas Jefferson's opponents tried to stir things up by suggesting he was a Muslim – so I was not the first, " Obama said. "No, it's true. It's true. Look it up. I'm in good company."

Like others, Obama had not taken Trump seriously at first. Trump was a sideshow, a carnival barker, an attention-addicted narcissist. His presidential campaign, Obama and his top advisers thought, was an exercise in vanity. It was not serious. "It's apparently open-mic day in the Republican campaign for president," David Axelrod, the president's longtime strategist, wrote mockingly on Twitter after Trump entered the race in the summer of 2015 with a politically divisive attack on Mexicans. David Plouffe, the other top strategist from Obama's two presidential campaigns, scoffed at the notion that Trump might succeed. He would eventually go on to predict that there was a 100 percent chance Trump would lose in a race for the presidency. In an interview before the primaries, Obama called Trump "a great publicity-seeker" but brushed off his chances. "I don't think he'll end up being president of the United States," he said. Trump's loss to Senator Ted Cruz in the Iowa caucuses a few days before Obama's mosque visit seemed to validate the early dismissals.

Obama's voice usually drips with disdain when mentioning Trump.

But that did not mean Obama could resist responding to some of Trump's more incendiary statements. During his visit to Africa shortly after Trump announced his candidacy, Obama denounced the candidate's blithe insult of Senator John McCain's war record. In a radio interview during his holiday in Hawaii, Obama accused Trump of exploiting the resentment of working-class men for his own political gain. In his final State of the Union address, he warned against trying "to scapegoat fellow citizens who don't look like us or pray like us or vote like we do."

Obama's voice usually dripped with disdain whenever he talked about Trump, leaving abundantly clear that he had no respect for the celebrity candidate. Obama may have disagreed with McCain and Mitt Romney during their contests, but they were both decent men, legitimate contenders and even plausible presidents. By contrast, Obama simply could not imagine a man whose most famous act was to flamboyantly fire contestants on his television show sitting behind the Resolute Desk in the Oval Office.

Trump, after all, was everything Obama was not. Bombastic and boastful, caustic, and crude, Trump reveled in ostentatious shows of wealth and playground style put-downs. A former co-owner of the Miss Universe Organization, he openly ogled beautiful women, denigrated those he did not consider attractive and discarded two wives who had been models before marrying a third, Melania Knauss, a model from Slovenia who once posed nude on Trump's plane for a *GQ* photo spread on sex at 30,000 feet.

President Obama meets families at the Islamic Society of Baltimore mosque, February 2, 2016.

DREW ANGERER/NEW YORK TIMES

President Obama enters the Oval Office following a visit with wounded troops at Walter Reed Military Medical Center, September 16, 2015.

The Supreme Court seat for Justice Antonin Scalia is draped in black following his death, February 13, 2016.

But rather than disqualifying Trump, his very outrageousness seemed to be key to his appeal. When he slighted a former prisoner of war like McCain or mocked a reporter with disabilities or called on supporters to beat up a heckler, Trump came across to broad sections of the country as a straight talker who was willing to throw off the shackles of political correctness and take on the oh-so-smug elites of the ruling political-media class. If he could make a fortune for himself, maybe he could fix a country where so many felt left behind. Maybe he really could make America great again.

At the heart of his campaign was a racial divide that had only opened even wider during the tenure of the country's first African-American president. Trump generated support especially from white men without college educations, many of whom were struggling in an era of globalization and vanished manufacturing jobs. While some were overtly racist and Trump did little to disavow the backing of white supremacist leaders, many voters attracted to him were simply feeling disenfranchised and lashing out at a system in which it seemed everyone else had special protections or attention. Whether real or not, it was a powerful perception.

Republicans refuse to consider an Obama nominee to succeed Antonin Scalia.

Paradoxically perhaps, racial comity in the United States had deteriorated under a black president. Where 66 percent of Americans surveyed by *The New York Times* and CBS News declared race relations in America to be good in April 2009, just three months after Obama took office, only 26 percent thought so in July 2016. Sixty percent of Americans that summer said race relations were getting worse.

Beyond race, the country was just in a foul mood. While the economy was growing and unemployment was falling, most Americans still told pollsters that the nation was on the wrong course. The wealthiest rocketed ahead after the Great Recession of 2008-09 but the rest of Americans barely kept even. And the atmosphere in Washington was as toxic as ever, if not more so. When it came to fixing that, Obama acknowledged he had failed. "Democracy breaks down when the average person feels their voice doesn't matter, that the system is rigged in favor of the rich or the powerful or some special interest," he said in his final State of the Union address in January 2016. "Too many Americans feel that way right now. It's one of the few regrets of my presidency – that the rancor and suspicion between the parties has gotten worse instead of better. I have no doubt a president with the gifts of Lincoln or Roosevelt might have better bridged the divide." But Obama was neither Lincoln nor Roosevelt.

President Obama announces Supreme Court nominee Merrick Garland at the White House, March 16, 2016.

I f he needed further proof of the breakdown between the parties, it came just weeks later when Justice Antonin Scalia died unexpectedly during a hunting trip to Texas. Scalia, the conservative intellectual powerhouse of the Supreme Court, had been a larger than life presence on the bench. But his sudden departure meant Obama now had a chance to shift the ideological balance for years to come.

Except that Senate Republicans were determined not to let him. They understood that a liberal Obama appointee in the mold of Sonia Sotomayor or Elena Kagan would be a disaster for conservative jurisprudence on a host of issues like abortion, gay rights, gun rights, religious freedom and government regulation. They were already disappointed that Chief Justice John Roberts had upheld Obama's health care program. So they looked at the calendar and gambled that they could hold out for a year. Within hours of Scalia's death, Senator Mitch McConnell, the Republican leader, announced that the Senate would not consider any Obama nominee, no matter whom he named, and would wait for the next president instead.

Obama was flabbergasted. While there were long vacancies during confirmation battles in the nineteenth century, only once in the past 150 years had a seat on the Supreme Court been kept open for a full year and never had the Senate flatly refused to consider any nominee from a president. Obama went ahead and nominated Merrick Garland, the mild-mannered and well-liked chief judge of the United States Court of Appeals for the District of Columbia Circuit. Considered a relatively moderate liberal with many friends among Republicans and conservative judges, Garland was, in effect, Obama's break-in-case-of-emergency choice, a nominee Republicans in any other context would have embraced as the best they could get from a Democratic president. But with several members of McConnell's caucus running for president and competing to show how tough they could be standing up to Obama, the Republican leader opted to shut down the process.

The impasse would have lasting effect. In June, the Supreme Court deadlocked, four to four, in a case challenging Obama's executive action sparing up to five million immigrants to remain in the country even though they were here illegally. Because a lower court had rejected Obama's action, the tie vote by the justices meant that ruling would stick. The high court offered no explanation but rendered its verdict in just nine words: "The judgment is affirmed by an equally divided court." Rarely have nine words impacted so many lives. Obama's efforts to revamp the immigration system were now over and millions of immigrants would have to await the result of the election to determine their future. Had Garland filled the empty seat, he likely would have provided the fifth vote to overturn the decision and uphold Obama's action shielding the immigrants. McConnell's gambit had worked.

Frustrated on the home front, Obama pointed Air Force One south to

President Obama and the First Lady mark Martin Luther King Day by
helping to paint a mural at a family shelter in Washington, January 16, 2017.

make history overseas. In March, he became the first American president to visit Cuba since Calvin Coolidge some 88 years earlier, a landmark trip meant to cement the diplomatic opening he had negotiated. Accompanied by Michelle and their two daughters, he strolled the streets of Old Havana, albeit drenched by a sudden rain, as Cubans called out "Obama!" Under sunnier skies, he attended a baseball game and joined the crowd in doing the wave, even as a clearly embarrassed Sasha stayed seated with her arm over her face. And Obama held a formal meeting with President Raul Castro, the first between leaders of the two countries in half a century.

Tired of hassles, Obama takes a trip to Cuba.

But his visit did not mean Cuba had changed. Before Obama arrived, the government cracked down on dissidents to prevent them from drawing attention. During a joint news conference by the two presidents, Castro brusquely dismissed questions about the lack of freedom in his country.

"What political prisoners?" he snapped at a reporter, demanding a list. He went on to argue that the United States should not lecture Cuba since it had its own human rights problems, including the prison it maintained at Guantanamo Bay. "It's not correct to ask me about political prisoners."

Obama, who would meet with dissidents during the trip, nonetheless replied with a deference that only confirmed to critics at home that he was going soft on Havana in the interest of pursuing a chimera of new relations. "Cuba's destiny will not be decided by the United States or any other nation," Obama said mildly.

He went on: "I actually welcome President Castro commenting on some of the areas where he feels that we're falling short, because I think we should not be immune or afraid of criticism or discussion as well." While an attempt to show that democratic leaders should be open to contrary views, Obama's comment fueled the conservative case that he often seemed intent on apologizing for America rather than appreciating its exceptionalism.

He encountered the same issue two months later when he became the first American president to visit Hiroshima, where in August 1945 the United States dropped the first nuclear bomb ever used in war. "Seventy-one year ago, on a bright cloudless morning, death fell from the sky and the world was changed," Obama told a crowd of appreciative Japanese at Hiroshima Peace Memorial Park and many more watching on national television. He did not apologize for Harry S. Truman's orders to drop the bombs that killed 200,000 at Hiroshima and Nagasaki, a morally fraught decision credited with helping to bring World War II to a swifter end. He did, however, meet with a few of the survivors. One ninety-one-year-old man gripped Obama's hand and would not let go for a long time until he

*President Obama joins Cuban President Raul Castro in a wave
during a baseball game in Havana, March 22, 2016.*

PETE SOUZA/ WHITE HOUSE

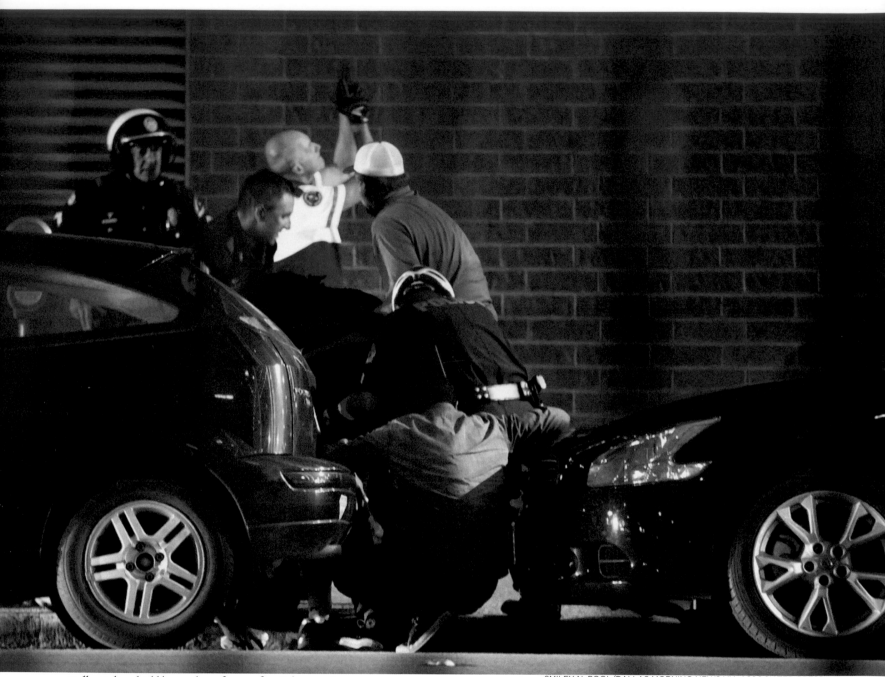

Dallas Police shield bystanders after gunfire, July 7, 2016.

had said what he wanted to tell the American president out of earshot of witnesses. A seventy-nine-year-old who spent years researching aspects of the bombing shared an embrace with the president.

Not long after returning home, Obama confronted violence of a different sort. In June, Omar Mateen, an American-born son of Afghan immigrants, opened fire in the middle of a gay nightclub in Orlando, Florida, after pledging fealty to the Islamic State, killing nearly fifty people and injuring dozens more in the deadliest terrorist attack in the United States since the World Trade Center and Pentagon were hit. Mateen had crossed the radar screen of the Federal Bureau of Investigation before without triggering alarm. He was investigated in 2013 after telling work colleagues that he had family ties to Al Qaeda and wanted to die a martyr. But the F.B.I. ultimately closed the case.

A few weeks after his attack, a spate of shootings reopened the country's fresh racial wounds. In separate incidents in July, police officers shot and killed black men in Baton Rouge, Louisiana, and Falcon Heights, Minnesota. The shooting of Philando Castile during a traffic stop in Minnesota was streamed live on Facebook by his girlfriend, who along with her young daughter was in the car at the time. Obama learned of the incidents while heading to Warsaw for a NATO summit. He holed up in his cabin on Air Force One composing a Facebook post expressing distress at the tragic events, but he told aides it was not enough. So when the plane landed, Obama went before cameras to personally issue a statement, immediately linking the shootings to race. "When incidents like this occur," he said, "there's a big chunk of our citizenry that feels as if, because of the color of their skin, they are not being treated the same, and that hurts and that should trouble all of us."

Shootings reopen the country's racial wounds.

Obama then headed to bed for a few hours before his diplomatic meetings. But as he slept, his country back home took an even darker turn. At a demonstration in Dallas protesting police shootings elsewhere – a protest guarded by the city's own officers – a heavily armed African-American military veteran opened fire at white men in uniform. The sniper killed five police officers, further convulsing a nation already torn between black and blue. Obama, who just hours earlier had lamented police mistreatment of African-Americans, now made a new statement denouncing the killing of the officers. "Let me be clear," he said. "There is no possible justification for these kinds of attacks or any violence against law enforcement."

Some in the law enforcement community thought it was too little too late, laying blame for the incident at the president's feet. William Johnson, the executive director of the National Association of Police Organizations, said that the Obama administration had appeased violent criminals in ways that "led directly to the climate that has made Dallas possible." It was a provocative accusation, one that the White House rejected. But Obama could hardly help wondering how the country had traveled from the highs of Chicago's Grant Park, where he proclaimed victory in the 2008 presidential election, to the lows of Baton Rouge, Falcon Heights and Dallas eight years later.

As the presidential campaign accelerated, Obama staked his legacy on electing the very person he had worked so hard to keep out of the White House just eight years earlier. Where once he portrayed Hillary Clinton as the embodiment of everything that was wrong with Washington, he now saw her as the only real chance of preserving the accomplishments of his administration.

Politics, of course, is the province of strange bedfellows and Obama was hardly the first president to end up embracing a rival – George W. Bush had been in the same position in 2008 when he backed John McCain, his vanquished primary opponent from eight years earlier. But the evolution of the relationship between Obama and Clinton went beyond mere political expediency. Somehow, Obama and Clinton had actually forged a friendship. Ultimately, they forgot all those campaign quotes, or at least forgave them, and teamed up in the White House Situation Room to guide the nation through one international crisis after another. It was not easy. In the early months of Obama's first term they remained wary of each other. Obama's White House saw Clinton's State Department as a rival power center. Team Hillary watched the new president's stumbles with a quiet told-you-so satisfaction. Team Barack made a point of blocking Clinton from bringing its least favorite partisan gunslinger, Sidney Blumenthal, into the administration.

Clinton, who nonetheless stayed in touch with Blumenthal, was insecure, fearful of being boxed out. "I heard on the radio that there is a Cabinet mtg this am," she emailed aides months into the administration. "Is there? Can I go?" Four days later, she showed up for a White House meeting that had been canceled. "This is the second time this has happened," she wrote aides. "What's up???"

Careful and deferential, Clinton eventually developed a rhythm of trust with Obama. She was the hawk on many of the big issues. She advocated a robust troop surge in Afghanistan, lobbied for intervention in Libya to prevent a massacre of civilians, supported the commando raid that would ultimately kill Osama bin Laden, and pressed for arming and training rebels fighting the Syrian government. She was the point person for the ill-fated reset with Russia and the more fitful pivot to Asia.

Obama took her advice much of the time but the end results were mixed at best. The war in Libya, her most prominent initiative, saved thousands of

Hillary Clinton and the president at the Democratic National Convention, Philadelphia, July 27, 2016.

DOUG MILLS/NEW YORK TIMES

civilians and toppled Muammar el-Qaddafi, but left the country in chaos.

Yet when she left office in early 2013, the two were surprised at how well they had gotten along. In a rare joint appearance on *60 Minutes* on CBS, they traded laughs and finished each other's thoughts, agreeing that five years earlier their collaboration would have seemed "improbable," as Clinton put it.

"I consider Hillary a strong friend," Obama offered.

"Very warm, close," Clinton responded.

The joint interview was seen as a blessing for her anticipated campaign to succeed him. When Vice President Joseph Biden began contemplating a late entry into the race in 2015, Obama gently helped steer him out of it, clearing the way, or so it seemed, for Clinton to clinch the nomination.

Clinton started the campaign eager to distance herself from Obama, who at the time was sagging in the polls. She repudiated the Trans-Pacific Partnership trade deal he negotiated, even though she was the one who got it started. She publicly split during the primaries with his policy of restraint in Syria and Ukraine. But as she came under fire from Senator Bernie Sanders on the left, she reversed course and wrapped herself around the president, trying to reassure liberals who were turned off by her interventionist foreign policy, close ties to Wall Street and been-around-forever staleness.

A full-throated endorsement of Hillary Clinton for president.

By the time Obama hugged Clinton on the stage of the Democratic National Convention in Philadelphia in July, the evolution was complete. "No matter how daunting the odds, no matter how much people try to knock her down, she never, ever quits," Obama said of his rival-turned-partner in his last convention speech as president. "That is the Hillary I know. That's the Hillary I've come to admire. And that's why I can say with confidence, there has never been a man or a woman – not me, not Bill, nobody – more qualified than Hillary Clinton to serve as president of the United States of America."

As a matter of politics, there was little wonder why Clinton would embrace Obama, literally as well as figuratively. His poll numbers were healthier, if not sky high, than they had been in a while. On the day before his convention speech, Gallup put his approval rating at 51 percent and his disapproval rating at 45 percent. More importantly for Clinton, liberals who were disappointed with Obama at times had come home to him when it mattered, and she needed to maximize turnout among his voters to win. Especially crucial were African-Americans, the stalwart base of the

Senator Bernie Sanders, Los Angeles, June 7, 2016.

Democratic Party, who came out in overwhelming numbers in 2008 and 2012 but might not have as much motivation in 2016.

Obama in those days was enjoying a resurgence of sorts, in part because of the contrast of the two seeking to succeed him. Donald Trump had rebounded from his Iowa defeat and outpaced sixteen other Republican contenders to capture the nomination for president, but much of the country was appalled by the insult-filled, racially charged primary battle. Many others were disenchanted with Clinton, who was investigated, though not charged, for her use of a private email server that potentially exposed classified information.

David Brooks, the center-right columnist for *The New York Times*, captured this sentiment early in 2016 with a column entitled, "I Miss Barack Obama." He wrote: "No, Obama has not been temperamentally perfect. Too often he's been disdainful, aloof, resentful and insular. But there is a tone of ugliness creeping across the world, as democracies retreat, as tribalism mounts, as suspiciousness and authoritarianism take center stage. Obama radiates an ethos of integrity, humanity, good manners and elegance that I'm beginning to miss, and that I suspect we will all miss a bit, regardless of who replaces him."

Obama started the fall campaign confident that Clinton would beat Trump. She led in the polls, she led in fund-raising, she led in experience. Despite her battle with Bernie Sanders, she seemed to have united the party leadership behind her while Trump was busy battling with Republicans like House Speaker Paul Ryan and Gov. John Kasich of Ohio as they renounced some of his more controversial statements or even announced they could not support him. By one count, Clinton received the endorsement of 240 newspapers, while Trump was supported by just nineteen. Even staunchly conservative newspapers like *The Arizona Republic, Dallas Morning News, San Diego Union-Tribune* and *Cincinnati Enquirer,* some of which had not backed a Democrat for president in more than a century, urged their readers to reject Trump and elect Clinton. So did magazines like *Foreign Policy* and *The Atlantic*, which rarely if ever endorsed candidates.

For Obama, it was hard to picture a President Trump. How could the country elect a man who insulted Mexicans, Muslims, women, people with disabilities and veterans, who refused to release his tax forms, who was being sued for fraud over a school he called Trump University, who got into a running feud with the Muslim father of a American soldier slain in Iraq and who handed down policy pronouncements in acerbic 140-character Twitter messages?

Obama took it personally. "This is not me going through the motions here," he said at a campaign rally in Philadelphia in September. "I really, really, really want to elect Hillary Clinton." A few days later, speaking at a

Hillary Clinton and Michelle Obama, Wake Forest University, Winston-Salem, North Carolina, October 27, 2016.

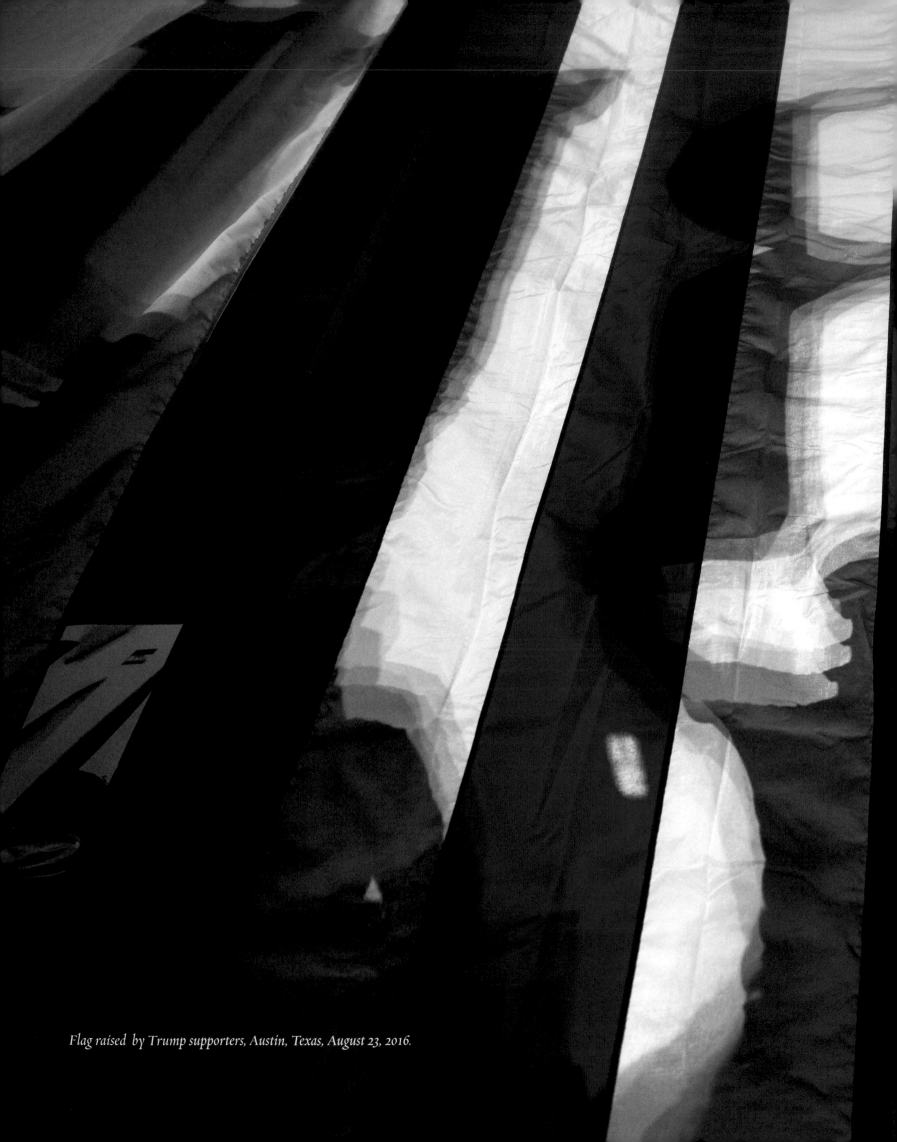

Flag raised by Trump supporters, Austin, Texas, August 23, 2016.

DAMON WINTER/NEW YORK TIMES

STEPHEN CROWLEY/NEW YORK TIMES

dinner of the Congressional Black Caucus Foundation, he elaborated. "My name may not be on the ballot, but our progress is on the ballot," he said. "Tolerance is on the ballot. Democracy is on the ballot. Justice is on the ballot." Obama told the crowd that black voters owed it to him to cast ballots for Clinton. "After we have achieved historic turnout in 2008 and 2012, especially in the African-American community, I will consider it a personal insult, an insult to my legacy, if this community lets down its guard and fails to activate itself in this election," he said. "You want to give me a good send-off? Go vote."

From Michelle Obama, impassioned speeches denouncing Trump.

Just how personal it was for Obama became clear that same week, when Trump finally reversed himself after years of promoting the false conspiracy theory that the president was not a natural-born American. "President Barack Obama was born in the United States, period," Trump said in terse remarks tacked onto the end of an unrelated campaign stop in Washington. "Now we all want to get back to making America strong and great again." Yet even as he retreated from the longstanding effort to question Obama's citizenship, he propagated another falsehood, claiming that it was Clinton's campaign that first stirred the so-called birther movement during the 2008 primaries.

At the black caucus dinner the following night, Obama joked that he had "an extra spring in my step" now that the mystery of his birthplace had been solved. "I mean, ISIL, North Korea, poverty, climate change – none of those things weighed on my mind like the validity of my birth certificate," he said, tongue planted firmly in cheek. "And to think, that with just 124 days to go, under the wire, we got that resolved."

Obama was not the only one in his household feeling personally offended by Trump's candidacy. Michelle Obama, who normally had little interest in campaigns, came out strongly for Clinton and gave impassioned speeches urging the country not to turn to Trump. She was especially offended after a tape emerged in which Trump could be heard boasting about grabbing women and having his way with them, followed by allegations by a number of women that he did more than talk about it. The First Lady expressed outrage. "I have to tell you that I can't stop thinking about this," she told an audience in New Hampshire in perhaps the most emotional speech of her time in public life. "It has shaken me to my core in a way that I couldn't have predicted."

Michelle Obama at the Democratic National Convention, July 25, 2016.

President Obama and President-elect Trump at the White House, November 11, 2016.

Trump taunted him with a tweet, he took the bait. "President Obama will go down as perhaps the worst president in the history of the United States!" Trump wrote.

By the end of the evening, the unthinkable happens.

Appearing on *Jimmy Kimmel Live!*, Obama read the tweet aloud and then responded by mocking Trump as a certain loser. "At least I'll go down as a president," he said, dropping his smart phone as a take-that punctuation.

He hoped he was right. The stakes for Obama could hardly be higher and at some points during the campaign he envisioned a bleak future for his legacy should Trump prevail. "All the progress we've made over these last eight years goes out the window if we don't win this election," he told one crowd.

His scorn for Trump grew more visceral in the final days of the campaign. In Florida, he said Trump only met working people when they were "cleaning his room." In North Carolina, he called Trump a "con artist and a know-nothing" who was "temperamentally unfit to be commander in chief." In Ohio, he mocked the idea that America could pick Trump. "This guy?" he said. "This guy? Come on." With just hours to go before Election Day, Obama pointed out that Trump's staff had, briefly, wrested away control of his Twitter account to keep him from sending out impolitic messages. "If your closest advisers don't trust you to tweet," Obama said, "how can you trust him with the nuclear codes?"

Obama woke up on Election Day convinced, like most of the country, that he would not be handing the nuclear football to Trump. Around 10 p.m., as returns rolled in, he turned on a television in the White House residence to watch. To avoid the stress of the evening, Michelle Obama opted to go to bed. She may have had the right idea. For Democrats, the stress levels climbed higher and higher as Trump won Florida, a key battleground state, and then captured the normally Democratic bulwarks of Pennsylvania, Michigan and Wisconsin.

By the end of the evening, the unthinkable had happened. While Clinton was significantly ahead in the popular vote, she had lost enough key states to hand Trump a victory in the Electoral College. The country that had twice elected Barack Hussein Obama as its president had now chosen as his successor a man who had questioned the very circumstances of his birth.

President Obama awards the Medal of Freedom to Vice President Biden at the White House, January 12, 2017.

President Obama stands behind his Oval Office desk for the last time as president, January 20, 2017.

"This stings," Obama said. "This hurts." The morning after the election, the president and his team were still trying to absorb the magnitude of what had happened. Sitting in the Oval Office, they mulled the prospect of President Donald Trump occupying that most powerful few square feet in the world. But the zen Obama, the never-too-hot, never-too-cold forty-fourth president tried to keep perspective. It hurt, he told his staff, but it was not the end of the world.

It was hard to convince short-timers in the West Wing of that. Many in the building were crying that day, shaking their heads in shocked disbelief. The place felt like a funeral service. As he talked with aides and advisers, Obama served as consoler in chief. The country had still moved forward on their watch, despite this obvious setback, he reassured them. Change does not follow a straight line, he said. It tends to zig and zag. He and others remembered David Axelrod's prescient observation that as a retiring president heads out the door, the country tends to choose a remedy, not a replica – someone who seems the opposite of the outgoing leader. There could hardly be someone more opposite of Obama.

The second-guessing and hand-wringing were unavoidable. "Never been as wrong on anything on [sic] my life," David Plouffe, who had stuck by his prediction that Clinton had a 100 percent chance of winning, wrote on Twitter. He was hardly the only one. Nearly every political and media outlet that engaged in game-show style predictions found itself humiliated. Only slightly less bullish than Plouffe, *The Huffington Post* thought Clinton had a 98 percent chance of winning. The web site FiveThirtyEight.com, which specialized in political prognostication, was more conservative but still put the likelihood of a Clinton victory at 71 percent. *The New York Times's* Upshot split the difference by pegging her chances at 85 percent – and many of the newspaper's online readers found themselves whipsawed when a graphic dial meter showing its presidential prediction suddenly flipped on Election Night to give Trump similarly lopsided odds.

No matter how much Obama tried to find the silver lining, Trump's victory imperiled many of Obama's achievements, including the health care law that extended coverage to 20 million more Americans even though it aggravated others who resented government intrusion and rising premiums. Trump vowed to scrap Obama's international climate change agreement and the Trans-Pacific Partnership trade pact, renegotiate his Iran nuclear deal, dismantle the Dodd-Frank regulations on Wall Street and reverse orders sparing illegal immigrants from deportation.

But while Obama just days earlier had said all of his progress would be "out the window," he and his team now argued that was not true. "Maybe 15 percent of that gets rolled back, 20 percent," he told David Remnick of *The New Yorker*, "but there's still a lot of stuff that sticks."

Trump, they argued, would find it harder to shift course than he expected. Taking health care away from millions of Americans would prove

STEPHEN CROWLEY/NEW YORK TIMES

problematic; indeed, within days of the election, Trump began saying he would find a way to ensure that they did not lose coverage. And many of Obama's successes – pulling the country out of the Great Recession, saving the auto industry, killing Osama bin Laden and promoting clean energy – could not be overturned.

Obama refuses to veto a U.N. resolution condemning Israeli settlements.

Remembering the gracious way George W. Bush handled his own transition eight years ago, Obama resolved to follow that example and reached out to Trump. They sat together in the Oval Office two days after the election, the first time they had ever met. Over the course of ninety minutes, Obama did his best to steer Trump toward seeing the world the way he had and the two tried to put the rancor of the campaign behind them. Obama called it an "excellent conversation" and said he was "encouraged" by Trump's interest in working together. Trump expressed "great respect" for Obama and called him a "very, very good man."

But if history had a way of zigging and zagging, so did the transition. When the United Nations Security Council took up a resolution condemning Israeli settlements in the West Bank and East Jerusalem and Obama would not commit to vetoing it, Prime Minister Benjamin Netanyahu reached out to Trump for help. Trump publicly called on Obama to block the resolution, but the president ignored him and had the United States abstain instead, allowing it to pass. Furious, Netanyahu accused Obama of conspiring against Israel by secretly orchestrating the resolution, an allegation the White House denied. But Trump used the moment to highlight how he would be different from Obama. "Stay strong Israel," Trump wrote on Twitter. "January 20th is fast approaching!"

The two also skirmished over intelligence reports that Russia had tried to tilt the election in Trump's favor by hacking into Democratic email accounts and leaking the contents. In retaliation for the interference, Obama expelled thirty-five Russian diplomats and closed two facilities used by Russians in the United States. But Trump repeatedly dismissed the notion that the Russians were responsible and accused the intelligence agencies of political maneuvering to undercut the validity of his election.

While Obama offered help to the incoming team, that did not stop him from using his final weeks to try to prevent his successor from reversing parts of his legacy. He used his presidential power to ban oil drilling off the Atlantic coast and set aside wide swaths of land as national monuments. He also issued more commutations to non-violent federal prisoners,

Hillary Clinton, with Bill Clinton and Tim Kaine, gives her concession speech,
New York, November 9, 2016.

transferred more detainees out of the prison at Guantanamo Bay, Cuba, and eliminated a long-suspended national registry program once used to track Muslim men to keep Trump from restarting it.

Obama could not resist tweaking Trump. During an interview with David Axelrod for his podcast, The Axe Files, Obama even boasted that had he not been barred from seeking a third term by the Constitution, he could have beaten Trump with a more inclusive message and appeal to the middle class.

"I'm confident that if I had run again and articulated it, I think I could have mobilized a majority of the American people to rally behind it," he said.

Trump fired back hours later on Twitter: "President Obama said that he thinks he would have won against me. He should say that but I say NO WAY! – jobs leaving, ISIS, OCare, etc." That, of course, would have been a contest for the ages. But it was not to be.

The next time the two met was Inauguration Day. The incoming president and his wife arrived at the White House in the morning for the traditional tea with the outgoing presidential couple. They chatted amiably on the North Portico and then went inside. After a while, Obama emerged from the White House for the last time as president to escort his successor in the motorcade to the Capitol for the ceremony.

After the oath was taken and the speech was given and the transfer of power was complete, the Obamas headed to the other side of the Capitol and boarded a white-topped Marine helicopter, which took one final loop over the White House before flying the forty-fourth president and his wife to Joint Base Andrews in the Maryland suburbs for a last farewell before leaving Washington on the presidential jet.

Addressing a crowd of several thousand former aides, advisers and supporters, Obama said they had reason to be proud of what they had accomplished. But history's paragraph, he said, was not done.

"This is not a period," he said, "this is a comma in the continuing story of building America."

President Obama delivers his farewell address, McCormick Place, Chicago, January 10, 2017.

STEPHEN CROWLEY/NEW YORK TIMES

The Obamas welcome the Trumps to the White House, January 20, 2017.

KEVIN DIETSCH/ EUROPEAN PRESS PHOTO AGENCY

MARK WILSON/GETTY IMAGES

STEPHEN CROWLEY/THE NEW YORK TIMES

*President-elect Trump and President Obama arrive for Trump's inauguration
ceremony at the Capitol, January 20, 2017.*

President-elect Trump walks to the podium, January 20, 2017.

PUTUS

POTUS

BARRON

FLOTUS

MRS. PENCE

MICHAEL

DON JR.

IVANKA

President Obama and President Trump at the
swearing in ceremony. January 20, 2017.

As Donald J. Trump is sworn in as president by Chief Justice John Roberts, family members look on. From left: Melania, Donald, Jr., Barron, Ivanka, Eric and Tiffany. January 20, 2017.

President Obama boards Air Force One at Andrews Air Force Base, May 18, 2016

DOUG MILLS/NEW YORK TIMES

The Obama Years by the Numbers

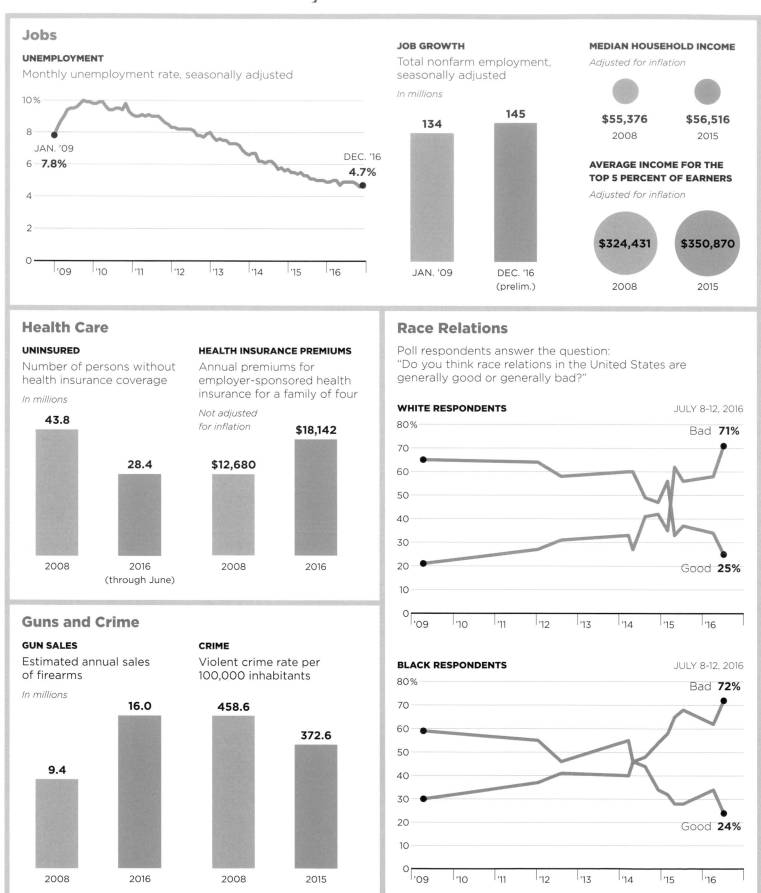

Jobs

UNEMPLOYMENT
Monthly unemployment rate, seasonally adjusted

JAN. '09 **7.8%**
DEC. '16 **4.7%**

JOB GROWTH
Total nonfarm employment, seasonally adjusted

In millions

134 JAN. '09
145 DEC. '16 (prelim.)

MEDIAN HOUSEHOLD INCOME
Adjusted for inflation

$55,376 2008
$56,516 2015

AVERAGE INCOME FOR THE TOP 5 PERCENT OF EARNERS
Adjusted for inflation

$324,431 2008
$350,870 2015

Health Care

UNINSURED
Number of persons without health insurance coverage

In millions

43.8 2008
28.4 2016 (through June)

HEALTH INSURANCE PREMIUMS
Annual premiums for employer-sponsored health insurance for a family of four

Not adjusted for inflation

$12,680 2008
$18,142 2016

Guns and Crime

GUN SALES
Estimated annual sales of firearms

In millions

9.4 2008
16.0 2016

CRIME
Violent crime rate per 100,000 inhabitants

458.6 2008
372.6 2015

Race Relations

Poll respondents answer the question: "Do you think race relations in the United States are generally good or generally bad?"

WHITE RESPONDENTS — JULY 8-12, 2016

Bad **71%**
Good **25%**

BLACK RESPONDENTS — JULY 8-12, 2016

Bad **72%**
Good **24%**

Sources: Bureau of Labor Statistics (unemployment, job growth); Census Bureau (income); Centers for Disease Control and Prevention (uninsured); Kaiser Family Foundation (health insurance premiums); New York Times analysis of NICS data (gun sales); Federal Bureau of Investigation (crime); New York Times/CBS polls (race relations)

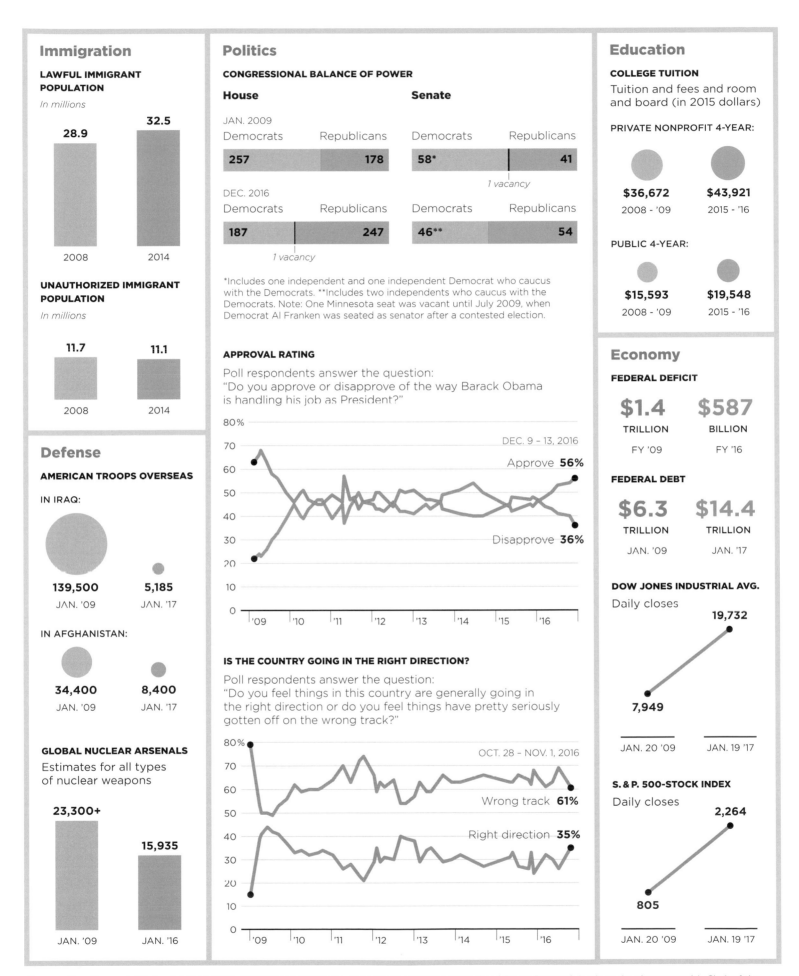

Immigration

LAWFUL IMMIGRANT POPULATION

In millions

28.9 — 2008
32.5 — 2014

UNAUTHORIZED IMMIGRANT POPULATION

In millions

11.7 — 2008
11.1 — 2014

Defense

AMERICAN TROOPS OVERSEAS

IN IRAQ:

139,500 — JAN. '09
5,185 — JAN. '17

IN AFGHANISTAN:

34,400 — JAN. '09
8,400 — JAN. '17

GLOBAL NUCLEAR ARSENALS

Estimates for all types of nuclear weapons

23,300+ — JAN. '09
15,935 — JAN. '16

Politics

CONGRESSIONAL BALANCE OF POWER

House

JAN. 2009

Democrats	Republicans
257	178

DEC. 2016

Democrats	Republicans
187	247

1 vacancy

Senate

JAN. 2009

Democrats	Republicans
58*	41

1 vacancy

DEC. 2016

Democrats	Republicans
46**	54

*Includes one independent and one independent Democrat who caucus with the Democrats. **Includes two independents who caucus with the Democrats. Note: One Minnesota seat was vacant until July 2009, when Democrat Al Franken was seated as senator after a contested election.

APPROVAL RATING

Poll respondents answer the question:
"Do you approve or disapprove of the way Barack Obama is handling his job as President?"

DEC. 9 – 13, 2016

Approve **56%**
Disapprove **36%**

IS THE COUNTRY GOING IN THE RIGHT DIRECTION?

Poll respondents answer the question:
"Do you feel things in this country are generally going in the right direction or do you feel things have pretty seriously gotten off on the wrong track?"

OCT. 28 – NOV. 1, 2016

Wrong track **61%**
Right direction **35%**

Education

COLLEGE TUITION

Tuition and fees and room and board (in 2015 dollars)

PRIVATE NONPROFIT 4-YEAR:

$36,672 — 2008 - '09
$43,921 — 2015 - '16

PUBLIC 4-YEAR:

$15,593 — 2008 - '09
$19,548 — 2015 - '16

Economy

FEDERAL DEFICIT

$1.4 TRILLION — FY '09
$587 BILLION — FY '16

FEDERAL DEBT

$6.3 TRILLION — JAN. '09
$14.4 TRILLION — JAN. '17

DOW JONES INDUSTRIAL AVG.

Daily closes

7,949 — JAN. 20 '09
19,732 — JAN. 19 '17

S. & P. 500-STOCK INDEX

Daily closes

805 — JAN. 20 '09
2,264 — JAN. 19 '17

Sources: Pew Research Center (immigration); Department of Defense (troops); Stockholm International Peace Research Institute (nuclear arsenals); Clerk of the House (House balance); Senate Historical Office (Senate balance); New York Times/CBS polls (approval rating, country going in right direction); The College Board (college tuition); Google Finance (stock market indices)

GRAPHIC BY GUILBERT GATES AND SUSAN BEACHY

EPILOGUE

The White House was not quite deserted in the twilight hours of the Obama administration but there were only a few dozen people left. Most of President Obama's aides had turned in their badges, packed their boxes and left to begin a new chapter. Obama gathered those who were still hanging around and invited them over to the State Dining Room, where hors d'oeuvres and drinks were served. On his last evening before leaving office, he ruminated on the meaning of his presidency.

"I have had an ongoing debate with Ben about whether individuals change the course of history or if structural changes happen on their own and people are just riding the wave," he told the last remnants of the team that had ridden the wave with him for the previous eight years, including Ben Rhodes, who had become one of his closest confidants on the staff. "What I know after working with this team and with our Cabinet is that in fact it is teams that change history."

More than just a final attaboy for his crew, Obama's observation on the way out the door touched on essential questions of his presidency. How much was he driving events and how much were they driving him? How much was he writing that paragraph in history and how much was it being written by forces of history far greater than he? He was propelled to power on a wave of yes-we-can determination in a moment of crisis, by a hunger for something new and different after years of struggle and a palpable desire on the part of many Americans to turn the page on an ugly racial past. But he left office with a country still deeply unsettled and bitterly polarized. While initially a figure of inspiration, he could not overcome the demons of division. At no point during his presidency did a majority of Americans tell pollsters that they thought the country was on the right track.

The election of 2016 was an earthquake that shook the Obama presidency to its core. How much Donald J. Trump's victory could be interpreted as a rejection of Obama will be debated for years to come but it was certainly a humbling end to his time in office. For many of his conservative critics, it was the welcome culmination of a grass-roots revolt against an elitist, big-government presidency that had already cost Democrats scores of seats in Congress and governorships, not to mention hundreds of state legislative seats across the nation. For many supporters of Obama, on the other hand, it was hard not to look at the results as a racially motivated backlash against the first African-American president. Language like "take our country back," in this view, was thinly veiled code for white Americans who felt threatened by the nation's rapidly changing demographics. Trump, who for years peddled the blatantly false conspiracy theory that Obama was not even born in the United States, appealed to racial resentment more overtly than any major party nominee in generations.

Yet the story was more complicated. Trump won the Electoral College in large part by capturing Midwestern states where Democrats had long prevailed but in recent years had lost their hold on working-class white voters, many of them past supporters of Obama who felt their own economic livelihoods slipping away along with the factories where their parents once worked. Even many of those who were not dislocated themselves felt the country was adrift. Hillary Clinton's campaign made little effort to appeal to less educated, working-class white voters who were once the backbone of the party, essentially writing them off as lost. Obama lamented this disconnect. "The challenge we had is not that we've neglected these communities from a policy perspective," he told *Rolling Stone* magazine the day after the election. "What is true, though, is that whatever policy prescriptions that we've been proposing don't reach – are not heard – by the folks in these communities."

An examination of exit polls suggested that despite this, and despite the racial overtones of the campaign, Trump did no better among white voters than Mitt Romney had done four years earlier. The difference was that although Clinton won overwhelmingly among African-American and Hispanic voters, she did not match Obama's stratospheric margins. In the end, haunted by an F.B.I. investigation into her email server, unable to dispense with conflict-of-interest questions about the family foundation and seen as the entitled embodiment of a stale status quo, she failed to energize Democrats as much as the outgoing president had. She was a flawed candidate and Obama partisans could make the argument that her fate was her own fault, not a reflection of the outgoing president.

Indeed, as the campaign climaxed and the country got the first taste of a President-elect Trump, Obama's own popularity kept rising. He left office with 59 percent of Americans approving of the job he was doing, his highest rating since the first months of his presidency nearly eight years before. Of the ten most recent presidents who lived to leave office, only Dwight Eisenhower matched Obama's final number and only Ronald Reagan and Bill Clinton surpassed it. The disappointment many felt toward Obama through much of his time in office, especially on the left, had to a large extent faded. In its place was a growing recognition, at least among erstwhile supporters, that Obama had accomplished a lot of what he had promised. In one liberal enclave in Washington, a storefront devoted its entire window space to handwritten thank-you notes to Obama. "Please don't go!" one wrote. In Blue America, at least, Obama nostalgia had begun.

To the extent that Obama had resolved to go down in history for more than just his original trailblazing election, he succeeded, for good or ill. He enjoyed two years of sweeping legislative victories arguably not seen since the days of Lyndon Johnson's Great Society, then spent six years fighting for inches against an opposition-dominated Congress that he barely bothered to woo and that did not want to work with him in the first place. He took great strides toward his goals in health care, financial regulation and climate change, only to fall short in immigration, criminal justice and income inequality. He turned around a nation teetering on the edge of depression and ultimately presided over the longest streak of job creation on record. More than 11 million new jobs were created on his watch, shy of the 23 million under Clinton or 16 million under Reagan, but still impressive given the hemorrhage of jobs he inherited. The stock markets more than doubled during his presidency, yet so did the national debt. Obama put two women on the Supreme Court and helped break down barriers for gay and lesbian Americans, even as racial minorities remained far behind in education and income.

In the end, he made progress, if sometimes halting, toward his broader ambition of fundamentally transforming the economy and breaking out of the boom-and-bust cycle he had sought to end. And in some ways, he put in place the building blocks for a new economy that he expected to pay off in the long run. The initiatives in his stimulus package and other policies, for instance, accelerated a clean energy boom that was already underway. But other elements of the plan never took hold. He temporarily spared many unauthorized immigrants from deportation but never overhauled a broken immigration system in a way that would outlast his tenure. His Trans-Pacific Partnership agreement with Asia that would have created the largest free-trade zone in the world was ultimately rejected by fellow Democrats, including Clinton, and would later be formally abandoned by Trump after he took office. He was brushed back by the courts for pushing the boundaries of executive power too far.

Overseas, Obama withdrew nearly all American forces from Iraq and Afghanistan although both countries remained mired in war as he left office. He dispatched Osama bin Laden, Anwar al-Awlaki and hundreds of other terrorists with relentless drone strikes, commando raids and other actions, breaking the core Al Qaeda organization, but a brutal new terrorist group rose to take its place in the form of the Islamic State. On his orders, American forces eventually reclaimed much of the territory captured by its black-flag-waving forces in Iraq and Syria, but Obama otherwise largely sat out the years of civil war in Syria that claimed hundreds of thousands of lives. His onetime model for a more targeted style of intervention in Libya devolved into a quagmire that he washed his hands of. He rallied Europe and much of the world against Russian aggression in Ukraine, arguably stopping Moscow from carving up more of the country, even though he could not roll back its seizure of Crimea. Perhaps his proudest foreign policy achievements were the diplomatic rapprochement with Cuba after more than a half-century of hostility and the arduously negotiated agreement with Iran to shut down its nuclear program for a decade in exchange for relief from sanctions – keeping his promise to reach out to hostile regimes even if some accused him of giving away too much to gain too little.

If the lesson he took from George W. Bush was to avoid foreign military entanglements – pithily summed up as "don't do stupid stuff" – the caution Obama exhibited struck some critics as an overcompensation, leaving an impression of passivity that sapped American leadership in the world. As they packed their boxes in the last days of the administration, some of his own senior officials ruefully concluded that the catastrophe of Syria would be a dark mark on their record – and his. But Obama judged that the American people were not willing to take the risks and pay the costs required to stop the slaughter and they did not consider it a high enough national priority. Tired of Bush's wars, Americans were not interested in getting involved in any new ones. In Trump's victory, oddly, Obama found something of a validation for this view, since the new president had made a point of promising to stay away from foreign military adventures, except for the war against the Islamic State.

Whatever the judgment on his policies, Obama's personal conduct in office over eight years stood him in good stead. Even some of those who opposed him bitterly agreed that he was a good family man and role model who carried the weight of the world's toughest office with dignity. And while he did not want to be judged solely by race, to young people especially, he changed the paradigm of expectations. "There are children growing up today who think it's perfectly normal to have an African-American president because that's all they have ever known," Valerie Jarrett, Obama's friend and adviser, said at one point. In a country long riven by race, that was no small matter.

Other than Clinton, Obama at age fifty-five was the youngest former president since William Howard Taft and hardly ready for a quiet retirement in the countryside. With his daughter Sasha still in high school, he and Michelle rented a house in the upscale Kalorama section of Washington where they could stay until her graduation in 2019 – as it happens, choosing a place just a stone's throw from the house that Trump's daughter and son-in-law, Ivanka Trump and Jared Kushner, would soon rent. In the process, Obama became the first president to remain in the nation's capital after leaving office since Woodrow Wilson, who was physically infirm. That put Obama just two miles away from the elegant mansion he had occupied for eight years and just as close to the action should he choose to engage.

At first, he planned to stay above the fray, much as Bush had done when he handed over power and retreated to Dallas. Bush had made a point of not criticizing Obama even when the new president reversed policies in areas that mattered to him, declaring that his successor "deserves my silence." Obama had always respected and appreciated this gracious approach, intending to follow Bush's example when his own time came.

But after the election, as Trump prepared to take the presidency, Obama's plans for his post-presidency were drastically upended. If it had been Hillary Clinton taking over, or even Jeb Bush or Marco Rubio, he likely would have slipped gracefully from the stage and kept quiet even when he disagreed with the new president. But Trump was a different case altogether. This was not a president who played within the usual boundaries. To Obama, Trump was not just vulgar but reckless, even potentially dangerous.

Given that, Obama vowed at his final White House news conference to speak out when he saw fit. "There's a difference between that normal functioning of politics," he told reporters, "and certain issues or certain moments where I think our core values may be at stake. I put in that category: If I saw systematic discrimination being ratified in some fashion. I put in that category explicit or functional obstacles to people being able to vote, to exercise their franchise. I'd put in that category institutional efforts to silence dissent or the press. And for me at least, I would put in that category efforts to round up kids who have grown up here and for all practical purposes are American kids, and send them someplace else, when they love this country."

It took just a week for one of his red lines to be tripped. When Trump opened his presidency with a hastily drafted executive order barring refugees from around the world from entering the country for ninety days and those from Syria indefinitely while also closing the border to visitors from seven predominantly Muslim countries for 120 days, the former president could not resist speaking out. Never mind that Obama had not yet even returned from his post-inauguration kite-surfing vacation, he released a written statement praising demonstrators protesting the new order for acting as "the guardians of our democracy." Issued in the name of a spokesman, the statement went on to say: "The president fundamentally disagrees with the notion of discriminating against individuals because of their faith or religion."

It was the beginning of a new chapter. There was much to do. He would establish a presidential library, build a foundation and expand his My Brother's Keeper initiative helping young Latino and African-American boys. He planned to write a memoir and team up with Eric Holder on a voting rights project. He wanted to work on health care and immigration. He would not miss the office, perhaps, but he was not ready to give up the work.

For Obama, history was still calling.

Promises and Results

President Obama came to office with an ambitious agenda to change America and redefine its role in the world. Not all of his campaign promises were kept, however, either because he changed his mind, was blocked by opponents or had to adjust to circumstances he had not foreseen. A look at ten top promises and how they turned out.

Fix the economy

Obama passed a stimulus package, bailed out the auto industry and took other measures to prevent a new Great Depression. Unemployment was cut by half, automakers roared back to life and markets shot back up. But the recovery was historically weak and most of the economic gains went to the wealthiest Americans, while income for the poor and middle class remained stagnant. His efforts to raise the minimum wage went nowhere in Congress, although many states took up the cause.

End the wars in Iraq and Afghanistan

Obama promised to end the war in Iraq and win the war in Afghanistan, neither of which quite happened. He withdrew American troops from Iraq at the end of 2011 but ended up sending thousands back in an advisory and support role to counter the rise of the Islamic State. He sent reinforcements to Afghanistan and then withdrew them after two years as promised but abandoned his plan to pull out entirely before leaving office. Overall, American troops in Iraq and Afghanistan fell from about 175,000 when he took over to just over 13,000 by late 2016.

Close Guantánamo

Obama signed an order to close the detention center at Guantánamo Bay, Cuba, within a year but was blocked by Congress. His administration did manage to transfer most of the detainees to other countries, bringing the population down from 242 when he took office to 41 when he left office. Obama signed an order banning torture in terrorism interrogations.

Reach out to enemies

Obama said he would be willing to sit down with the leaders of Cuba, Iran, North Korea, Syria and Venezuela within his first year in office. While he did not meet with any of them in his first year, in his second term he did restore diplomatic relations with Cuba and met with President Raul Castro while reaching agreement with Iran to curb its nuclear program.

Expand health care

Obama enacted a program to expand health care coverage by creating state-based marketplaces and offering subsidies while enrolling additional working poor Americans in Medicaid. He dropped a promised alternative government insurance plan known as a public option and imposed a mandate requiring individuals to obtain coverage even though he opposed it in the campaign. His promise that anyone could keep their doctor turned out not to be true, but the program provided coverage to 20 million more Americans.

Regulate Wall Street

Obama did not break up any of the big banks and generally did not prosecute top banking executives implicated in the financial crash of 2008. But he pushed through Congress the Dodd-Frank law that set up a consumer financial protection bureau and imposed rules meant to curb abusive practices.

Liberalize immigration

Obama could not convince Congress to pass legislation overhauling the immigration system, so instead he turned to his executive authority to try to enact some of the changes. He allowed young people brought into the country illegally as children to stay without fear of deportation, but his program to extend that protection to as many as 5 million immigrants was blocked by the Supreme Court.

Tackle climate change

Obama could not convince Congress to pass a system known as cap and trade to limit the gases blamed for climate change while allowing businesses to trade pollution credits. But he used regulatory power to increase gas mileage for cars and restrict power plant emissions. He also forged an international climate change agreement, drawing in fast-developing nations like China and India.

End Bush tax cuts for rich

Obama promised to make tax cuts enacted by George W. Bush permanent for most Americans but reverse them for those making $250,000 a year or more. He was forced to extend all the tax cuts for his first term but in the end accepted a compromise raising the rates again on income over $400,000 a year.

Change the culture of Washington

Obama, who as a candidate said, "I can bring this country together," acknowledged that he had failed to bridge the partisan divide and in fact it "has gotten worse instead of better." He faulted Republicans for obstructionism but agreed that he bore some of the blame. "I'll take my share," he said.

President Obama, August 25, 2016.

DAN WINTERS FOR NEW YORK MAGAZINE

INDEX

Abadi, Haider al-, 206

Abbottabad, Pakistan, 104, 105

ABC, 151, 257

Abdulmutallab, Umar Farouk, 64, 74–75

Abortion rights, 129, 272

Adult children, on insurance plans, 34

Affleck, Ben, 253

Afghanistan, 11, 13, 41, 42, 44–51, 53, 55, 59, 69, 73, 88, 115, 123, 127, 155, 178, 180, 182, 200, 204, 278, 307, 310

Al Arabiya television network, 67

Al Qaeda, 49, 54, 64–66, 69, 73, 74, 103, 119, 139, 178, 195, 196, 198, 277, 310

Alaska, 259–260

Alcatraz prison, 162

Aleppo, Syria, 178, 179

"Amazing Grace," 223

American Civil Liberties Union (ACLU), 65, 70

American Muslims, 265, 294

American President, The (movie), 160

Andrews, Troy "Trombone Shorty," 236

Ansar al-Sharia terrorist group, 137

Apprentice, The (television show), 172

Arab League, 115

Arab Spring, 103, 105, 135, 196, 255

Argo (movie), 253

Arizona Republic, 283

Arlington National Cemetery, 42

Arms control, 88, 91, 92, 127, 200

Assad, Bashar al-, 116, 135, 141, 176, 178, 180, 184, 257

Assault rifles, 157

Associated Press, 158

Atlantic, The, 283

Austin, Lloyd, 120

Australia, 257

Automobile industry, 10, 21, 22, 29–30, 127, 129, 292

Awlaki, Anwar al-, 65, 75, 119, 158, 160, 310

Axelrod, David, 22, 32, 36, 44, 55, 67, 88, 93, 107, 140, 145, 234, 266, 290, 294

B-2 bombers, 106

Background checks, 157

Baghdad, Iraq, 135, 205

Bahrain, 103, 112, 114, 115

Bain Capital, 129, 140

Baltimore, Maryland, 230

Banking system, 21, 22, 38–39

Basketball, 217–219

Baton Rouge, Louisiana shootings, 277, 278

Bay of Pigs operation, 247

Beatty, Warren, 160

Beck, Jeff, 236

Benghazi, Libya, 115, 116, 136–139, 158, 178

Bergdahl, Robert "Bowe," 204–205

Berlin Wall, fall of, 105, 247

Bernanke, Ben, 153

Beyoncé, 237

Biden, Beau, 123

Biden, Joseph R. Jr., 11, 59–60, 93, 129, 150, 206, 227, 230, 244, 280

    Afghanistan and, 49, 123

    background of, 123

    bin Laden raid and, 100, 106, 123

    death of son and, 123

    education of, 123

    Egyptian crisis and, 112, 114

    gaffe-prone style of, 123

    Gates and, 123

    gun control issue and, 153

    Iraq and, 120, 123

    Libyan crisis and, 115, 123

    Medal of Freedom awarded to, 290

    Obama and, 122, 123

    personality of, 123

    photographs of, 35, 52, 72, 122, 290

    same-sex marriage and, 130–131

    as vice president, 123

bin Laden, Osama, 10, 12, 101–111, 119, 123, 129, 278, 292, 310

Bipartisanship, 69, 86, 127, 189, 235

Birth certificate issue and, 106, 109, 172–173, 213, 224, 234, 265, 287, 308

Black Hawk helicopters, Somali downing of, 105

Black Lives Matter, 225

Black site prisons, 69

Blair, Dennis, 45

Blinken, Antony, 180

Blumenthal, Sidney, 278

Boehner, John, 27, 37–38, 94–96, 98, 99, 163, 173, 189, 211, 242, 257

Bosnia, 182

Boston Marathon bombing, 158–159

Boston Tea Party, 35

Bowles, Erskine, 94, 95

BP oil spill, 76–79

Brazil, 183

Brennan, John, 69, 71, 102, 105

Brooks, David, 283

Brown, Michael, 224, 226, 228

Brown, Michael Sr., 226

Brown, Scott, 36

Bulworth (movie), 160

Bundy, McGeorge, 49

Burma (Myanmar), 155

Burns, Ken, 237

Burns, William, 250

Busey, Gary, 109, 172

Bush, George H. W., 182, 237

Bush, George W., 11, 22, 34, 55, 100, 106, 110, 119, 123, 155, 158, 196, 204, 208, 217, 237, 250, 278, 310, 311

    Afghanistan and, 44, 47

    counterterrorism strategy of, 65–66, 69, 86, 102–103

    drone strikes and, 70

    economic issues and, 29, 30, 94

    Haitian earthquake and, 75

    Hurricane Katrina and, 78

    Iraq and, 44, 45, 50, 66, 119, 163, 182, 205, 206

    midterm elections (2006), 209

    photograph of, 60

    Presidential Library and Museum, 157

    press and, 193

    September 11, 2001 terrorist attacks and, 265

    tax cuts and, 88, 91, 153

    transition to Obama administration and, 292

Bush, Jeb, 311

BuzzFeed, 172, 173

Cameron, David, 180

Camp David summit, 112

Camp Lejeune, North Carolina, 45

Camp Victory, Baghdad, 40

Canada, 34, 35, 257

Cantor, Eric, 26, 27, 96, 189–190

Cap-and-trade climate change program, 22, 38, 188

Caprio, Leonardo di, 237

Carbon emissions, 189, 210

Carney, Jay, 93, 131

Carr, Bill, 234

Carter, Jimmy, 11, 87, 105, 112, 139, 242

Carville, James, 79

Castile, Philando, 277

Castro, Fidel, 241, 247

Castro, Raul, 241, 247, 250, 273, 275

CBS, 138, 271, 280

Celebrity Apprentice (television show), 109

Chemical weapons, 135, 175, 176, 178, 182–184, 210

Cheney, Dick, 65, 70, 73

Chicago, Illinois, 21, 25, 66

China, 183, 210, 242, 259

Chinese Uighurs, 73

Christie, Chris, 143

Christmas airline bombing attempt, 64, 65, 74–75, 119

Chrysler Corporation, 30

CIA (Central Intelligence Agency), 67, 69, 70, 102, 103, 105, 119, 137, 139, 178

Cincinnati Enquirer, 283

Citizens United, 147

Civil liberties, 160

Civil Rights Act, 228

Civil rights era, 25, 227–228, 234

Civil unions, 130

Clark, Gary Jr., 236

Clean Air Act, 189

Clemency power, 235

Climate change, 12, 22, 37, 38, 127, 154, 188–189, 210, 237, 244, 259–260, 290

Clinton, Bill, 11, 34, 55, 60, 78, 94, 131, 162, 182, 217, 237, 280, 309, 310

    Foster's death and, 224

    gays in the military issue and, 44, 92

    Haitian earthquake and, 75

    health care and, 35

    midterm elections of 1994, 87, 88

    Obama and, 87–89

    photographs of, 60, 89, 293

Clinton, Chelsea, 137

Clinton, Hillary Rodham, 45, 107, 112, 155, 178, 193, 311

    bin Laden raid and, 100, 106, 278

    Egyptian crisis and, 112, 114

    election of 2008, 25, 34, 87, 213, 241, 309

    election of 2016, 11, 259, 278–280, 279, 282, 283, 289, 290, 293

    health care and, 38

    Libyan crisis and, 116, 119, 136–138, 278, 280

    Obama, Barack and, 278–280, 283, 287

    Obama, Michelle and, 282

    photographs of, 100, 279, 282, 293

    as secretary of state, 29, 49, 50, 100, 200, 208, 278

Clooney, George, 237

CNN, 132

Colbert, Stephen, 123, 166, 172

Colbert Report, The, 172

Cold War, 199, 241

Cole, Tom, 182

Collins, Susan, 70

Columbia University, New York, 25

Comedy Channel, 166

Communism, 49, 65

Congressional Black Caucus Foundation, 287

Constitution of the United States, 92, 132, 182, 294

    First Amendment to, 147

    Second Amendment to, 157

Consumer Product Safety Commission (CPSC), 162

Contraceptives, insurance coverage for, 147

Coolidge, Calvin, 275

Corker, Bob, 184

Costco, 188

Craig, Gregory, 67, 73

Crimea, 199, 310

Criminal justice system, 227, 230–233, 235

Crumpton, Henry, 66

Cruz, Ted, 163, 225, 266

Cuba, 13, 241, 242, 244, 246–247, 250, 273, 275, 310

Cuban Five, 247

Cuban missile crisis, 241

Cutter, Stephanie, 93

Daley, William, 93, 95, 155

Dallas, Texas shootings, 277, 278

Dallas Morning News, 283

Damon, Matt, 237

Daqneesh, Omran, 178

Daschle, Tom, 29

De Parle, Nancy-Ann, 93

Debt ceiling, 95, 96, 163

Deepwater Horizon oil rig, Gulf of Mexico, 76–79

Defense of Marriage Act (1996), 130, 131

Democratic National Convention
  2004, 26, 155
  2012, 129, 131
  2016, 133, 213, 279, 280

Dempsey, Martin, 210

Derivatives, 38, 87

Disney Company, 188

Dodd, Christopher, 38

Dodd-Frank law (2010), 38–39, 290

Doherty, Glen, 137, 139, 178

Domino theory, 49

Donilon, Tom, 49, 106, 114, 115, 120

"Don't ask, don't tell" policy, 44, 88, 92

Douglas, Michael, 160

Dow Jones industrials, 21

Dowd, Maureen, 11, 160

Draper, Robert, 26

Dream Act, 92–93, 132

Dreams From My Father (Obama), 26, 225

Drone strikes, 11, 42, 53, 67, 69, 178, 237, 310

Dunham, Ann, 24, 25, 225

Dyson, Michael Eric, 228

East Jerusalem, 292

Economic issues, 10, 12, 21, 22, 27–30, 32, 34, 38, 87, 94–96, 127, 130, 153–154, 160, 162–163, 187–188, 225, 271, 292, 307–310

Edmund Petrus Bridge, Selma, Alabama, 222

Egypt, 103, 112, 114, 116–117, 135, 137, 184–187, 196, 255

Eikenberry, Karl, 45, 49

Eisenhower, Dwight D., 53, 209, 217, 309

El Salvador, 190

Electoral College, 145

Elkhart, Indiana, Obama's town hall meeting in, 30–31

Emanuel, Rahm, 13, 29, 30, 34–36, 49, 93

Emanuel African Methodist Episcopal Church, Charleston, South Carolina, 220, 223, 230

Energy industry, 189

Environmental issues, 12, 22, 37, 127, 154, 188–189, 210, 242, 259–260, 290, 309

Environmental Protection Agency (EPA), 188–189, 210, 259

Ethiopia, 246

Euphrates River, 205

European Union, 199

Executive orders, 188, 235, 272

Facebook, 193

Falcon Heights, Minnesota shootings, 277, 278

Fallon, Jimmy, 172

Fallujah, Iraq, 196, 198, 199

Families of Flight 93, 110

Favreau, Jon, 39, 150

FBI (Federal Bureau of Investigation), 74, 137, 277, 309

FCC (Federal Communications Commission), 209

Federal Correctional Institution, El Reno, Oklahoma, 232, 233

Felt, Gordon, 110–111

Ferguson, Missouri, 228, 230

First Amendment to the Constitution, 147

FiveThirtyEight.com, 290

Flickr, 193

Flynn, Michael T., 199

Foley, James, 208

Food and Drug Administration (FDA), 162

Foreign Policy magazine, 283

Fort Hood, Texas shooting, 73–75, 119, 153

Foster, Vincent, 224

Fox News, 132, 145

Foxx, Virginia, 38

France, 183, 242

Francis, Pope, 241, 245–247, 250

Frank, Barney, 38

Freedom Works Foundation, 147

Fried, Daniel, 69

Friedman, Thomas L., 217, 242, 244, 255

G 20 (Group of 20) summit meeting, 183

Galifianakis, Zach, 172, 192, 193

Gandhi, Mohandas, 54

Gang of Eight, 189

Gap, the, 188

Garland, Merrick, 99, 147, 271, 272

Garner, Eric, 230

Gates, Henry Louis "Skip" Jr., 227

Gates, Robert M., 29, 44, 67, 75, 92, 109, 251
  Afghanistan and, 49, 50, 59, 60
  Biden and, 123
  bin Laden raid and, 100, 106
  Egyptian crisis and, 112, 114
  Iraq and, 120
  Libyan crisis and, 115, 116
  photograph of, 45

Gay rights, 123, 129, 155, 272, 309
  gays in the military, 44, 88, 91 92, 130
  same-sex marriage, 130–131, 228–229, 234

Gaza, 186

Geithner, Timothy F., 20, 29, 155

General Motors Corporation, 30, 129

Georgia, 200

Germany, 183, 242

Ghouta, Syria, 176, 178

Gibbs, Robert, 55, 59, 75, 93

Giffords, Gabrielle, 93–95, 158

Gig economy, 188

Gingrich, Newt, 88

Goldstein, Gordon, 49

Golf, 216, 217

Google+, 193

Government shutdown, 163–167, 190

Gray, Freddie, 224, 230

Great Britain, 34, 180, 242

Great Depression, 21

Great Society, 34, 309

Green, GloZell, 193

Green Revolution, 112

Greenhouse gas emissions, 22

Gregg, Judd, 29

Gregory, David, 130

Grenada, 182

Gross, Alan, 247, 250

Group of Eight, 200

Group of Seven, 256

Group of 20, 183

Grylls, Bear, 260

Guantánamo Bay prison, Cuba, 37, 68, 69, 73, 127, 204–205, 210, 275, 294

Guardian newspaper, 160

Guatemala, 190

Gun control, 12, 93–94, 123, 156–158, 187, 272

Gun sales, 306

"Guns of August, The" (Stevens), 137

Guns of August, The (Tuchman), 137

Haditha Dam, 205

Hagel, Chuck, 155, 180, 182, 210

Haitian earthquake of 2010, 59–61, 75

Hamilton (musical), 237

Harvard Law Review, 21, 26, 225

Harvard Law School, 25, 66, 78, 147

Hasan, Nidal Malik, 73–75

Hasson, Maureen, 111

Hastings, Michael, 59

Hawaii, 25, 36, 44, 64, 93, 106, 109, 228

Headley, David Coleman, 74

Health care system, 10, 12, 22, 34–38, 127, 132, 134–135, 147, 149, 162, 163, 166, 167, 172, 202, 204, 225, 272, 290, 292, 306, 309

Heritage Foundation, 34

Hill, Grant, 217

Hiroshima, 275, 277

Hispanic voters, 189

Holder, Eric, 70, 73, 106, 227, 228, 230, 311

Homegrown extremists, 74

Honduras, 190

"Hope" poster, 86

Huffington Post, 290

Hughes, Charles Evans, 146

Hurricane Katrina, 78, 79

Hurricane Sandy, 142–143

Hussein, Saddam, 205

"I Miss Barack Obama" (Brooks), 283

Ifill, Sherrilyn, 224, 225

Ikea, 188

Immigration, 12, 22, 34, 37, 38, 88, 91–93, 127, 131–132, 147, 154, 189–191, 211, 272, 307, 310

Inaugural Address (Obama)
  2, 25, 241
  2013, 155, 227

India, 183, 242, 259

Indonesia, 25, 66, 228

Instagram, 193

International Monetary Fund (IMF), 96

Internet regulation, 209–210

Interrogation techniques, 67, 70, 103

Iran, 11, 13, 200, 210, 241, 242, 252
  Green Revolution in, 112
  hostage crisis, 242, 250, 253
  hostage rescue mission, 105, 106
  nuclear program of, 183, 242, 250, 251, 253, 290, 310
  U.S. negotiations with, 242, 250, 251, 253, 290

Iraq, 13, 41, 42, 44, 45, 47, 50, 66, 69, 88, 115, 119, 120, 127, 135, 163, 182, 195, 196, 198, 199, 205, 207, 259, 307, 310

IRS (Internal Revenue Service), 158, 202

Islam, 67, 74, 105, 205

Islamabad, Pakistan, 104, 105

Islamic extremism (*see* Terrorism)

Islamic Society of Baltimore, 265

Islamic State (ISIS, ISIL), 12, 195, 196–199, 205–208, 257, 259, 260, 277, 310

Israel, 112, 155, 184, 186, 187, 210, 242, 253, 292

Italy, 183

Jackson, Andrew, 145

Jalalabad, Afghanistan, 109

James, LeBron, 217

Japan, 255, 257

Jarrett, Valerie, 59, 223, 225, 310

Jay Zee, 237

Jefferson, Thomas, 265

Jimmy Kimmel Live!, 172, 289

Johnson, Lyndon B., 11, 34, 49, 237, 309

Johnson, Magic, 217

Johnson, William, 278

Joint Chiefs of Staff, 49, 67

Joint Special Operations Command, 106

Jonas Brothers, 172

Jones, Booker T., 236

Jones, General James, 45, 49, 59, 106

Jones, James Earl, 237

Jordan, Michael, 217

Justice, U.S. Department of, 67, 119, 130, 158, 211, 235

Kagan, Elena, 72, 78, 147, 272, 309

Kaine, Tim, 293

Kappes, Stephen, 67

Karzai, Hamid, 49

Kasich, John, 283

Katzmann, Robert, 146

Kelly, Mark, 94, 95

Kennedy, Edward M., 33, 35, 37

Kennedy, John F., 11, 49, 241

Kenya, 234, 244

Kerry, John, 155, 178, 180, 181, 184, 236, 251, 255, 260

Kessler, Glenn, 166

Key, Keegan-Michael, 172

Keynes, John Maynard, 22

Keystone pipeline, 260

Khan, Samir, 119

Kharkiv, Ukraine, 203

Kiev, Ukraine, 199, 202

Kimmel, Jimmy, 172, 173

King, B. B., 236

King, Martin Luther Jr., 54, 155, 225, 227, 234

Kirkham, David, 84, 85

Korean War, 60

Kosovo, 182

Kroft, Steve, 138

Kurds, 205

Kushner, Jared, 302, 311

Kuwait, 114

Lady Gaga, 163

LaPierre, Wayne, 157

Lavrov, Sergey, 184

Leahy, Patrick, 187

Leiter, Michael, 67

Leno, Jay, 163

Lessons in Disaster (Goldstein), 49

Levey, Curt, 147

Levey, Stuart, 69

Lew, John, 155

Lewis, John, 222, 234

Libya, 103, 112–113, 115, 116, 123, 125, 127, 135–139, 158, 178, 182, 196, 200, 278, 280, 310

Lincoln, Abraham, 11, 12, 21, 25, 85, 154, 271

Lincoln Memorial, Washington, D.C., 234

Locke, Gary, 29

Lute, Douglas, 45, 69

MacArthur, Douglas, 60

Malaysia, 257

Malaysia Airlines Flight 17, 202

Maliki, Nuri Kamal al-, 120, 198, 206

Manchin, Joe III, 157

March on Washington (1963), 225, 228

Maron, Marc, 217

Martin, Trayvon, 224, 225, 228

Mastromonaco, Alyssa, 93

Mateen, Omar, 277

McCain, John, 22, 25, 35, 155, 241, 266, 278

McCarthy, Kevin, 26, 211McChrystal, Stanley A., 44, 45, 47, 49, 50, 53, 59–60

McConnell, Mitch, 98, 99, 272

McDonough, Denis, 49, 59, 64–65, 75, 155, 176–177, 180

McFaul, Michael, 200

McKiernan, David, 44, 45

McKinsey & Company, 29

McLaughlin, John, 65

McLeod, Mary, 186

McRaven, William, 106, 109

Medicaid, 34, 36, 132

Medicare, 134

Medvedev, Dmitri, 92, 116, 200

Meet the Press (NBC), 130, 131

Merkel, Angela, 160, 161, 256

Messina, Jim, 93

Metadata, 160

Mexico, 257

Meyers, Seth, 107

Midterm elections
　1994, 87, 88
　2006, 209
　2010, 12, 83–86, 93, 208–209
　2014, 208–209

Migrants, 190–191

Military commission system, 69

Minimum wage, 188

Miss Universe Organization, 266

Mohammed, Khalid Sheikh, 73

Morsi, Mohammed, 184, 186

Mosul, Iraq, 205

Mourning, Alonzo, 217

MSNBC, 145

Mubarak, Hosni, 107, 112, 114, 115, 184, 186

Mullen, Mike, 49, 50, 67, 92

Mumbai, India, 74

Murguia, Janet, 189

Murray, John, 190

Muslim Brotherhood, 135, 187

My Brother's Keeper, 235, 311

NAACP (National Association for the Advancement of Colored People), 230

Nabors, Rob, 93, 180

Nagasaki, 275

Nairobi, Kenya, 246

Napolitano, Janet, 64

National Association of Police Organizations, 278

National Council of La Raza, 189

National Counterterrorism Center, 67, 69, 139

National debt, 91, 127

National Rifle Association (NRA), 157

National Security Agency (NSA), 64, 160, 161

National Zoo, 162

NATO (North Atlantic Treaty Organization), 50, 277

Nazism, 65

NBC, 130, 131, 163

Nelson, Ben, 36

Net neutrality, 209–210

Netanyahu, Benjamin, 155, 173, 242, 244, 253–255, 292

New Covenant, 34, 39

New Deal, 34

New Foundation, 34

New Nationalism, 130

New Start nuclear arms control treaty, 92, 200

New York Stock Exchange, 23

New York Times, The, 13, 28, 70, 86, 105, 108, 123, 131, 136, 143, 160, 217, 227, 242, 244, 253, 258, 271, 283, 290

New York Times Magazine, The, 26

New Yorker, 198, 290

Newtown, Connecticut shooting, 12, 71, 149–153, 155

9/11 terrorist attacks, 42, 64, 66, 70, 73, 74, 102, 110–111, 137, 224, 265, 277

Nixon, Richard M., 34, 147

Nobel Peace Prize, 53–55, 58

North Korea, 241

Northwest Airlines Flight 253, 64

Nuclear weapons, 88, 92, 127, 200, 241

Obama, Auma, 244, 246

Obama, Barack Hussein
　address to joint session of Congress (2) by, 36
　advisers to, 21, 55, 59, 69, 93, 251
　Afghanistan and, 11, 13, 41, 42, 44, 45, 47, 49, 50, 53, 55, 59, 127, 155, 178, 180, 310
　Africa, visit to, 234, 244, 246
　Alaska, visit to, 259–260
　"Amazing Grace" sung by, 223
　American Muslims and, 265, 294
　approval ratings of, 10, 37, 102, 129, 187, 208–209, 280, 307–309
　Arab Spring and, 103, 105
　arms control and, 88, 91, 92, 127, 200
　automobile industry crisis and, 10, 29–30, 127, 129, 292
　Awlaki killing and, 119
　Bergdahl trade and, 204–205
　Biden, Joe and, 122, 123
　bin Laden raid and, 10, 12, 102, 105–111, 129, 139, 292, 310
　bipartisanship, hope for, 26, 29, 38
　birth certificate issue and, 106, 109, 172–173, 213, 224, 234, 265, 287, 308
　Boehner, John and, 99, 211, 216
　cabinet of, 29, 155
　Cairo speech (2) by, 67, 112
　character and personality of, 11–13, 25, 26, 123, 129, 290, 310
　childhood and youth of, 24, 25, 44, 66, 225, 228
　China, visit to, 210
　cigarette smoking and, 99
　civil rights and, 224, 227–228, 234
　clemency power, use of, 235
　Clinton, Bill and, 87–89
　Clinton, Hillary and, 278–280, 283, 287
　commencement speech at West Point (2014) by, 201, 206
　as community organizer, 21, 42
　compared to predecessors, 11, 55, 59, 65–66
　criminal justice system and, 227, 230–233, 235
　Cuba, opening of, 13, 241, 242, 244, 246–247, 250, 310
　Cuba, visit to, 273, 275
　Deepwater Horizon oil spill and, 78–79
　Democratic National Convention speech (2004) by, 10, 26, 155
　drone strikes, use of, 11, 42, 53, 70, 178, 237, 310
　economic issues and, 10, 12, 21, 22, 27, 29, 30, 32, 34, 38, 87, 94–96, 127, 130, 153–154, 160, 162–163, 187–188, 225, 292, 307–310

education of, 25–26, 66, 147

Egyptian crisis and, 112, 114, 115, 186–187, 255

election of 2008, 21, 22, 25, 34, 228, 278, 287

election of 2012, 21, 22, 25, 34, 93, 99, 102, 125, 127–131, 139–143, 145, 287

election of 2016, 10, 278–280, 283, 287, 289, 294, 308

entertaining in White House by, 236–237

environmental issues and, 12, 22, 37, 127, 154, 188–189, 210, 242, 259–260, 290, 309

executive orders of, 188, 235, 272

as family man, 12, 169

final news conference of, 311

final weeks in office of, 292, 294

Fort Hood, Texas shooting and, 73–74, 153

Gates, Robert and, 44

gay rights and, 123, 130–131, 155, 234, 309

gays in the military issue and, 44, 88, 91–92, 130

George Washington University speech (2011) by, 95

grandparents of, 25, 225

Guantánamo Bay prison and, 37, 67, 69, 73, 127, 294

gun control and, 12, 93–94, 123, 148, 153, 155, 157–158, 187

Hagel resignation and, 210

Haitian earthquake and, 59, 75

Harvard Law Review, president of, 21, 26, 225

at Harvard Law School, 25, 66, 147

health care and, 10, 12, 22, 34–38, 127, 132, 134–135, 147, 149, 162, 163, 166, 167, 172, 202, 204, 225, 272, 290, 292, 309

Hiroshima, visit to, 275, 277

humor and, 172–173

Hurricane Sandy and, 143

as Illinois state senator, 21, 26, 66

immigration and, 12, 22, 34, 37, 38, 88, 91–92, 127, 131–132, 147, 154, 189, 211, 272, 310

inauguration of (2), 22, 25, 26, 66, 147, 241

inauguration of (2013), 144, 154–155, 227

interrogation techniques issue and, 67

Iran and, 11, 13, 239, 242, 244, 250–251, 255, 310

Iraq and, 13, 41, 42, 44, 45, 47, 119, 120, 127, 198, 205–206, 208, 210, 310

ISIS and, 196, 198, 199, 205–206, 208, 257, 259

Israeli settlements issue and, 292

lame duck priorities of, 88, 91–93

Libyan crisis and, 115, 136–139, 178, 182, 310

McChrystal resignation and, 60

McConnell, Mitch and, 99

memoir of, 26, 225

Michelle and, 24, 171, 213

midterm elections of 2010, 12, 83, 85–86, 93, 209

midterm elections of 2014, 208–209

national security issues and, 64, 65, 69–70, 73–75, 160–161

net neutrality and, 209–210

Netanyahu, relations with, 253, 255, 292

Newtown school shooting and, 12, 71, 150, 152–153

Nobel Peace Prize awarded to, 53–55, 58

operating style of, 55

as orator, 12, 26

Osawatomie, Kansas speech by, 129–130, 188

parents of, 25, 225

photographs of, 18, 20, 24, 31, 33, 35, 40, 45, 52, 55, 58, 60, 62, 71, 72, 80, 81, 82, 89, 97, 100, 115, 122, 124, 126, 128, 131, 133, 134, 136, 143, 144, 148, 152, 168, 170, 171, 173, 174, 177, 181, 192, 194, 215, 216, 218, 219, 220, 222, 231, 232, 236, 238, 240, 243, 245, 254, 256, 261, 262, 267, 268, 271, 273, 274, 279, 288, 290, 291, 295, 296, 297, 298, 300, 303, 305

physical appearance of, 10, 13, 25, 154, 172, 217

popular culture and, 236–237

post presidency of, 311

press and, 193

Putin, relations with, 181, 183 184, 200, 202

racial tensions and, 12, 221–225, 227–228, 230–235, 271, 277–278

"red line" remark by, 135, 178, 184, 210

Republican opposition to, 26–27, 37, 38, 86, 88, 91, 99, 129, 154, 155, 190, 209, 211, 224, 272, 309

Roberts, John and, 147

September 11, 2001 terrorist attacks and, 66

social media and, 193

sports and, 26, 216–219

State of the Union addresses by, 37, 135, 155, 187, 266, 271

Supreme Court nominations of, 30, 32, 72, 78, 99, 127, 147, 271, 272, 309

Syria and, 13, 116, 135, 137, 175, 176, 178, 180–184, 200, 205, 206, 208, 210, 310

tax cuts and, 22, 27, 86–87, 91, 153–154

terrorism, approach to, 65–67, 75

timeline of presidency of, 14–17

Trans Pacific Partnership and, 244, 257, 280, 290, 310

transgender rights and, 234

transition to Trump administration, 290, 292

Trump, Donald and, 266, 288, 292

Trump's inauguration and, 294, 296–298

Tucson, Arizona shooting and, 93–94, 153

Ukrainian crisis and, 199–200, 202, 310

as U.S. senator, 26

veterans affairs and, 202, 204

as wartime president, 42, 44, 53–54

at White House Correspondents' Association dinners, 107, 109, 160, 172, 173

Obama, Barack Hussein Sr., 24, 25, 225, 234, 244

Obama, Malia, 12, 78, 154, 172, 275, 311

childhood in White House, 169, 213

photographs of, 126, 168, 170, 171, 212, 222, 273, 275

Obama, Michelle, 223, 235, 286, 294, 311

Clinton, Hillary and, 282

election of 2016, 213, 286–287, 289

as first lady, 213

as mother, 169, 213

photographs of, 24, 126, 144, 150, 170, 171, 212, 214, 215, 222, 273, 274, 275, 281, 282, 286, 296, 297

Obama, Sasha, 12, 154, 172, 275, 311

childhood in White House, 169, 213

photographs of, 126, 168, 170, 171, 212, 222, 273

Occidental College, Los Angeles, 25

Occupy Wall Street sit ins, 130

Odierno, Ray, 67

Office of Management and Budget (OMB), 49

Olsen, Matt, 139

Oman, 251

Orlando, Florida nightclub shooting, 277

Osawatomie, Kansas, Obama's speech in, 129–130, 188

Ownership Society, 34

Pakistan, 46, 53, 74, 123

bin Laden raid in, 101–109

U.S. drone strikes in, 42, 53, 67, 69

Palin, Sarah, 84, 85

Panetta, Leon, 45, 102, 103, 105, 106, 109, 110, 155, 178

Panetta, Sylvia, 110

Paris terrorist attacks (2015), 257–260

Patriot Act, 69

Pawlenty, Tim, 107

Payroll taxes, 91

Pelosi, Nancy, 244

Pentagon, 47, 50, 66, 120, 137, 178, 205, 277

Perriello, Tom, 85

Petraeus, David, 47, 49, 50, 52, 53, 60, 69, 178, 208

Pfeiffer, Dan, 88, 109, 110, 141, 145, 180, 188, 193

Pharmaceutical industry, 35, 36

Philadelphia, Carlton, 80

Philadelphia, Jacob, 80–81

Pierce, Franklin, 11

Pinckney, Clementa C., 230

Plouffe, David, 59, 93, 96, 110, 160, 266, 290

Podesta, John, 67, 96

Poland, 184

Police shootings, 277–278

PolitiFact, 166

Power Africa initiative, 244

Pre-existing conditions, 34

Presidential elections

2008, 21, 22, 25, 34, 87, 213, 228, 241, 278, 283, 287

2012, 21, 22, 25, 34, 93, 99, 102, 125, 127–131, 139–143, 145, 283, 287

2016, 10, 11, 213, 259, 264–266, 271, 278–280, 282, 283, 286–287, 289, 290, 292, 293, 294, 308–309, 311

President's Council of Economic Advisers, 22

Prince, 237

Prison system, 232–233, 294

Public option, 35, 91

Public works spending, 27

Punahou Academy, Hawaii, 25

Putin, Vladimir, 116, 135, 160, 161, 181, 183–184, 199–201

Qaddafi, Muammar el-, 115, 116, 118, 119, 137, 178, 280

Qatar, 205

Race relations, 12, 221–228, 230–235, 271, 277–278, 310

Ramadi, Iraq, 196, 198, 199

Rasmussen, Nick, 69

Reagan, Ronald, 87, 145, 182, 237, 309

Recess appointments, 147

Reddit, 193

Reid, Harry, 209

Remnick, David, 13, 198, 290

Renditions, 69

Rezaian, Jason, 253

Rhodes, Benjamin, 59, 80, 112, 180, 247, 250, 308

Rhodes, Ella, 80

Rice, Susan, 115, 139, 180, 210

Richardson, Bill, 29

Roberts, John, 132, 146, 147, 272, 303

Roberts, Robin, 131

Robinson, Amelia Boynton, 222

Robinson, Marian, 213

Rolling Stone magazine, 59, 309

Romer, Christina, 22, 27
Romero, Anthony, 70
Romney, Mitt, 125, 129, 132, 139–141, 143, 145, 266
Roof, Dylann Storm, 230
Roosevelt, Franklin D., 11, 34, 271
Roosevelt, Theodore, 54, 130, 241
Ross, Dennis, 135
Rouhani, Hassan, 250, 252, 253
Rouse, Pete, 85, 93
Rubin, Michael, 139
Rubio, Marco, 157, 250, 311
Ruemmler, Kathryn, 132
Russell, Bill, 217
Russia, 11, 12, 88, 91, 92, 127, 135, 160, 180, 183, 184, 199–203, 242, 256, 257, 278, 292, 310
Russo-Japanese War, 54
Ryan, Paul, 38, 94–97, 98, 129, 257, 283

Sadat, Anwar, 112
Salman, King of Saudi Arabia, 255
Same-sex marriage, 130–131, 228–229, 234
San Bernardino, California shooting, 257, 259
San Diego Union Tribune, 283
Sanders, Bernie, 280, 281, 283
Sandy Hook Elementary School, Newtown, Connecticut, 12, 71, 149–153, 155
Sarin gas, 176, 178
Saudi Arabia, 114–115, 183, 187
Scalia, Antonin, 147, 271, 272
Schiliro, Phil, 36
Sebelius, Kathleen, 166, 167, 204
Second Amendment to the Constitution, 157
Secret Service, 193
Seinfeld, Jerry, 172
Selma, Alabama, 222, 228, 234
September 11, 2001 terrorist attacks, 42, 64, 66, 70, 73, 74, 102, 110–111, 137, 224, 265, 277
Sequester process, 96, 153
Sharpton, Al, 237
Shear, Michael, 13
Shiite Muslims, 206, 255
Shinseki, Eric, 202, 204
Simpson, Alan, 94, 95
60 Minutes (CBS), 280
Small-bore grants, 188
Smiley, Tavis, 227
Smith, Jacqueline, 84, 85
Smith, Sean, 137, 139, 178
Snapchat, 193
Snowden, Edward, 160–161, 183, 200
Social Security, 134, 158

Solitary confinement, 233, 235
Somali-Americans, 74
Somali extremists, 66–67
Somalia, 42, 105
Sorkin, Aaron, 160
Sotloff, Steven, 208
Sotomayor, Sonia, 30, 32, 35, 78, 147, 272, 309
Souter, David, 30, 32
South Korea, 120
Soviet Union, collapse of, 247
Spotify, 237
State, U.S. Department of, 49, 137–139, 186, 278
State of the Union addresses by Obama, 37, 135, 155, 187, 266, 271
Staten Island, New York, 230
Statue of Liberty, 162
Steele, Michael, 54
Stevens, Christopher, 137, 139, 178
Stevens, John Paul, 78
Sudan, 182, 237
Sui Kyi, Aung San Daw, 155
Sullivan, Jake, 250
Summers, Lawrence, 29, 161
Sunni Muslims, 195, 196, 198, 205, 206, 255
Supreme Court of the United States, 30, 32, 72, 78, 99, 127, 270
    Citizens United case, 147
    environmental issues and, 189
    health issues and, 132, 134, 135, 147
    Obama's nominations to, 30, 32, 72, 78, 99, 127, 147, 271, 272, 309
    same sex-marriage and, 228–229, 234
Surveillance programs, 69, 160
Syria, 13, 103, 112, 116, 135, 137, 175, 178–184, 195, 196, 198–200, 205–208, 210, 241, 257, 259, 278, 280, 310, 311

Taft, William Howard, 311
Tahrir Square, Cairo, 112, 116–117, 186
Taliban, 47, 49, 73, 204
Tate, Bill, 234
Tax cuts, 22, 27, 86–88, 91, 153–154
Tea Party movement, 12, 35, 84, 85, 129, 162, 189–190
Terrorism
    Benghazi, Libya, 115, 116, 136–139, 158, 178
    Boston Marathon bombing, 158–159
    Christmas airline bombing attempt, 64, 65, 74–75, 119
    Fort Hood, Texas shooting, 73–75, 119, 153
    homegrown extremists, 74
    Islamic State (ISIS, ISIL), 12, 195, 196–199, 205–208, 257, 259, 260, 277, 310

Mumbai, India bombing, 74
    Orlando, Florida nightclub shooting, 277
    San Bernardino, California shooting, 257, 259
    September 11, 2001 terrorist attacks, 42, 64, 66, 70, 73, 74, 102, 110–111, 137, 224, 265, 277
    Somali extremists, 66–67

Terry, John, 55
Thorne, Adande, 193
Tikrit, Iraq, 205
Tonight Show, The, 163, 172
Toomey, Pat, 157
Torture, 65, 70, 103
Trans-Pacific Partnership, 244, 257, 280, 290, 310
Transgender rights, 234
Trucks, Derek, 236
Truman, Harry S., 34, 60, 147, 275
Trump, Barron, 302
Trump, Donald J., 10, 11, 193, 310
    election of 2016, 173, 213, 264–266, 271, 283, 287, 289, 290, 292, 308–309
    health care issue and, 292, 294
    inauguration of, 294, 296–303
    Obama and, 266, 288, 292
    Obama birth certificate issue and, 106, 109, 172–173, 213, 234, 265, 287, 308
    personality of, 266
    photographs of, 264, 288, 296–299, 301, 302
    transition to presidency, 290, 292
    travel ban of, 311
Trump, Donald Jr., 302
Trump, Eric, 303
Trump, Ivanka, 303, 311
Trump, Melania, 266, 294, 296, 297, 302
Trump, Tiffany, 303
Trump University, 283
Tsarnaev brothers, 158
Tuchman, Barbara, 137
Tucson, Arizona shooting, 93–94, 153, 158
Tumblr, 193
Tunisia, 111–112
Twain, Mark, 160
Twitter, 193

Ukraine, 199–203, 256, 280, 310
Unemployment, 12, 21, 27, 88, 91, 127, 154, 188, 225, 271, 306
United Arab Emirates, 114, 115
United Nations, 180, 183, 200
    Security Council, 115, 116, 292
United States Border Patrol, 190

United States Fifth Fleet, 114
United States Military Academy at West Point, 53, 199, 206
United States Navy Seals, 102, 104–106, 109, 110
USS Carl Vinson (aircraft carrier), 110, 206, 207
Universal health coverage, 34
University of Chicago, 26

Van Duzer, Scott, 131
Vanity Fair, 172
Venezuela, 241
Versailles Treaty, 54
Veterans Affairs, U.S. Department of, 202
Vickers, Michael, 67
Vietnam War, 25, 44, 49, 53
Vine, 193
Virginia Tech shooting, 158
Voting rights, 227
Voting Rights Act of 1965, 147, 222

Wagoner, Rick, 30
Walmart, 188
Walter Reed National Military Medical Center, Washington, 42, 269
Warren, Elizabeth, 257
Washington, George, 11
Washington Post, The, 109, 160, 166, 253
Waterboarding, 67, 69, 103
West, Cornel, 227
West Bank, 292
White House Correspondents' Association dinners, 107, 109, 160, 172, 173
Wilson, Joe, 36
Wilson, Woodrow, 54, 311
Wisner, Frank, 114
Wonder, Stevie, 237
Woods, Tyrone, 137, 139, 178
World Trade Center, 66, 137, 277
World War I, 54
Wright, Jeremiah, 230

Xi Jinping, 210, 243

Yanukovych, Viktor, 199
Yazidis, 205
Yellen, Janet, 160
Yemen, 42, 64, 74, 103, 119
YouTube, 193, 225

Zazi, Najibullah, 74, 75
Zero Dark Thirty (movie), 103
Zine el Abidine Ben Ali, 112
Zuniga, Ricardo, 247

ACKNOWLEDGMENTS

More than most, this book has been a team effort, the product of a decade spent chronicling the rise and tenure of the forty-fourth president by the best journalists in the business. Much of the text is drawn from my own reporting for *The New York Times* but also that of my amazing colleagues, while the bulk of the pictures were produced by the paper's all-star photographers.

This book would not have been possible without Nicholas Callaway, who came up with the idea and nursed it lovingly from conception to reality. At *The Times*, Alex Ward was an unflagging champion of this project whose wisdom and patience at every step of the way were truly invaluable. David Stout brought his sharp eye and good judgment to reviewing every page, every paragraph and every word to make sure the book was the best it could be.

The rest of the crew at Callaway was indispensable, including Manuela Roosevelt, the incomparable designer Toshiya Masuda, Ivan Wong, and Danielle Sweet.

Veteran photo editor Vin Alabiso, along with Phyllis Collazo at *The Times*, chose many of the images that brought this book to life, and Maggie Berkvist and William P. O'Donnell assisted on the early photo research. Susan Beachy and Guilbert Gates put together the compelling graphic summarizing the Obama presidency through telling statistics. Jane Farnol produced the index amid constant design tweaks. Lee Riffaterre provided wise legal counsel and Danielle Rhoades-Ha helped with promotion. We are thankful for the expert assistance of Andrew Wylie and Jeffrey Posternak of The Wylie Agency in the contractual negotiations. We have also been extremely fortunate to work with the dedicated people at Abrams, led by Eric Himmel, Paul Colarusso, Jennifer Brunn and Maya Bradford.

All of us at *The Times* are fortunate to work for Arthur Sulzberger, Jr., the steward of a storied tradition of excellence in journalism that he has preserved and strengthened despite all the challenges, and we are grateful to have A.G. Sulzberger to lead us into the future. Our coverage of the Obama presidency was produced under the stalwart leadership of Bill Keller and Jill Abramson in New York; David Leonhardt, Carolyn Ryan and Elisabeth Bumiller in Washington; and Dean Baquet in both places. Gerald Marzorati, Megan Liberman and Chris Suellentrop edited pieces for *The New York Times Magazine* that shape part of this book. Special thanks to Bill Hamilton and Richard Stevenson, who are profoundly great editors and mentors.

Over eight years, I was blessed to team up with the most talented White House reporters in journalism, especially my friend of a quarter century, Michael D. Shear, as well as, at various points, the fabulous Jackie Calmes, Helene Cooper, Julie Hirschfeld Davis, Gardiner Harris, Mark Landler, Sheryl Gay Stolberg and Jeff Zeleny. Maggie Haberman and Glenn Thrush have joined the beat with great things ahead of them. On top of the daily coverage, journalists at *The Times* have already produced a library of insightful books about President Obama, his family, his team and his time in office, authored by Michael R. Gordon, Jodi Kantor, Mark Landler, James Risen, David E. Sanger, Charlie Savage, Eric Schmitt, Janny Scott, Scott Shane, Thom Shanker and Rachel Swarns. Every one of us has benefited from the research assistance of Kitty Bennett.

The backbone of this book, though, are the compelling images, most of them by the *Times* photography staff. Between them, Stephen Crowley and Doug Mills were there for nearly every minute of the Obama presidency, skillfully capturing history in real time. They were also astute and endlessly generous partners for the writers, helping us do our job better. Damon Winter and Tyler Hicks produced some of the most eye-catching photographs in this volume. Others who contributed gripping pictures include Drew Angerer, Nicole Bengiveno, Ruth Fremson, Todd Heisler, Richard Perry, Moises Saman, Brendan Smialowski, and Zach Gibson, who took the cover photograph.

Finally, I am grateful to my parents, family and friends for their love and support. In particular, my wife, Susan Glasser, the most extraordinary journalist of our generation and the best partner anyone could have, was a boundless source of inspiration. At a young age, our son, Theo Baker, has already become an incisive student of Washington but more importantly the joy of his parents' lives.

A special recognition to the photographers who contributed their work to the book:

Esam Al-Fetori, Ameer Alhalbi, Monica Almeida, Thaier Al-Sudani, Christopher Anderson, Philip Scott Andrews, Drew Angerer, Scott Applewhite, Nicole Bengiveno, Andrea Bruce, Narciso Contreras, Andrew Craft, Stephen Crowley, Michael Czerwonka, Linda Davidson, Gabriella Demczuk, Kevin Dietsch, Larry Downing, Al Drago, Adam Ferguson, Ruth Fremson, Zach Gibson, David Goldman, Todd Heisler, Tyler Hicks, Michael Kappeler, Meredith Kohut, Chang W. Lee, Saul Loeb, Mauricio Lima, Kirsten Luce, Tannen Maury, Doug Mills, Karsten Moran, Olivier Morin, Tauseef Mustafa, Mandel Ngan, Warrick Page, Richard Perry, Sergey Ponomarev, Smiley N. Pool, Craig Ruttle, Moises Saman, Ivan Sekretarev, Brendan Smialowski, Chris Somodevilla, Pete Souza, Linda Spillers, Justin Sullivan, Kayana Szymczak, John Tlumacki, Jim Watson, Kirsty Wigglesworth, Jim Wilson, Mark Wilson, Damon Winter, Dan Winters.

PETER BAKER is the Chief White House Correspondent for *The New York Times* and covered President Obama's tenure from its inception. Previously he covered the White House for *The Washington Post* during the presidencies of Bill Clinton and George W. Bush. He is the author of three other books, including *Days of Fire: Bush and Cheney in The White House,* which was named one of the five Best Non-Fiction Books of 2013 by *The New York Times Book Review.* He has won the Gerald R. Ford Prize for Distinguished Coverage of the Presidency twice, the Aldo Beckman Memorial Award for White House Reporting twice and the Merriman Smith Award. He lives in Washington with his wife, Susan Glasser, and their son, Theo.

ALSO BY PETER BAKER

The Breach: Inside the Impeachment and Trial of William Jefferson Clinton

Kremlin Rising: Vladimir Putin's Russia and the End of Revolution
(With Susan Glasser)

Days of Fire: Bush and Cheney in the White House

CALLAWAY

Printed in the United States

Distributed by ABRAMS Books

2 3 4 5 6   17 18 19 20

Library of Congress Cataloging-in-Publication Data available.

ISBN 978-0-935112-90-0

Visit The New York Times at www.nytimes.com   Visit Callaway at www.callaway.com

Produced by
CALLAWAY ARTS & ENTERTAINMENT
41 UNION SQUARE WEST, SUITE 1101 NEW YORK, NY 10003

Nicholas Callaway, President and Publisher   Manuela Roosevelt, Editorial Director
Danielle Sweet, Managing Editor   Toshiya Masuda, Art Director   Ivan Wong, Production Manager
Sue Medlicott and Nerissa Vales, The Production Department

FOR THE NEW YORK TIMES
Alex Ward, Editor
Vin Alabiso and Phyllis Collazo, Photo Editors
David Stout, Copy Editor